# The *Right* Thing

# Dr. Celia Banting

Wighita Press
P.O. Box 30399
Little Rock, Arkansas 72260-0399

www.wighitapress.com

The events of this story occurred over a four-month period. All names have been changed to protect privacy.

Library of Congress Cataloging-in-Publication Data

Banting, Celia
The Right Thing
p. cm.

ISBN 9780984976300

1. Autobiography   2. Community care   3. Abuse   4. Healthcare

Library of Congress Control Number: 2012903209

A CIP catalogue record for this book is available from the British Library.


Layout by Michelle VanGeest
Cover production by Susan Harring



Printed by Dickinson Press, Grand Rapids, Michigan USA

# The *Right* Thing

## Also by Dr. Celia Banting

*I Only Said I Had No Choice*

*I Only Said "Yes" So That They'd Like Me*

*I Only Said I Couldn't Cope*

*I Only Said I Didn't Want You Because I Was Terrified*

*I Only Said I Was Telling the Truth*

*I Only Said I Could Handle It, But I Was Wrong*

*I Only Said It Didn't Hurt*

*I Only Said I Wasn't Hungry*

*I Only Said I Wanted To Kill Myself; I Didn't Really Mean It*

*I Only Said Leave Me Out of It*

*This book is dedicated to dearest "Ellen" and to all the forgotten infirm and elderly who are abandoned by the state and who are mistreated by their carers. It is also dedicated to all children who suffer the same fate.*

# Acknowledgements

The acknowledgements for this book are many and varied. As always, my proofreader and typesetter, Michelle VanGeest, is first to be mentioned because she continues to "replace my mother's voice." By that I mean that I learned English grammar and punctuation not through formal education but from my mother; I learned "her rules." I suffered from what is now known as dyslexia, though there was no diagnosis for dyslexia in the late fifties. "If you need to take a breath, put in a comma." I've been on a 20 year journey to educate myself and all of it has been hard, but I'm helped by my mother's voice telling me where the punctuation symbols have to go. After she died in 1997 and I started writing novels, Michelle replaced my mother's voice, yet without the reprimand. When I get things wrong or "talk funny" because I'm English, she straightens me out. She's honest and has great integrity. She will always be my proofreader and typesetter.

In order for "The Right Thing" to reflect my Englishness and our countries' differences, I needed the manuscript to be proofread by an English teacher (she's actually Irish). Marie Callinan took the manuscript first and proofread it her way, clarifying the differences between the way America and England dictate grammar—it's very different. The confusion adds to the fog in my dyslexic brain. Marie did a great job, thank you!

The manuscript was then sent to Michelle, not to change what Marie had done, but to look for phrases that we English use that Americans don't know the meaning of. In response, I added a glossary to address the different uses of our common language, English. There are many differences and I find them amusing.

The next person to acknowledge is Susan Harring, whose creativity amazes me, along with her character, her love and acceptance of everyone. Her design of the cover for this book says is all: all nations, races, and creeds worldwide should join hands to do the right thing. She epitomizes holiness—yet equally womanhood and motherhood—and has the most amazing sense of humour. She is an inspiration to everyone.

My next acknowledgements are equally as important, yet in different ways. Thank you to my precious friend, Vicki, for her continued "guiding sense of style," and her profound "one-liners" that guide me in my personal and professional life. She always gets it right. She and my work partner, Dwayne, both helped me through those terrible four months. Indeed they have been my work partners since 1996 when we all first met. Another precious friend I have to acknowledge is Jeremy Daniel who taught me "American" nursing in 1990 when I was fresh out of nursing school and very naïve. He tragically died in 2011 of A.L.S., a horrific death, leaving three gorgeous children. Jeremy has always been an inspiration to me; in fact, he is the one who came with me—as described in the beginning of this true story— to help me put fliers in neighborhood mailboxes so that I could find lodgings. I want every reader to know that Jeremy spent his life doing "the right thing," and he impacted thousands of lives in the Children's Cardiac Unit, and all those with whom he came into contact. He also gave in death by leaving his body to science.

Additionally, I owe so much to my psychotherapist supervisor, Dr. Maria Gilbert. During my training she guided, challenged and forced me to grow through questioning myself and everything I thought or felt. She asked the vital question that changed everything for me and my own personal journey, "Who is going to take care of you?" Her input in my life has been huge, always extracting the right questions, which forced me to find the right answers. So this book reflects the journey she forced me to willingly take, and I am forever grateful that she agreed to "take me on" as a student psychotherapist when she was so very busy. Thank you to Dr. Claude Steiner, who renamed positive and negative Strokes as Warm Fuzzies and Cold Pricklies to make a complicated concept accessible to all.

The next acknowledgements, equally important, belong to the characters in that four-month period of my life: Darling "Ellen," a precious lady, a gift I was honoured to meet; "Brenda" for her welcome home greeting she gave me at the airport; "Alex" for all his support, advice at work with the children (they loved him); and dear elderly "Ben" for helping me on that awful day. Although I'd never met "Ben" before that terrible morning, I found him to be an absolute gentleman despite his poor health. I will honour him forever, because he taught me what it really means to "Pay it forward."

I thank "Mark" who was a ship in the night, a gentleman who anchored me to a sane place when insanity was all around me.

I wish to acknowledge my love of those Americans who "do the right thing," through the care I received from Barbara Tiffany, a semi-retired registered nursed who loaned me $200 when I was absolutely destitute. Barbara understood what was going on and had faith that I was trying to do "the right thing." God bless the fabulous Americans I've met in this great country.

Last, but never least, I acknowledge my darling husband, Dessy, who embarked upon the same four-month journey I did, yet differently, with neither of us knowing what the outcome would be. He grew, as I did, and forevermore he has shown the strength and tenacity that makes our marriage stronger.

# Preface

THIS IS A TRUE ACCOUNT OF a four-month period of my life when I returned to America from England and lived as a lodger with people I'd "met" on the Internet.

I have been as honest as I can be and I'm aware that the book is harrowing and raises some pertinent issues about life and politics in America. Cultural differences enthral me, and I embrace them. Although what I discovered highlights a side of America that few see or wish to acknowledge, I want to emphasise that I love America. I know so many wonderful Americans and they have enriched my life more than I can say.

The issues I was forced to face throughout that four-month period, and since, are presented as a respectful challenge to all those who govern at federal and state levels.

Thus, this book has three purposes:

- To highlight the plight of children, the forgotten infirm and elderly, and abuse that may be going on in the house next to yours.
- To honestly explore my own internal processes as I recognised that I was a "mandatory reporter" of abuse, and how that impacted upon myself and the dear lady I was trying to save.

- Lastly, to highlight that despite the United Kingdom and the United States both speaking English we are, as Sir Winston Churchill once quoted, "Two nations separated by a common language," I wish to show how differently we use the English language.

\* This four-month period occurred many years ago prior to iPhones and iPads, and the computer programme constantly referred to was an obscure one in its infancy that was quickly outdated and replaced by more efficient means of communication.

# The Right Thing

"Always do the right thing," was the phrase my mother instilled into me before I knew that I was learning about life or what it would cost to live up to those words and ideals. It's always been a part of me and I've lived to curse it at times—and now is one of those times.

As I sit on my bed in this unfamiliar room I feel far from home and very alone, only I know that I'm not *really* alone, my family loves me wherever I am in this world, even if they miss me, but I do know someone who is really alone. The thought of her curdles my stomach and muddles my senses, as I strive not to picture her frail, helpless, and frightened in her bed just feet away from me in the next room in this strange house so far from home.

# 1

I'M SITTING IN MCDONALDS at Gatwick Airport eating a sausage McMuffin, in fact I eat two, and feel guilty having just completed an eating disorder training course that says I should put "distance between the impulse and the action." Why am I doing this; waiting for a plane? I look at Dessy, my husband, doing his "paperwork": signing cheques and paying bills. I wonder if neither of us *can* say goodbye, since eating is my way out and paying bills is his. It's bizarre and my stomach plays a crazy game with the sausage McMuffins as I see the second hand speed around my watch—it's almost time to go to the departure gate and that means saying goodbye. Dessy gathers up his bills and neatly encrypted envelopes, looking really pleased with himself. "Well, that's a good job done," he says, with a satisfied smile that belies his distress at my impending departure.

The goodbye is brisk—just a brushed kiss, almost like kissing a maiden aunt or a stranger. We both know that to linger any longer would be too painful and this pact we've made will seem insurmountable.

I'm exhausted from trying to manage three university courses, so I'm taking a year off to go to a well-paid job in America. This will allow me to repay my tuition fees without having to beg Dessy to loan me the money. When I suggested taking the job, I think he was so relieved that I wasn't going to ask him for the money that he said, "Well, I won't like it but it'll solve a problem, won't it?" His end of the deal is to finish decorating our house. During the four years we've lived there, we've become complacent and the type of people that neither of us likes, and our house reflects our exhaustion and complacency.

"Are you sure you've picked out the colour for your study?" he asks, and I wish he'd just say "I love you" instead.

"Yes. I've put a cross on it," and when I think of a cross I think of kisses, and long for a proper kiss that would tell me that he loves me and is going to miss me, but it doesn't happen and I understand. It's too hard to go anywhere near our love, for I might not be able to walk through the departure gate, and I know that it's the same for him.

"Don't wait," I say, urging him away. Before I married him, I'd go to America several times a year and normally he'd wait until neither of us could see each other anymore by stretching and craning our necks, and I'd make him laugh by pulling silly faces or strongman poses. This time, however, I can't bring myself to do those things since I want him to go quickly. He does as I ask, and when I turn around to see if he's still there as I queue to have my bags and my shoes searched, he's gone and I feel abandoned and alone. Does he have to take me at my word, this time of all times?

My shoes pass the test and I'm allowed to go through the metal detector as nothing bleeps. I guess I'm a safe person. I don't *feel* safe, in fact I feel far from safe. Beyond the security checkpoints there are crowds of people in a holiday mood and I feel even more alone, wondering if I haven't just made the worst mistake of my life.

I'm going to be away from home for ten months. How on earth am I going to do this? I get homesick after just two weeks away from Dessy and England's green and damp countryside each time I go to America.

Yet it seems that I've developed an uncanny knack of being able to blot out unpleasant feelings or thoughts, because I walk along the moving walkway without thinking about how I'll manage without my soul mate, my friend and lover, for *so long*. Instead, I get to the departure lounge panting, and fumble for my phone so that I can leave messages for the other people in my life that I care about.

"I'm just about to get on the plane and in case it crashes you need to know just how much you mean to me," I say, with panic and a tinge of hysteria in my voice that is not tempered by the Valium coursing through my body.

I miss what's said overhead and watch people walk so confidently towards the boarding gate, and when I'm the last one left, still making last minute love phone calls, I feel an incongruous sense of urgency to get on the plane, thinking *Hey, don't go without me!* I am terrified of flying and always hang back, but this time I rush towards the gaping open mouth of the plane, stifling my terror with indignation that I'm the last in line.

My handbag bumps into the people who are already seated. "Sorry...sorry...oops...sorry," I say to mildly irritated passengers, seasoned travellers who, from the tortured look on my face, must think I'm either neurotic or a relative of Mr. Bean. I kick my cabin bag under the seat in front of me and as the captain tells the stewards to prepare for take-off, I frantically search for my seatbelt, praying that it's big enough to go around me, and accidentally run my hand along the thigh of the man sitting next to me.

"Sorry," I say again, as his boyfriend, who's holding his hand across the aisle, glares at me while I yank the belt as tight as I can, trying desperately to stop a gruesome thought rolling around my head: *If this plane goes down then at least I'll still be in my seat.*

I guess the Valium must be kicking in for I manage to smile at the lady sitting on the other side of me as I feel the plane revving beneath me and the overhead lockers judder...*They're loose. Someone should screw them down. Oh God, I hope nothing else is loose.* I can't help but remember the time I stuffed myself into a tiny plane a year ago, terrified as usual, and certainly not prepared for the Captain to announce that a wire had "come loose." I mean, what does that statement do to someone who is terrified of flying? To retain my sanity I chase those thoughts away.

Before too long we're in the air and I'm asleep. Disjointed figures float before my eyes as I dream of the last few weeks and all the goodbyes I've dreaded and endured. I awake to an irritated, over-painted air stewardess who would look more at home babysitting her grand-children than flying the skies with her glamorous cohorts.

"Pardon?" I say.

"I said, 'fish or chicken'?" she says slowly as if I'm stupid.

"Chicken, please." As she hands me a tray, I notice that this will probably be the last time I'm given a knife and fork to eat my dinner before having to cope with merely a fork and my fingers as Americans seem to use a fork in their right hand and not bother with a knife. I hate plastic cutlery (in England, "tableware" refers to place mats and cruets, table decorations and candle stick holders; cutlery is the collection of utensils you use to eat with). However, little do I know that within hours of landing all my *cutlery* will be plastic and my plates, paper.

I try to use my knife and fork but give up as my elbows offend my neighbours, and the boyfriend is still glaring daggers at me across the aisle as I accidentally nudge his lover. "Sorry," I grin inanely at them, dropping my knife and swapping my fork into my right hand, resigned to the fact that when with Americans, do as Americans do, even though I'm not on their soil just yet. I pass my tray back to the harassed, painted lady and nestle back into the seat and think of the changes I've been forced to make in order to sort my life out.

• • •

My ambition has always been to be a chartered clinical psychologist, but after finishing an honours degree in psychology, at that time in England there was a waiting list of eight years for a place to study clinical psychology. There was also a cut-off age limit of forty years and, as I was forty-four when I finished my first degree, it seemed as if my ambition was beyond my reach. I was fifty-one when I saw an advert offering the same course in Australia with no age limit, and after reaching the final interviews I'd already started packing. I was devastated when I wasn't offered a place. Undeterred, I decided to enrol at a college in London to complete my psychotherapy training, having already done three years at another college. However, within a few months an advert appeared in the *Psychologist* magazine offering the same Australian course in London, so I applied for a place. I never expected to be accepted but I was, and I found myself in a situation where I was nearly at the end of a PhD researching psychological and sociological factors implicated in teenage suicide attempts, and at the end of a Masters programme in psychotherapy. I couldn't give up either, having spent so much time, determination and money just so that I could be a clinical psychologist in order to help children and young people.

"*Always do the right thing,*" rang in my head. *Okay, I can do this*, I thought. *I'll juggle three university courses for this year and at the*

*end of the year I'll have finished my Masters' training in psychothera-*
*py and my PhD. Then I'll only have this one course to do and that'll be*
*a piece of cake by comparison.*

Only I didn't realise just how awful it would be. My life had
begun to resemble a hamster frantically running on a treadmill
going nowhere. I was tearing on and on, driving for hours to get
to Greenwich—the eastside of London a few miles away from the
Millennium Dome—attending classes in body only, and then racing across a traffic-congested London to my next psychotherapy
supervision appointment. Then there were course assignments that
needed to be handed in on time, and all this as well as working
full-time as a probation officer, which was a difficult and challenging job with sixty open cases between two offices. I was exhausting
myself and getting further and further into debt, with only a smidgen of time for my poor, patient husband, and none for myself.

I remember exactly the moment when I decided I had to
change my life. The National Probation Service decided that one
person from each office had to be trained to work with sex offenders and they chose me, particularly as I worked between two
offices, so from their perspective I'd be twice as valuable. I know
that sex offenders have their issues as well, need to be treated with
respect, and need help too—but my ambition has always been to
help children, and I couldn't bring myself to work with perpetrators of crimes against them.

I tried to explain to the office supervisor that I had my own
issues about these perpetrators, having inadvertently allowed a
family friend into my home, who then went on to attempt to *groom*
some of my children. I knew I couldn't be objective, but the needs
of the National Probation Service in the United Kingdom were paramount—I was the one chosen to train in sex offender treatment
and that was that.

I felt hopeless, as if all the years of studying were going to be for nothing. I made my decision easily, almost as if it had been made for me and I had finally listened to what I needed to do. I had finished the fifth year of my psychotherapy training, was at the write-up stage of my PhD and had completed the first year of the clinical psychology course at Greenwich University. The decision was crystal clear to me—I was going to take a year out, go back to work in America with children in a behaviour health care facility, pay off my debts, and finish writing up my PhD thesis.

However, unbeknown to me at that time, my PhD supervisor had found another job and left the university without telling any of his students. So far from being at the write up stage of my thesis, I still had two years to do to catch up with all that he'd let slide. I found this out the week before I flew out to America and I was in despair. At least I got to meet my new PhD supervisor and she was mortally embarrassed that this could have happened at a prestigious English university. She was so outraged, she had her department pay for my tuition fees, and she drove me relentlessly—for which, looking back, I am eternally grateful, although at the time I couldn't see it and cried every day. My husband had no idea what to do other than pat my head helplessly, wondering why women are so emotional. (I didn't do a lot for female-kind. Sorry.)

I have always wanted to work with children, so when after qualifying as a Registered Nurse on the Isle of Wight (a small island on the south coast of England) I discovered that there were no vacancies to do so, I looked further afield. I found an advertisement in the UK's *Nursing Times* to work for a large children's hospital in America. My five children were ecstatic at the thought of going to America, and so we all travelled to this wonderful country in 1990. I was terrified to leave the sleepy, safe, tiny island but I followed my dreams to work with children. It was an amazing experience, but initially I only stayed just over a year because the city had a terrible gang problem, and I was scared for my teenagers. However, I made lifelong friends there and America has been an important part of my life ever since. Each year, in order to retain my Green Card, I'd return and I was lucky that the hospital valued me enough to allow me to work for them during my annual trips.

For years I've stayed with a colleague who accepted my presence in his home with the same nonchalance as his two pet lapdogs. "Oh, you're back," they would yap for thirty seconds, and then go about their business of nestling into laps. Eighteen months ago, after a family emergency, this friend had to move from the area, so suddenly I had nowhere to stay. It was a turning point for me. I had to ask myself whether America meant anything to me and if it did, I had to find myself new lodgings. I thought about it a lot and decided to take control of my life and make things happen *for* me rather than just sit there and let them happen *to* me.

Twelve months before I left England, I took a week off from my English treadmill with a mission in mind—to find new lodgings in America. I walked down a leafy subdivision behind my beloved hospital and put an orange flier in every home's mailbox. It said: *Registered Nurse seeks lodgings. I'm quiet and respectful and when I'm not working or sleeping, I'll be studying and completing my PhD. Let's share each other's cultures.*

I flew home a week later, my heart in my mouth, my future in the hands of strangers, and wondered and waited. Days later an email arrived and suddenly there appeared to be the perfect answer and the perfect situation: a daughter taking care of her mother with Multiple Sclerosis needing "financial help and a change of face to amuse her mother."

Greta and I chatted over the Internet in the months before I was due to leave England and she seemed so perfect, so friendly, and I couldn't wait to meet her. When she told me that she had given up her English fiancé in order to care for her mother, I thought, *What an amazing human being, one who obviously knows how to do the right thing.*

So, armed with a place to stay that was mutually beneficial to each of us, I left my English treadmill and my dear husband, who promised faithfully to finish decorating the house while I was away. I set out to follow my destiny: to work with children, to write up my PhD, and to clear my tuition debts.

• • •

The Valium's wearing off, and I sense an uneasy tremor in my stomach, which lurches horribly every time the captain turns on the "fasten your seatbelt" sign and we plummet through turbulence.

*Please let this be over soon,* I pray; my head is so full of bargaining prayers that I can't even begin to fret over what might be waiting for me when I touch down. I become neurotic as I watch the flight information that shows exactly where we are. As the plane edges towards Atlanta on the screen and begins its descent, my nails leave a permanent indentation on the armrests. I mumble hurried prayers, and as the ground swings up to meet us and the tyres screech, a sigh wheezes from me. The engines slow as we taxi to the terminal and I display the blasé cockiness of a seasoned traveller, which belies my terror and my profound relief.

Now that the business of flying is out of the way and I'm safely on the ground, I allow myself to wonder what might be awaiting me. Will Greta turn up? I mean, I don't know her from Adam even though I have her address, and I could take a taxi if she doesn't turn up. But if she changes her mind about having a lodger she could just turn me away, and then I'd truly be alone with nowhere to go and no one to care about me. It's not a nice thought. I long for Dessy and tears prick my eyes, but when the longing threatens to engulf me, I try to ignore it.

*Don't be so daft*, I chide myself and force my feet to walk to the barrier where I think I see her. It takes me a second to work out which of the few people waiting at the barrier has to be her, for she is not waving and hugging the weary passengers. I force a bright smile on my face and give a cheery wave.

I am amazed at my ability to squash all the warning bells that ring through my head. It started last night—last night seems a world away, which it is. Dessy and I had wasted our last night together in an attempt to ignore our impending goodbyes by logging onto the Internet. Finally after all the months of *chatting* on the Internet, Greta had allowed us to see her image on the computer, and I'd had a sinking feeling in my stomach when I saw her straggly hair and bloated body. I had instantly reprimanded myself and thought how outraged I'd been at the eating disorder training programme I'd attended a few weeks ago, when someone had said that fat people have no control over their lives. I've always stuck up for the underdog, tried to do the right thing, and in the past have ignored my gut instinct in the pursuit of being fair. And last night when I saw Greta's appearance was one of those times.

Greta lifts her hand in some sort of greeting as I walk towards her to give her a hug. I try to ignore the way her body instantly freezes with human contact.

I'm anxious—maybe she is too.

"It's so good to meet you," I gush. "You're so kind to come and meet me." I mean it. It *is* good of her to meet me, but every part of my body and instinct is screaming at me to run and book into a Holiday Inn.

"Good flight?" she asks curtly, walking away before I can answer her. "Come on, walk this way. Baggage is down here."

I feel so uncomfortable as she marches off in front of me. I sneak a look at my new landlady and automatically think of the sentiments that woman at the training session had voiced. I had frowned at her at the time, and I'd known that my nostrils were flaring with distaste when she had said that she wouldn't consider offering therapy to a person who was very overweight, for it would indicate a profound level of psychopathology. Yet watching Greta waddle off towards the baggage claim, I can't get the woman's words out of my head.

I don't know what to say, so I chunter on about the flight and how I managed to stop myself feeling afraid, but as she raises one eyebrow at me, I feel stupid and weak.

"Go over there," she orders, "then you'll be the first to get your bags."

I do as I'm told, stifling the thought, *Hey, I've been waiting around for nearly twelve hours, five more minutes isn't going to hurt!* But I do as she says, trying to squash the image I have of her being the sort of person who would beat her way to the front of a jumble-sale queue or—more appropriately now that I am on the other side of the Atlantic—garage sale line. I don't want to push in—it's not me, and I know that my bags are very heavy—so to get them off the conveyer belt will mean that I'll have to swing them to gather momentum, and I'll be just as likely to beat some poor old person over. Luckily my bags come out last, rattling their way towards me after the old folk have moved away.

Greta storms off ahead with one of my suitcases and I tug at the other, wishing Dessy was here to help me. She is already in the distance and I start to feel really girlie as my hand hurts with the weight of my bag. I need my man. I try to keep up and feel as if I'm three feet tall with my mother about to shout at me to hurry up and stop dawdling. As I try to ignore the pain in my hands and shoulders, I begin to wheeze in the humid heat and tell myself that now is not the time to have an asthma attack.

"Oh, thank you," I wheeze, lifting the end of one suitcase as we try to haul it over the electrical wiring in the back of her car.

"Oh, maybe it's a bit close to the wiring?" I say, full of concern, having once knocked out the wiring in my friend's car with my heavy suitcases.

"No!" she says emphatically, and I feel silenced and stupid.

*Come on, Celia, get a grip*, I think, tears springing into my eyes. *You're exhausted. It'll be all right, you're just too sensitive*, and so I smile and say "Thank you," which she ignores.

I try to focus on the drive. I've missed the trees and landmarks that all hold sweet memories for me.

"It's so beautiful," I say, feeling awkward, desperate to dispel the anxiety in my stomach and to bridge the gap between us. I realise that it's likely to seem strange. After all, despite chatting on the Internet, we don't really know each other, but I'm troubled because I know deep down that I'm capable of feeling really close to complete strangers if they are capable of reaching out to me. I try again.

"I just love autumn; the trees are so beautiful. I'm never here during the fall. The airfares change on the first of November back home so I always miss it. I always miss Halloween, too. I can't wait to experience Halloween. Do you have many children in your neighbourhood? Oh, I do hope so as I long to be a part of Halloween," I gush.

She looks at me sideways.

"There are some, I think," she says, "but I don't really *do* children. I prefer animals."

I remember last night when Dessy and I were on the computer and she had written, "I hope you like pets." My heart had sunk even further for I don't *do* pets. It's not that I don't care about living creatures, I do. It's just that as a child I had some unfortunate experiences with horny dogs that kind of put me off fur and slipperiness. I've never quite managed to get past the idea that any creature with its genitals on show should be wearing underpants, and not doing its business in public or on the road.

"Animals don't seem to like me," I say, lying, for they like me rather too much. I recall taking my toddlers to our church's "cream tea" years ago and the vicar's small dog escaping from the house, making a beeline to hump my leg. The vicar was very embarrassed, but I just wondered what it was about me that brought out such behaviour in dogs. A sentiment that was reinforced years later when I sat on the esplanade pavement, hanging my legs over the sea wall watching children building sand castles. A dog ambled along, cocked its leg and peed down my back. *Why me*? I thought.

Greta jolts me from my musing. "Give me animals over people any day," she says. "Oh, that reminds me, I must pick something up for my mother."

"What's your mother's name?" I ask, ignoring her slight against human beings and the association between animals and her mother.

"Ellen."

"How is she?" I ask, full of concern. I deduced from Greta's emails that she was up to her eyes in responsibilities, being the sole carer of her fifty-four-year-old mother, having no brothers or sisters to share the burden. She had told me that she had given up her fiancé and a life in England to care for her mother, and while reading those emails I felt as if I was in the presence of someone very special and self-sacrificing. So why don't I feel that now?

"She's a bitch, always calling for something. I'm sick of her. D'you know that the other night she woke me up in the middle of the night and asked me to get her a breath freshener. Can you believe that? I told her to fuck off. I can't believe it, a breath freshener!" She shakes her head. I'm shocked and don't know what to say. "The evil bitch just thinks that I'm being mean to her, but she's so lazy and a liar. She says that she does things but she doesn't at all. You know, her friend is just as bad. She's crazy, you know. I told her! She asked if Ellen could stay for a weekend, but when she brought her back she hadn't done the things I'd told her to do. I told her that she'd never stay with her again 'cause if she can't look after my mother in the way I tell her to, then she's not going again. You don't mind if I smoke in the car, do you?"

*Well actually, I'm asthmatic so I do mind*, I think, but I say nothing, already feeling…I want to say intimidated, but I think *scared* would be nearer the truth.

She lights up and sucks the polluted air into her lungs and opens the windows.

"Pretty day," she says. "I love it when it's like this. I love to have the windows open and have the fresh air in my hair." (I'm confused by Americans calling a *day* "pretty." To us English the word "pretty" refers to flowers, faces and frocks.)

She opens the windows by remote control and suddenly my hair, which hasn't been combed for almost a whole day, is flying out behind me like an advertisement trailer from a prop plane. Those bits that are not flying out behind me are in my mouth, stuck there by G force. I try to retrieve them from my throat and maintain my dignity at the same time, but it's not easy and I don't manage it.

"Well, actually, I'd prefer it if the wind was not directly in my face." I fiddle with the controls and she shoots me a disapproving look.

A sigh escapes her as she presses a button that sends my window shooting skywards. Suddenly I feel very anxious, but I'm so exhausted from the flight and the awful unfulfilled goodbyes that I can't trust my judgement. Yet deep down I know something isn't only incongruent, it's just plain wrong. My head is so befuddled with jetlag that I can't figure it out, so I try to ignore my sense of disquiet and fall silent.

"Y'know, I've given my life for that woman. I was engaged to be married, but no, she got sick and I had to give him up and come back to look after her full-time."

"How awful," I say, thinking what it would feel like for me if I'd had to give Dessy up in order to go and look after someone else, but then I think of alternatives. I'd have done anything in order to be with Dessy and look after the person who needed me. "Couldn't he have come out here to be with you?" I venture.

Something horrid flashes across her face. "I don't *think* so. I couldn't inflict my mother on anyone else."

"But if he loved you surely it wouldn't have been an issue?" I ask, feeling confused.

"Oh, he wanted to come," she says scathingly, "but he didn't have a degree and didn't seem to realise how important having a degree is here in America. I wasn't going to end up taking care of him if he couldn't provide the kind of life I wanted."

I fall silent again for I don't know what to say. There seems to be a chasm between us. I don't feel like telling her that I married for love, not money, and that I have to work full-time because I made a choice to marry a man I loved, despite him only being able to earn a low wage. She isn't going to understand it and so I don't waste our precious love story on her. It feels as if she's only told me part of the picture, and I'm sure there's more that she'll reveal later because it doesn't really make any sense to me—love is love, just that and nothing more.

She flicks ash outside the car as she drives, swerving in front of cars and bawling at the other drivers for being in her way.

"Does your mother smoke?" I ask in order to make conversation to reduce my growing anxiety.

"Huh, she used to but I put a stop to that. There's no way that she's going to smoke," she says, taking a hard drag on the cigarette between her lips and breathing in deeply. "The stupid bitch would set fire to the house if I let her smoke, so I put them where she can't reach them."

An image flashes into my mind back to the days when I was training as a nurse and caring for a wizened young man lying awkwardly on a waterbed: bony and shaking as Multiple Sclerosis ravaged through him. Blind and incapable of doing anything for himself, his only pleasure was to smoke a cigarette, and we student nurses would take turns lighting up for him and guiding his hand to his mouth. The thought serves to increase my anxiety, for if we could do that for him, a person who we weren't emotionally attached to, why couldn't Greta do that for her mother, even if smoking may cause cancer—the poor woman's dying anyway. I try to dispel my dismay and slip into a persona where I try to please, and I hate myself for it.

"It must be hard," I say, trying to be empathetic but feeling as if I'm giving her permission to be abusive about her mother. While I want to let her know that I realise the strain she's under, I don't want to collude with her, but as she talks it sounds like a mother-bashing bonanza, so I change the subject.

"You know, it's kind of a tradition with me to go from the airport straight to Burger King," I laugh shrilly. "My friend used to pick me up and we always went to the same place. I was amazed when the assistant remembered my name, for most people can't even say my name properly in America. Isn't that strange?" I'm talking too fast and I know it.

There's that sideways look again and I feel chastised and stupid once more, but in a split second she smiles the sort of smile that turns my stomach. "Well, we best not break with tradition," she says, swerving the car around the corner, making the wheels screech.

*Ah*, I think, *I'm wrong. That's a really sweet thing to do. Bless her.*

I flirt with the assistant who's long since forgotten my name but valiantly tries to remember, and Greta rides along on my crest with American humour that I don't understand but which feels better than mother-bashing. With a bagged burger in my hand and a few warm fuzzies from the assistant who has no teeth, I get back into the car.

"Your mom does know I'm coming, doesn't she?" I ask.

"Of course," she says, with *duh* written on her face. Then she giggles the same little sweet laugh I'd heard over the Internet, which I'd found so endearing. The only word I can think of right now is *incongruent*, and as goose bumps spring onto my arms in the humid heat, I immediately wipe the word out of my mind.

As she drives I'm lost, even though I know this neighbourhood, and when she swings into her driveway I truly can't remember having put one of my orange fliers in her mailbox almost a year ago. She says nothing and I wonder if she's feeling as nervous as I am. I know that *I* would be if someone was coming to stay in my house for the first time, even if I knew them—let alone a stranger. I stand there feeling rather helpless as she orders me around, telling me which bags to take out first, and what she's planning to do to the garden.

"That's the car," she says.

"Pardon?" I ask, not knowing how to respond, and there's that *duh* look on her face again.

"You know, the car I emailed you about, the one I said I'd hang on to in case you wanted to buy it before I get rid of it elsewhere."

I suddenly feel a rush of gratitude that wipes away the previous hour of misgivings.

"I didn't get any email about a car," I say, ignoring her deep drawn-out sigh.

"I wrote saying I'd hang on to it, even though I could sell it several times over, to see if you wanted it," she says, with impatience, biting at me like a het-up terrier.

"How much are you asking for it?" I ask steadily, trying to control myself.

"Two thousand dollars," she says. "You can pay me four lots of five hundred dollars if that would help you out." She glances at me. "I wondered why you didn't say anything about it."

"Thank you so much," I gush, genuinely grateful for being given the means of transport and instalments to pay for it. I hadn't expected to be able to buy a car for many months, which is why I chose this neighbourhood so that I could walk to work. I'm also grateful that the car comes recommended. I mean, a car that is only worth two thousand dollars is likely to be loaded with troubles, but to be offered one that comes with a history of good behaviour is a godsend. "Is it running okay?" I ask, trying to sound as if I know something about cars when I know absolutely nothing other than where to put the key and the petrol—I mean gas—I'm in America now.

That *duh* look is on her face yet again and says, "I'd hardly sell you a car that was a pile of crap when you're living in the same house, would I?"

Now *I* feel incongruent. I feel reassured about the car being okay but completely chastised and ridiculed, but decide to ignore it. Anxiety and exhaustion wash over me and I long to be alone so that I can cry for my man, be alone with my thoughts, my sorrows and my fears. Although everything inside me yells that this is all wrong and I should run far away, I ignore it because I'm exhausted and have nowhere to go. What helps me to grasp a remnant of sanity is knowing that there's a parcel waiting for me somewhere in this house, one that I'm desperate to open. But feeling as anxious and bereft as I do, I don't want to open it right now. I want to open it slowly, on my own, because the contents are utterly precious to me and I don't want to share them until I'm ready to, quite aside from the fact that it would be the height of rudeness to rush into my new home, ignore Greta and her mother, and rip the parcel open. I have to do the right thing.

I follow Greta into the house, scanning around as I go through the door with my heavy suitcase, aware that my wheezing has returned with the exertion. I let it sit on the floor while I get my breath back. Greta waits for me, rolling her eyes. As I attempt to slow my breathing, I feel confused. The room feels odd. The front door opens straight into this room where I'm standing and I can't tell whether it's a hall or a living room. I decide that it's a hall but then I change my mind when I see in the corner of the room a huge pile of merchandise: odd things, totally unrelated. There's a hideous old-fashioned flowered bedspread in a see-through plastic zip-up bag, an orange storage box, a tapestry footstool, various gardening tools and household tools all still in their boxes all dumped in an untidy pile. There's also a television sitting in an oak unit, and in front are two chairs placed either side of a small, white marble table, which confirms my decision that this must be a living room. But why is there so much rubbish in the corner of the room?

I feel nervous about meeting Ellen. What happens if she doesn't like me, or if I don't like her? This is my future for the next ten months and possibly more. This is an arrangement that should be beneficial to each of us, but it needs to be comfortable for all of us.

I feel nervous and disorientated as I step into the house. Something is *really* wrong but being jetlagged and exhausted, I can't discern what it is. Greta barges through the door and pulls my suitcase into a room at the side of a short corridor.

"This is your room," she says, dumping one of my cases against a wall. "Let me show you the bathroom," she orders, turning me around and hustling me into a tiny room opposite that has a really repugnant smell about it. She points to the toilet bowl that has a plastic contraption under the seat with a pile of something very nasty beneath it in the bowl. "I'm trying to potty train the cat," she says proudly.

I know that my face is betraying me but I can't help it. I'm reminded of my youngest daughter who once tried to draw attention to one of my failings when she said with horror and shame in her voice: "Mum, put your face away." I know that everything I feel is like a beacon on my face.

My face has always been an open book and right now I know that my nostrils are flaring, showing what's on my mind. *That's disgusting. I've never seen anything so disgusting.*

A cat has pooped leaving a *parcel* resting sedately on a pile of kitty litter blocking the toilet. I feel grossed out as I've never seen anything like it before, and the sight of it makes me want to run a million miles away. Clutter I can just about deal with, but cat doings and kitty litter in the toilet is just about more than I can stand. I'm plagued with a bizarre image that pops into my head and, try as I might, I can't get rid of it. If the cat's *parcel* is too big to flush away, then what on earth will happen to one of mine? It'll be like the Titanic run aground, and I know right now as I stare down the toilet with my nose assaulted and my nostrils flaring, that I will never be able to use this bathroom. Constipation is already my bedfellow.

She pushes past me saying, "Just think of it, with training, the cat will be able to use the bathroom just like you or I and there'll never be any need for filthy kitty-litter boxes in this house." She says it with pride and I know that I'm not keeping up with her, for I'm still having trouble with my flared nostrils. I truly never expected to have to share a bathroom with a cat—sharing one with a man is bad enough, but not a cat—and again my imagination starts to run riot. If a cat is expected to emulate a human's bathroom habits, am I expected to copy the cat's bathroom habits? Oh lord! All that licking and grooming...Oh no, I just can't even begin to go there so I shut down my imagination as soon as it begins to take flight. Gross! But not only do I shut down my imagination, I shut down everything else that would have compelled me to run.

She pushes past me. "This is my mother's room," she says, standing in the adjacent doorway, which I assume is an invitation for me to enter, so I do. The sight that reaches my eyes makes my heart lurch. A frail lady, who is only months older than me, lies in the bed, shaking all over with the involuntary movements that Multiple Sclerosis inflicts upon its unwitting victims, and my heart hurts as she reaches out a trembling arm in an attempt to shake my hand. I love her immediately and I try desperately to silence the glaring incongruity between this open, sweet, courageous woman before me with the derogatory ways in which her daughter has described her. I try to ignore my thoughts, for they tell me that something is seriously wrong in this house, but I'm so exhausted and distressed that I can't work it out right now.

"Hi, my name's Celia," I say, smiling at her.

Her voice shakes as she welcomes me. "Well hello, Celeste. It sure is a pleasure to meet you."

I want to giggle but I grin instead and say, "It's a real pleasure to meet you, too." I grasp her hand, giving it a squeeze, and hang on to it so that it doesn't shake away from me.

"Welcome," she says, and I thank her while Greta walks off.

We chitchat for a while and then I leave Ellen to go to my room, writing four post-dated cheques for the car. I retrieve the gifts I've brought: a catering pot of Lemon Curd for Greta, as she said she loved it when she was with her fiancé in England, and Belgian chocolates for her mother. *Weird gifts*, I'd thought, but I know how one culture longs for the taste of another. I remember having German students each summer when my children were little, and they always brought a gift related to their culture—a big juicy sausage!

I feel a bit better as I see my things laid out, never realising just how much comfort I would get from the sight of my knickers. I start to put things away in the skinny little drawers that are not really big enough to hold all my not so skinny drawers. I put my precious pot of Marmite on the window sill, salivating at the thought of it on toast. The pot of lemon curd is huge and very heavy, so I take it to Greta.

If I'd been confused about whether the lounge was a living room, the next room confuses me even more. The floor area is completely covered with filth and clutter. I can't even begin to take in what's on the floor. I think I see a piece of bottle-green carpet that's completely covered in crumbs and clods of dust underneath a mountain of stuff. At first I think I've stepped into a garage. There are no tables or chairs but around two corners of the room are kitchen cupboards and a cooker. So it must be a kitchen, but how could anyone let their house be such a mess, especially if they knew someone was coming to stay? To hide my embarrassment, I hand Greta the lemon curd and babble on about how scared I'd been that my bags would be stopped for being too heavy. She smiles a little grin that is sicklier than the lemon curd, and it makes my stomach turn.

"I brought your mother some chocolates, I hope she's allowed to have them," I say, suddenly worried that she might have diabetes added to her list of troubles.

"Oh, she loves chocolate," and she points to a large box of truffles on the counter.

"Oh, good," I say, and follow her back into Ellen's room.

"Celia's brought you a present," Greta announces and I thrust the parcel into her shaking hands. She looks like a child at Christmas, with delight and surprise in her eyes. Concentration screws up her face as she attempts to hold the box and find an edge to rip. Greta comes to the rescue and says, "Hey, shall I get it started?" She rips an edge of wrapping paper.

Ellen's face is a picture when she realises that the coloured shells on the box reflect the exquisite shell-shaped chocolates inside.

"Ooh," she said, her eyes sparkling, and there's something between us immediately, "Oh, thank you."

I grin and rip the rest of the cellophane off showing her the chocolate shells inside the box, and she dives into them with the desperation of a dry alcoholic. I feel a bit humbled—it's only a little box of chocolates and she's slightly too grateful.

Leaving Ellen tucking into chocolates, Greta urges me to follow her out into the lounge.

"This chair is *so* comfortable," Greta says placing her broad hips into an armchair and reaching down beside her ankles. "Here, if you really want to relax, pull this," and suddenly without warning she's flat on her back: head back, legs up, with her belly shimmering, not knowing where to settle.

I'm surprised and embarrassed, and pray that she's not going to try to force me to have a go, so I quickly sit in the other chair, a Victorian armchair.

"Well, *this* chair is really comfortable," I say slightly too fast. "Good for my back," daring her not to challenge me to a turn in the booby chair.

"*I* want this chair," she says, to my relief, "so that I can relax in it, then Ellen can wheel herself into this space in her wheelchair."

I'm relieved but vaguely confused. When Dessy comes out at Christmas, where's he going to sit? I guess there's always the orange storage box which looks sturdy enough to support his weight. I thought that living rooms were supposed to have chairs in them, but once Greta takes her chair there'll only be the one chair left, which I guess will be my chair. I can't even imagine finding the space in this cluttered room to put another chair. I want to ask, "Where will Dessy sit?" but I say nothing.

I'm still confused. Where does Greta sleep? I know I'm jet-lagged, distressed and missing my man, not to mention my five kids and four grandchildren, but my brain doesn't seem to be working properly. Everything seems to be a little off whack. My heart also plummets, for one of the things I've longed for after living in our "builders' yard" house in England is cleanliness, tidiness and a lack of clutter; yet this place makes our house seem like a show home. Again I stifle my gut instinct—why do I do that?

I put my psychologist's hat on in order to try and make sense of it all, yet as I do so, I justify all my concerns away, and do what we humans are good at: denial and reframing things to fit the way we want or need to see them. It's obvious to me that poor Greta needs help and she's not coping at all well, *but never mind, I'm here now* I think with bravado, and I'm going to help her.

I return to my room, which has been cleaned, and retrieve my teabags (an English *must have)* and my Marmite (again, a staple English foodstuff) and return to the kitchen. I step over the clutter to put my things in a cupboard to try and help me feel as if I belong. I'm scared that in the low lighting I might trip and break a bone—until I start working I don't have any health insurance, and even then not for ninety days. Fear induces a sharp longing for the home I've left only hours ago. If I were to fall and break a bone in England, all my treatment would be free under our National Health Service, paid for by every employed citizen buying a national insurance stamp. Not only that, but I'd receive my full wage while I recovered. These things flash through my mind, and again I wonder if I've just made a huge mistake, even though it's the only way out of my situation as I see it. Enough sense seeps into my thoughts and tells me that I'm exhausted and I'm not thinking straight. Everything feels really strange and I'm uneasy, so I apologise for myself, saying that I need to go to bed.

"Aren't you going to open your parcel?" Greta says, with an edge in her voice that I can't quite place.

I grin at her. "You haven't peeped, have you?" trying desperately to play with her and entice her Free Child ego state out of hiding. That's what's wrong! It dawns on me in my exhausted, stressed state that the core of herself—her Free Child ego state—is absent. I'm too tired to acknowledge what that means to me or to her mother, for all I want to do right now is to lock myself away in my room and allow the oblivion of sleep to embrace me.

"No, of course I haven't peeped," Greta says. "Well, I'll see you tomorrow. Sleep well."

"'Night, and thanks again for picking me up. I really appreciate it," and I do.

She disappears through a door leading from the kitchen down a flight of stairs. I guess that's where she sleeps. So, suddenly alone, I step over the mounds of clutter and filth to go to my room.

I poke my head into Ellen's room and she's busy tucking into the Belgian chocolate shells. *Her* Free Child ego state is set free to play and enjoy. I squeeze her hand to say goodnight, and as I smile at her, there's something in her eyes that I can't quite fathom. I was to later discover that it was the feeling of relief that she was no longer alone in this house with her daughter.

I shut my door and notice the parcel safely delivered in order to be here waiting to welcome me. It was the one thing that I'd focused on during all the goodbyes and the long journey—my precious parcel waiting for me—but I'm so exhausted, scared and bereft that I can't open it. I feel so sick that I throw my bagged burger into the trash, lie on my bed and silently sob into my pillow with grief and exhaustion until sleep steals me away.

# 2

IT'S PITCH BLACK OUTSIDE AND I'm desperate to go to the loo, but thoughts of what lurks in the bathroom force me to hold on to my water as long as I can, which really hurts. I don't want to open my door in case I wake Ellen, although her television is on and the light is flashing through the one inch gap under my door, shining crazy moving shadows over my stark white walls. I can't be sure that she's awake and I don't want to scare her. I turn over and force my earplugs into my ears and will the pain in my stomach and back to stop, not to mention the pain in my heart as I think of Dessy and my precious children.

I awake again several hours later and this time I'm so desperate that I have to ignore the marooned cat's *parcel* and hold my breath for as long as I can while the water escapes from me. Ellen is knocking on the wall and I have a sudden flash of insight of how wearing it must be for Greta to have her mother constantly knocking, wanting attention. It seems to take ages for me to finish and throughout, the knocking continues, so after I wash my hands, I poke my head around Ellen's door.

"Well, good morning, Celeste. Did you sleep well?" she stammers.

"Yes, I did thanks. Can I get you anything?"

"Why, no, not a thing," she smiles at me.

I feel shame flow through me as I realise that her knocking isn't trying to gain mine or Greta's attention. It is merely because her bed is too close to the wall and she's shaking so badly that her bed knocks as she shakes. I feel sick.

"We need to move your bed a little bit away from the wall," I say, "otherwise it'll keep you awake."

"I know it," she drawls. "I hope it didn't keep you awake."

"Oh no, not at all," I say, humbled that she should be concerned about me and *my* comfort when she obviously has so little of her own.

I look at her water bottle. It's empty, so I ask, "Can I get you some water?"

"That would be nice."

As I step over the pile of clutter in the kitchen—trying to be quiet and feeling like an intruder—I fill her bottle and Greta bursts through the cellar door.

"Hello," I prattle, feeling caught, as if I shouldn't be there.

She ignores me. "Oh, so she's got you fetching for her already, has she?"

"Truly, I don't mind. I've just come out to make a cup of tea, so it's no trouble."

"Listen," she says, snuffing out the words on my lips. "She's to get her own water. If you let her she'll have you running about all over the place and she really can do this for herself."

I want to say "How?" looking at all the junk on the floor and wondering how on earth she'd be able to get to the sink in her wheelchair, but the look on Greta's face tells me that it's dangerous to answer back. She takes the filled bottle from me and marches off to take it to Ellen, and I hear her as I wait for the kettle to boil.

"Now, you know that you can get your own water. Don't be so lazy. You know what the Occupational Therapy (OT) lady says. 'You're quite capable of doing these things for yourself.' We're not here to wait on you, and don't you be going to put on Celia, now."

*It's just a bottle of water*, I think, trying to suppress the anger I feel at Greta for being so short with her mother, and at myself for being so passive and subservient. This really isn't me. I've always had a lot to say for myself and can say my piece when I need to, but standing here at the mercy of Greta and having nowhere else to go or any means of getting there, I feel disempowered. I decide to try and shame Greta into being nice to her mother.

I walk into Ellen's room and Greta is sitting in Ellen's wheelchair by the side of her bed, still lecturing her mother.

"I was just saying to Ellen that we'll have to move her bed a little further away from the wall so that it doesn't keep knocking and you think that she's constantly calling you," I say.

Greta rolls her eyes. "There's nowhere in this house that I can't hear her."

I feel that I've missed the mark somehow and that my attempt at rescuing Ellen from her daughter's relentless tongue has backfired and given her permission to carry on.

"Do you like Marmite?" I ask Greta, trying to steer the conversation away from chastising her mother. She gets up from the wheelchair and I follow her back into the kitchen.

"Yuk, no," she says. "You're quite safe there, I won't be touching that, and *she* only likes sweet things."

She toasts a piece of bread and spreads lemon curd on it and takes it to Ellen. "Try that," I hear her say in Ellen's bedroom. "It's from England. Celia brought it." She walks back into the kitchen and I smile at her, thinking: *Well, that was a nice thing to do; perhaps she's okay after all.*

"I have to go out to the shops later," she says. "Would you like to come?"

"Yes, please, that'll be great. Will Ellen be okay to leave on her own though?"

She looks at me scathingly, and says, "She'll have to be. I'll go mad if I have to stay in this house every second of the day with her."

I say nothing, assuming that she knows her mother well enough to know whether it's safe to leave her alone or not.

She giggles and I'm surprised.

"Did you open your parcel?" she smiles, with her head tilted to one side. Her smile seems like an identity kit feature placed in the wrong position.

"No, let's go and do it."

My Free Child ego state is suddenly set free and I almost run to my room, excitement flaring through me, and I reach for the box on top of my chest of drawers, feeling shocked at how heavy it is. Greta watches as I slide a knife along the tape and gently lift the contents out of the box. I'm stunned—it's beautiful—but Greta gives a gasp of revulsion and backs away.

I laugh—I can't help it.

"That's too real," she says, "much too real for my liking."

"She's a collector's item," I say, holding the baby doll in my arms and smoothing down her ruffled hair. I don't want to share this moment with Greta, especially as she's making derogatory noises, but she's here in my room so I can't ignore her.

"Would you like to hold her?" I ask, walking towards her, but as she backs even further away I giggle, enjoying the momentary transfer of power.

"Oh, no, I don't do kids. That's revolting." She leaves my room and I'm left alone with my purchase.

• • •

I'm a psychologist and a psychotherapist, and throughout my training the one criticism constantly levelled at me is that I spend my whole time caring for others but not for myself. I remember, scathingly, when a psychotherapy supervisor challenged me, saying, "And who's going to take care of you while you're out in America?" I know I frowned and my face told her that I thought the question was stupid. I've never had anyone take care of me since the age of seven, so I've always relied on myself to get through things. I remember my mother drumming it into me to "do the right thing" and I've always tried, even though others may have questioned my perception of what is right, or even what being *right* actually means. So yes, I looked scathingly at the supervisor when she asked me who was going to take care of me, but I did think about it.

I have to give credit to my precious sister-in-law Moya—who tragically died recently, leaving a huge hole in my heart—for showing me a way to answer the supervisor's nagging question. When Dessy and I visited Moya, there on her lap was a beautiful "one of a kind" collector's item: a baby doll, looking so real it was uncanny. I was instantly drawn to hold the doll and felt a powerful wave of emotion to nurture it. It was overwhelming.

I'd been writing a paper about attachment theory and how both the mother's and baby's verbal communication and non-verbal behaviours make lasting changes to the baby's brain development and to the strength of attachment between mother and child. The teachings of Transactional Analysis developed by Dr. Eric Berne in the 1960s focus on strengthening the nurturing part of our person-alities; therapeutic change comes about by learning to nurture not only other people but also ourselves. I've spent a lifetime nurturing other people and have had to learn how to treat myself in the same caring way, which has not been easy. It's one thing to *say* "take care of yourself" but quite another to actually do it, and after finding the task of actually doing so extremely difficult, Moya showed me the perfect way to make it seem real to me.

I bought a "reborn" baby doll from the Internet: a unique collector's item that would represent the core of me; a tangible, concrete way of reminding me to nurture myself. It's an extremely powerful therapeutic tool, and one that overrides parental reprimands that say it's wrong to consider yourself.

I arranged to have the doll delivered to my new lodgings so that as I steeled myself against saying goodbye to my precious husband, and bracing myself against my fear of flying—let alone flying into the unknown—the thought of this beautiful doll waiting for me in my new lodgings sustained me. I wondered what having her with me would mean to me when I was battling with homesickness and being alone, and whether or not this therapeutic analogy *really* would help me to finally take care of the core of myself. I'd seen pictures of her on the Internet but to see her in *person* was amazing. She'd been lovingly restored from a basic factory item to a lifelike baby with eyelashes, blue eyes, and white tips to her little finger and toe nails, and it was obvious to me that she had been lovingly created. She is the personification of me; a symbolic image I found surprisingly easy to accept. She was a reminder to me that I must take care of myself and not allow others to hurt or abuse me. She is "Little Cely."

• • •

I hold her in my arms and she's heavy; her head flops like a real baby and the sight and feel of her stirs something deep within me, something that I have no adequate words for, something beyond me.

I'm glad that Greta finds the doll repugnant, for a wave of protectiveness washes over me and I steep myself in this new feeling that I'm unaccustomed to. As I stand here, with the metaphoric extension of myself in my arms, and watch Greta back out of the room, an image flashes into my mind. The look on her face is such that she resembles a Satanist backing out of a room when faced with a cross, and the image disturbs me. One of my passions is babies and I can't imagine what degree of pathology would cause such a repugnant, almost fearful, reaction in a human being that is programmed by nature to love infant creatures. I was to find out in a big way in the weeks to follow.

I take "Little Cely" into Ellen's room and her reaction is the same as mine.

"Oh, she's just beautiful, and she looks so real," she says.

"Would you like to hold her?" I ask, amazed at the affinity between us already.

"Oh—yes, please."

I place the doll in her arms and she beams at me.

"She is just beautiful," Ellen whispers as she shakily tries to hand "Little Cely" back to me after a minute. I don't tell her the purpose the doll plays for me but just tell her that she's a collector's item, and she drawls, "Well, she's just beautiful."

I set the doll down gently in my room and go to find Greta.

"I'm ready when you are," I say, a little tickled that she's showed a chink in her armour.

She's recovered though and starts ordering me around again. "We've got everything here," she says, and begins to throw open the kitchen cabinets revealing row upon row of cereal packets, boxes of snacks and sachets of sauces. She walks over to a pine shelf storage unit and points to stacks of canned goods that stand in regimented rows, all of which have blue stickers on them.

"We have every vegetable you can imagine, and fruit as well."

"My, you've done well," I say, not knowing what to say for it seems alien to me. There isn't any way that she and her mother will ever be able to eat all this stuff before it's out of date or goes off, but from her tone of voice I know that I'm required to praise her for her thriftiness rather than point out the pitfalls in her shopping habits.

"Come with me," she orders, and I follow her through the *out of bounds* cellar doorway and down into a pit that is worse than upstairs. "I'm in the middle of sorting things out," she explains.

She leads me into a dingy room that is chock-a-block with everything you could imagine and covered with laundry in varying stages of being laundered. She ignores all of it and I'm embarrassed for her, but it's a wasted emotion for she seems oblivious to it and heads for the cupboards above the washing machine and dryer. She yanks the doors open, and there in front of me is row upon row of bathroom tissue, deodorants, combs, brushes, washcloths and everything you could imagine that would last for years. I get a sense that she's preparing for a siege, but don't say so. Instead I mutter, "Wow."

She looks proud and pleased with herself, and says, "The silly bitch constantly asks me for things when I go shopping even when I tell her repeatedly that I've already got everything she needs, but she doesn't listen and asks for the same things every time I go out. You wait, when we go out in a minute she'll ask for something I've already got." I say nothing but follow her up the steps, past a dog imprisoned in a tiny cage, who cowers as we pass.

She goes into Ellen's room and says, "We're just going shopping, is there anything you want?"

"I wouldn't mind some deodorant," she replies, and Greta looks at me, rolling her eyes and says scathingly, "See!"

I feel sick.

"We won't be long," I say, in my most cheery voice. "See you later."

"Okay," she shakes.

Greta backs out of the drive talking about the car she's going to sell me.

"It's got a lawn mower in the front seat," she says, "and I have to take the damned thing back, but I'm damned if I'll put it in my car 'cause it's all dirty."

I don't say anything but think that she's pretty insensitive to say it, even if she thinks it, because what she's said is that it's okay to mess up the car she's selling me but not okay to mess up her own.

"What's wrong with it?" I ask, making small talk.

"It's just a piece of crap, it's never worked from the moment I bought it and the store won't take it back, so that means I lose two hundred bucks." I cringe when she says the word "bucks" and I'm reminded of just how English I am. It's like using the slang word "quid" for pounds, and I hear my mother's voice telling me to speak properly.

"I've got to take it to a person who mends them and if they can say that it was a faulty design then I'll get my money back; if not, then I'm fucked."

*NICE*, I think. *I wouldn't be able to take this woman home to meet the Queen, or my mother.* I shudder involuntarily.

"You hungry? I am," she asks and asserts, swerving around a corner; and without waiting for a reply she pulls into a Chinese restaurant.

I feel guilt wash over me, thinking of Ellen lying in bed: un-dressed, having only eaten a slice of bread with lemon curd on it with a bottle of water—which she must surely have finished by now—and here we are not going shopping but going out for a treat.

It's a Chinese buffet, the best I've ever tasted and for a while Ellen's forced out of my mind as my taste buds explode and my stomach expands. Again I think of the woman attending the eating disorder course, and I feel a sense of shame at my own gluttony.

My stomach's extended to the hilt when we leave and begin our tour of shop after shop, and I notice that she hasn't got a list of what she needs. What could she possibly need? The house is full of food already, and so I quickly realise that this a bargain hunt. She shows me things I've never come across before, like the shelves at the back of the store with items that are past their sell-by date, battered and dented, that wear blue stickers marking down the price to almost nothing. It means, though, that in her pursuit of bargains she never buys what she wants or needs. It takes me to a bad place when I was a child, being so poor that my mother would do the same, stockpile items but never use them. Greta's pathology is becoming glaringly obvious—she has scarcity issues, never getting enough, so being compelled to hoard and buy more and more to defend against the emptiness.

I try so hard to put my psychologist's hat on and remain compassionate but she makes it very difficult for me to do that. In her need to defend her wounded self she pushes people away, so try as I might to befriend her I know that I'll never succeed. But heck, I'm going to try, for if she's happier, then that dear, sweet lady stuck in bed at home will be happier and better cared for.

Greta buys a packet of chocolate pudding, which is marked down, and when she realises at the check-out that it's knocked down to just twenty-five cents she holds up the queue, what Americans call a line, by going back to the bargain basket and digs through to find all the remaining packets of chocolate puddings. I feel embarrassed but try to stifle it. As we walk back to the car she's over the moon having just humiliated the teenage assistant by accusing him of forgetting to knock off ten cents on a packet of cut-price tissues. I pray a silent prayer that I never get to be so poor that I have to resort to behaving this way, but as my face flushes bright red, I forget the fact that her behaviour has nothing to do with poverty but everything to do with her fear of scarcity, need for power and seeming pleasure in humiliating others.

She goes on and on about Ozzy Osbourne and marvels over the coincidence that he is singing every time she puts on the radio. Could it even be a message, she ventures…I sit and wonder what's going on in her head that would make her think Ozzy was sending her a message. The notion makes me feel very uneasy, for this is magical thinking and not the thoughts of a rational person.

We are gone forever and I'm becoming more and more anxious thinking about Ellen lying in bed with her catheter bag filling, with a water bottle that must now be empty and with no food; yet I say nothing and I'm ashamed of myself.

"This is the first day I've been out forever," Greta says.

"Do you have any friends that you can visit or who can visit you?" I ask, genuinely concerned about her being so stroke deprived. Everyone needs strokes (attention and validation) to be emotionally healthy.

"Nope, none. I used to work at night in a store, but frankly I'd rather be away from people. I don't really *do* people."

"I think it's great that you have so many friends on the Internet," I say, but she interrupts me.

"Those aren't people," she snaps.

I think she's just missed the point that the strokes she gets from them is better than not receiving any, but I don't really feel like explaining it. I'm beginning to feel that every time I say anything, she seems to shout me down and make me feel stupid. From what I've seen of Greta so far, she seems unable to be close to people.

Perhaps interacting with *people* on the Internet is a safe way of getting some of her needs met. I leave it alone though and go back to worrying about Ellen.

After several more shops, she drives home. I'm jetlagged and my swollen feet are killing me. I don't think I've ever been more pleased to see a house, and I help Greta take in all her *bargains*, which add up to a lot—all funded by money taken from Ellen's bank account. All things that I would have put out in a car-boot sale, things that she doesn't need, and most of which will find their way into the pile of return merchandise in the living room. The pile of jackdaw treasures; none truly belonging to her but each one an emblem of her bland and empty life.

"Greta, where have you been?"

My stomach does a double summersault and knots with anxiety. While we've gorged ourselves and Greta has shopped at her mother's expense—she doesn't have a job—the poor woman has been lying in bed having only eaten one slice of bread seven hours before, and has since been left without water. I want to cry, but it gets worse.

Greta launches into a tirade of venom. "You fucking evil bitch. The first day I've had to myself, the first day I do something nice for me, you have to ruin it."

She's beside herself and I'm scared at the change in her demeanour since we met just twenty-two hours ago. She has been brusque, sarcastic and demeaning but she hasn't been out of control like this in an instance and without warning. She's raging like a maniac and is such a frightening spectacle that I'm too scared to say anything or to try and get her to see that *we've* been unreasonable, not her mother, and that the poor woman is hungry and thirsty.

I don't know what to do so I go to my room and shut the door.

I pick up "Little Cely" and I'm suddenly so grateful that she's here and for everything that she stands for. I feel vulnerable and frightened, and as I hold the doll, I am able to reassure myself that I *will* be able to take care of me, and that I won't let this monster hurt me or her mother. And although I try to comfort myself as I hear Greta raging, I couldn't know that over the next few weeks I wouldn't be able to take care of me or Ellen, and I'd even turn my back on the symbolic core of myself.

I suddenly feel desperate to speak to Dessy. After a while, I hear Greta in the kitchen banging around, and I venture out of my room to try to strike up a conversation with her.

Since she contacted me after finding my flier in her mailbox, she has gone on and on about how wonderful it would be for me to use her computer and stay in contact with my family through the Internet. It sounded wonderful, so I set up Dessy, my eldest daughter and my brother with web cams so that we could see and talk to each other.

After Greta's outburst I feel desperate for Dessy's gentle voice in my ear, but the computer is downstairs and there's something unspoken that says it's her space and out of bounds, her domain, a dungeon. My desperation compels me to ask her if I can sit at her computer, as she promised, although I'm not sure how to handle her. It's obvious to me that she's not coping with her life in any way, shape or form, so despite her instability I decide to try and befriend her. But I was about to learn that her life was going exactly the way she wanted it to go. I also learned that I'm too stupid and too compassionate for my own good.

I enter the kitchen. "Is there anything I can help you with?" I ask tentatively, waiting for her to bite my head off. I feel a bit like a creeping insect, scared that she'll pounce and gobble me up, but I'm even more scared when she turns around and smiles that sweet, saccharin smile with her head cocked to one side. It's as if she's someone else and not the person that has just raged like a maniac at her frail, starving mother.

"I was just thinking about what colour to paint the kitchen walls. What d'you think? I'd like to do the ceiling black." I try not to cringe, but I know that my face is an open book so I try my hardest to *put my face away* like my daughters tells me to do.

"Green's nice," I venture, meaning it. Green is one of my favourite colours.

I dare to hope that she's warming to me.

"I did think about burgundy," she says, "for this wall and maybe the ceiling, but *she* says it'll be too dark. What does she know?"

"I guess I've always been a white ceiling person myself," I say, not feeling able to agree with her because I get the feeling that she's testing me out. I mean, who'd want to paint their kitchen ceiling black or burgundy? She pulls a face at me and I know I'm wrong. She's not trying to test me out, she's serious, and she's just made a judgement about me and my obvious lack of taste.

"Black's good," I say, revolted by my creeping. "Burgundy, too."

"I think I'll just paint it all the same as the green walls," she says as if I'm not there.

I'm ashamed of the silent sarcasm that rides through me. Everywhere throughout the house where she has tried to paint the walls, she has splattered paint all over the door linings, ceilings and windowsills. None of the ceilings has been "cut into" as we say in England, and she's left the paint an inch or two short in a jagged line from the ceiling. I wonder why she bothered; it would have looked better if she'd left it plain white. As she's toying with her options of bottle green, black or burgundy, I think: *Well, if she chooses green for the ceiling at least there won't be any cutting in to do and it will look better than it does now.* And I know what I'm talking about because my precious first husband, Joey, a perfectionist, taught me how to decorate homes properly. "It's all in the preparation," he would say as he drove me to sand down walls and paintwork so that they would be perfect surfaces.

Perhaps being taught by a perfectionist has made me critical and I suddenly feel bad. I have antennae inside me that tell me when I'm becoming bitchy. I hate giving way to that innate feline thing that cuts more keenly than a warm knife through butter. I feel confused though, for everything she's said during the months that we were communicating on the Internet, and during the previous twenty-four hours, would lead me to believe that she's spent every second working to provide a home for her mother. Yet what I see is minimal effort, a slapdash "can't be bothered" effort and "that'll do you" half-hearted affair. Dessy's brother calls such shoddy workmanship "Hack it, Bash it and Leg it." The whole thing is *incongruent*, and there's that word again.

"I really like the green," I say.

She smiles that sickly smile again and I think she may be calm enough for me to ask her if it's okay to go and log on to the computer so that I can talk to Dessy.

"Do you think it would be possible if I... if I was able to... that's if it's not too much trouble... I realise you're busy, but it would be great if I could try and get through to Dessy." I take a deep breath. I've said it now and for a split second I don't know which way it's going to go. Her shoulders stiffen and I brace myself, but then she turns around and marches off down the stairs without saying anything. I follow, feeling apprehensive.

The dungeon truly is a mess, and what it must have been like before she'd allow me to see it, I cannot even begin to imagine. Every step is full of clutter—crazy things that have no rhyme or reason to be on a stair. I tread really carefully trying not to trip, and follow her into the bowels of the basement to the corner of the huge room. Her computer sits under layers of dust, cigarette butts, stale crumbs on paper plates and too much clutter for me to be able to discern what else is there. She orders me to sit down and then hovers over me, pressing and clicking the mouse. Being barely computer literate, I have no idea what she's doing... and she then walks away barking an order at me as I peer into the screen wondering what to do next. I have no idea. I'm dyslexic and it takes me a long time to read anything. At home I've come to recognise the colours and shapes of my own computer, but this one is a new and unfamiliar territory where nothing makes any sense.

"I don't know what to do," I say, feeling very dumb, but my desperation to see and speak to Dessy forces me to suffer the humiliation of begging for her help. She sighs loudly and walks back over to the computer, standing over me whilst she does something to the mouse and says, "You only have to read it." I say nothing but want to cry almost as much as I want to punch her. I'm also beginning to feel a creeping self-loathing for not standing up for myself but there's also a small voice inside of me telling me this is a dangerous place for "Little Cely," and she'd best be quiet or else something bad could happen. I sit helplessly in front of the computer having no idea what to do, and no idea how best to approach Greta, for she's the only hope I have of seeing and hearing my Dessy.

My desperation grows by the minute, and yet deep inside me I know that no matter what I say or do, I'm set up to stumble. I shake away the image of a huge spider's web, yet it's one that suddenly sharpens when I glance over my shoulder and see her sitting on the cluttered stairs waiting ominously for me to struggle and entangle myself. I know that I have no choice but to surrender.

"I don't know what to do," I say, waiting for her to come scrabbling over the web to saturate me in humiliation that will slowly consume me, and come she does.

Her sigh is venomous. "Celia, you *need* to read what it says. It's very *simple*." It hurts less than I thought it would, at least she's going to come and help me, and if humiliation and denigration is the price I have to pay to speak to and see my Dessy, then I'll gladly pay it. But deep down inside of me is a little voice that says, *But why do you have to pay such a price for something that's as free as the air, kindness?*" so I speak up.

"Greta, I'm dyslexic, I have real trouble reading what's on the screen. I know my computer at home but this is all different."

I try and say it with some authority in my voice but I think it probably sounds like bleating. She pushes me out of the way and I jump up like a scalded cat (did I mention that there's a second cat locked in the dungeon bathroom that's not allowed out until it can learn to poop in the toilet like a human being?) and she presses something on the keyboard. Suddenly there is my husband's face, smiling and blowing kisses at me and the price I've paid is worth it.

I can hear him and I can see him, and he can see me and he can hear me, too. It's a miracle. Greta suddenly fades as I blow kisses to my man and feel the love I've always felt for him all over again. She hovers, and I notice later that every time I speak to Dessy from that computer she is there: hovering, wanting to hear or be involved in our banter. No sooner had I logged on (once I learned how to do it) than she would be there, standing over me and talking about what she'd seen on television or about the things she'd lost by sending all her possessions to England in the hopes of marrying her fiancé—anything to prevent me from speaking to my man.

After we blow our last goodbye kisses, nothing can touch me, and I smile at her and ask her to come and share a beer with me, which she does. As I start to feel more mellow having just had my man in my ear, I slip into place where "pleasing" is my name. I listen attentively.

Her voice is a whisper. "She's doolally. You wouldn't believe what I've been through. She's so fucking selfish that she won't sign the house over to me so that we can get help from the government, but I'm trying to transfer all her assets into my name so that we can get help. D'you know her prescriptions are at least $2000 a month? I can't afford them. And that doesn't include the cost of care for her, which is a fortune."

I again think of England's National Health Service and that if Ellen lived in England, her prescriptions would be free and the term "pre-existing condition" would be unheard of.

I try to sound intelligent and ask her to explain the system for the care of the elderly and infirm in America. I try and explain how at home in England if the elderly are unable to take care of themselves and they have to go to a nursing home, the government takes their home to pay for it. They leave the family with the equivalent of $25,000 assets and take the rest to pay for their care. She begins to describe a similar situation and says that because Ellen won't sign her assets over to her, she's unable to receive the same help that someone who had no assets would be entitled to. I understand what she's saying but I can see both sides of the argument, for it would be a difficult decision to make: to relinquish all control over your money and home. It would be like accepting the inevitable too soon, either waving goodbye to your independence or having it ripped from you.

"She's a selfish bitch, she doesn't seem to care that, thanks to her stubbornness, I'm left to do everything for her," Greta whispers. "But there are some things I can do and that's reduce the amount of money she has, as my name is on her credit cards, and then I can speak to the financial advisor and get her certified as being unfit to manage her own affairs. I mean, two thousand dollars a month for medications is too much. Now, if she had no money the government would help and my inheritance wouldn't be going down the drain."

"Don't you have medical insurance?" I ask, confused.

"We used to when she worked as a nurse before getting sick, but the stupid hospital didn't renew her insurance and when I kicked up a storm about it, because it was their fault, they said that her Multiple Sclerosis would now be a pre-existing condition and they wouldn't renew the policy. Private health insurance costs a fortune and *her* illness wouldn't be covered, so what's the point of wasting more money if they're not going to cover the cost of anything?"

I feel a bit confused because I don't know anything about renewing health insurance in America; either you're insured or you're not. I think about England's National Health Service and if Greta and Ellen lived there, all Ellen's care and medications would be free while she lived in her own home.

I understand the financial dilemma Greta and Ellen have, and realise that Greta must feel very stressed having put her life on hold to take care of her mother, but there is something that feels very nasty about it all, a rottenness that is reflected in her whispering.

"Does she understand all that's at stake?" I say, my voice a normal volume, and she's horrified and hisses at me.

"Sssshhh! She'll hear you." She takes a second to compose herself and replace her reprimand with a sickly grin. "She gets very funny about money. Don't let her hear you."

I feel even more uneasy now, for if Ellen's coherent enough to be affronted about discussing money, then surely she's coherent enough to be able to have a say in how her money and assets are consumed. Something feels very wrong but I say nothing, and self-doubt flows through me. Is her animosity towards her mother something I would have felt towards mine if I'd been her sole carer and had to give up the love of my life? Would my compassion be eroded by isolation and an oppressive sense of duty? I don't know, but as I walk into my room with my head reeling and Greta heads towards the dungeon, I see "Little Cely" lying on the bed, and the sight of her ignites the compassion that is always at the surface of my soul, and I am reminded of what is right. I know that no matter what, I could not treat another human being the same way that Greta treats her mother. There are always other ways out, ways to solve problems so that everyone's needs are met or addressed through compromise.

But as I pick up the doll and remind myself of the promise I made to my supervisor to keep myself safe, I feel even more afraid and am not comforted by her weight in my arms. I feel desolate. Deep down, somewhere in a place where voices are mute, yet loud if you listen, I realise that I'm not doing the right thing because everything feels wrong, and the doll's symbolism is conveniently lost on me right this minute.

# 3

I WAKE UP TO MY ALARM AND it's still dark outside. I try and gather up my wash kit without making any noise because I don't want to wake Ellen, but as I poke my head out of the door she's already awake, watching the television that's been on all night.

"Well, good morning Celeste. Did you sleep well?"

"Not really," I say. "I've been waiting for the alarm to go off. I've got to go the hospital today to do orientation."

"Oh, my," she stammers. "How exciting."

"Yes, I'm looking forward to it. I'll see you later and tell you how it went."

"Well, okay, you have a good one."

I go into the bathroom and am assaulted again by a fresh kitty poop and this time I have to surrender to it for I need to take a shower. Greta told me yesterday that I could take a shower in her bathroom down stairs, which is big and more luxurious, but there's another cat locked in that bathroom because it poops on the floor. It's the thought of accidentally treading on soft, ripe, warm kitty poop and seeing it squeeze through my toes that forces me to attempt to use the upstairs bathroom. The bath is dirty and has a bathing aid stuck in it. I wonder if I'll break my neck if I try to take a shower by placing my legs in between the metal chair legs. I have no choice but to place my feet through the contraption and pray I don't slip on the soapsuds, because I'll break both my legs if I do, and I don't have health insurance yet. I feel more than a little irritated and confused that this greatest nation on earth can't develop a National Health Service like we have in Britain where healthcare is free for everyone. After the Second World War the NHS was born and paid for in part by workers out of their monthly wage. It works because tests aren't abused, medications are only used as a last resort and there is a reasonable ceiling limit to the cost of services.

I have metaphorically stepped onto my soapbox as I step through the invalid bath contraption, praying as I steady myself, chasing sleep away lest I tangle myself up and break both my legs in three places. The water's hot, so that's a bonus, and I scrub as quickly as I can in order to try and erase the experience from my head and nostrils. It's good to feel clean though. I get ready and leave the house without even having a cup of tea. I feel a pang of homesickness as I think of waking up to the teabag Dessy always leaves in my cup before he leaves the house to go to work.

I can't use the car because I have to sort out the insurance and buy licence plates; a strange procedure to us English folk. In England cars are sold with their number plate and keep the same throughout their lifespan, a bit like a child keeps his name throughout his life. In America, however, sell the car and it gets a new *name*, much like children who are repeatedly adopted and who assume multiple identities.

I've seen many things that have made my hair curl and my toes shrivel. Seven years ago I tried to adopt a child who had been abused, but the DHS (Department of Human Services) wouldn't let me because I was English. I was able to stay in touch with this precious child for several years and watched as her name was changed so that she became someone else and was forced to abandon who she really was. Then, when her new adopted mother had enough of being a *hero* and put her back into the foster system as a failed adoption, I was dismayed by my feelings of disgust and anger. The woman wouldn't tell me where the child was and my heart was broken. It's a wonder I'm not bitter and twisted.

My mind's wandering, like it always does, and I chase my thoughts away and look up the road as I walk past my nameless car and stride up the hill. The leaves are beginning to fall—it's beautiful. My heart feels light and I'm excited. I'm going to the hospital and know that my friends, who I haven't seen for a year, will be there, so I walk with a spring in my step. I know the sight of me walking up the road causes a stir—people don't walk here, they drive everywhere, even for the shortest of distances. They look at me as they drive past with an expression on their faces that shrieks: "Bag lady." I try really hard to look like the professional person that I am and nod a congenial "good morning," trying to ignore the catcall from Redneck Billy in his truck.

It's a quiet road, for which I'm grateful, but by the time I get to the intersection the traffic is flying by in all directions. I stand at the lights, waiting for them to change so that I can cross the road. I wait forever and become embarrassed by the drivers who are all driving blind as they watch me and try to figure out why I'm standing there at this time of the morning. I feel like whistling and looking everywhere but at them. It dawns on me as I watch the lights change in sequence that I've pressed the wrong button and I'm glad that no one can see my humiliation. I press the right button and the lights change almost immediately. I cross as sedately as I can, knowing that all eyes are on me, and suddenly as I'm half way over the wide highway, a hand starts flashing—telling me to stop walking. I begin to run and curse under my breath, as my breasts start bouncing and I give a free show to the waiting drivers.

I cross the road to avoid a sprinkler that's just burst into action and quicken my step, having wasted ages waiting for the lights to change. I don't want to be late on my first morning.

The receptionist opens the door for me and I go in, feeling instantly at home. I'm excited and go to the front desk, saying, "I'm here for orientation."

She looks at me blankly. "There's no orientation here today. It's next week."

"You're joking," I say. "I phoned to make sure of the date so that I could plan my flight. I've just flown in from England."

She looks unimpressed and tells me to sit down.

All of a sudden an old colleague comes round the corner and it's like a family reunion. She takes me to meet new colleagues, and the anxiety I've felt during the past thirty-six hours fades away. I'm home. We sit and work out a schedule, and everywhere I go I see my friends and they hug me, making me feel like a million dollars. I'm so excited because I've just walked into the shift I really like, three to eleven, on my favourite unit with the little kids. God is smiling on me and my destiny is unfolding as it should. I'm to start shadowing staff on Thursday and attend full orientation next Monday. After that I'll be ready to roll, back with my old work partner of seven years, Dwayne, who I have more respect for than I can possibly begin to say, and with a new big, gentle guy called Alex.

I walk back to the house, past the traffic lights, which I press properly this time, and down the road, smiling at anyone that drives past me. Nothing can mar the happiness I feel right now.

Ellen is in her wheelchair, parked by the marble table in the living room, and Greta is putting a potted plant on a table in front of the door when I go in. I tell them what's happened and how there was a mix up about the orientation day so that means I'll be able to have three days off before starting my new life. It seems like a luxury to me. I also tell her that I need to get a drug test done before I can start working.

"Oh good," she says. "I need to go to Walgreens. Wanna come? We can get your urine test done at the same time."

I'm so happy that nothing can faze me, so I say yes and hope that some of my excitement will rub off onto her. Maybe I got her wrong. Perhaps she's just so tired and bogged down that her lights have gone out. Perhaps all she needs is a bit of attention and to be around someone with their lights on, and I *know* that my lights are on. Any other time I might have noticed that thoughts like these could mean stepping onto the slippery slope towards co-dependence, but right now, I'm so excited having been given the shift and unit of my dreams, and seeing so many of my old friends, that I can't detect anything even glaringly abnormal.

I'm in my room and Greta says to Ellen, "We're just going out. Is there anything you need?"

As I walk out of my room she says, "Duh, we've already got a whole cupboard full," and she shakes her head in disbelief as she ushers me through the front door.

"See you later," I call over my shoulder, feeling uneasy again at Ellen being left in her wheelchair all alone. She looks so frail and it takes such an effort for her to wheel herself along with her thin, depleted arms. Her water bottle is on the table and I pray that she has enough until we get home because there's no way that she'll be able to wheel herself through the clutter on the kitchen floor to refill her bottle.

"She is so out of it," Greta says in a sweet lilting voice. "Y'know she's feeble minded and hasn't got a clue."

I want to say, "Well, humour her," but I don't. I don't want anything to spoil the feeling I have of being valued and cared for. Everyone in management that I met this morning had said, "Well, we've heard so much about you and we're so thrilled that you're back with us," and although it sounded corny I believe that they meant it. I don't want Greta and her mess to tarnish how I'm feeling, so I try to ignore the nasty things she's saying. It's impossible for my feelings not to be tarnished though, because I'm ashamed of myself for not sticking up for Ellen.

I know that I'm playing a game, the "Please Others" psychological game, and I hate it. I already know that I've been sucked in because I'm dependent upon Greta at the moment. I've always hated being dependent upon anyone, for it brings back memories of being manipulated and fearing for my life and that of my boys years ago. I say nothing.

She says, "You hungry?"

It's only 1100. Why's she always thinking about food?

"Well, I haven't eaten," I say, evading her question.

"Well, where do you want to eat?"

"Oh, God, I don't know."

"Jeez, I hate people who don't know their own minds," and she twists her face and mimics, "'I don't mind, you choose.' It drives me crazy."

I quickly say that I like Chinese, which she already knows from yesterday, and Indian.

"You like Indian? Cool. We'll go there."

Once again all I can think of is Ellen sitting at home with nothing to eat, with just a bottle of water, and I feel ashamed. I don't want to do all this eating; it feels immoral to be indulging myself so much. I don't *do* consuming goods that I don't need, or food that's too much for me—books maybe, but not food or material things.

She swerves across lanes and into the Indian restaurant's parking lot. I've been here before and they make fabulous curried spinach and feta cheese. She giggles her little girlie giggle and starts to tell me about how she'd humiliated the owner once after he'd gushed all over a new patron saying "Hi, how are you? We haven't seen you for a long time." Then she adds, "And I told him, 'She's never been here before.' He's so fake," she says, and I wonder what pleasure she got from humiliating him so.

I'm amazed at how much food she can eat and I have to dig my heels in when she insists that I try their rice pudding. Now, I *know* rice pudding and I'm not eating theirs. Mine's to die for and I refuse to fill my poor extended stomach with something other than spinach and feta cheese just because she's bullying me. I stand my ground and she scoops her rice pudding into her mouth looking at me as if I've betrayed her. I make small talk to lighten the heaviness in my stomach, which isn't only due to curried spinach.

As we leave, the owner gushes all over us, saying, "Don't stay away so long next time," and I shout out, "We won't," to silence Greta before she lashes him with her tongue.

"Idiot," she says, putting her car into drive. "Let's shop."

I'm grateful that she's agreed to drive me across town to do a drug test. I can't work without having one, and I say so, but she doesn't seem to be able to take a compliment, and says, "Well, I wanted to go to the Salvation Army Store anyway."

I try to ignore it and tell myself that just because some people can't accept positive strokes doesn't make them bad people, but I feel deflated nonetheless. She pulls up to the second-hand shop and I try to share her enthusiasm but it's impossible. It takes me straight back to my childhood where dirty, raggedy old second-hand clothes were given to us by a social worker. Ever since then I've had a problem coping with other people's clutter and dirt.

She's wearing that little girl look with an excited grin and I just know that she's going to find a bargain at any moment. Sure enough, she rushes up to me with a dirty, tacky necklace.

"Look what I found. That'll make a great Christmas gift for my mother. Isn't it pretty?"

I look at her and I don't know if she's joking, so I say, "Hmm."

She cocks her head on one side and rests her hands on her hips, and says, "One day I'll know what that 'Hmm' means," and I know that she's trying to read me as much as I'm trying to read her. I hope she doesn't "read" the disgust I feel that she would consider giving her mother a trashy, second hand necklace that cost her cents for Christmas. She must really hate her.

I wander off looking at aisle upon aisle of other people's cast off junk and hope that she takes the hint that I'm really bored. She picks up a large black scarf, and skilfully, in one fluid movement, she wraps it around her head and flashes her eyelids at me.

"I used to be Muslim," she says sweetly.

I'm confused, and the reason for my confusion is that she draped the cloth so easily, as if she'd done it a thousand times before, and with confusion etched on my face I say, "Really?" She laughs at me. Then I'm more confused. If she isn't a Muslim, then what would she gain from telling me that she was, other than to make a fool of me? Why would she want to do that just forty-eight hours after meeting me? She starts to speak in what I assume is Arabic. This is getting just too complicated and scary. I back pedal.

"Well, you certainly know how to put one of those on," I say, nodding to the scarf, which hangs expertly in folds around her head and neck. I know that she's done it over and over to be that sure of herself.

"Actually, I'm a Jehovah Witness," she laughs, and by now nothing would surprise me.

"Really? Several of my friends are Jehovah Witnesses," but my line of conversation is obviously not where she wants it to go, for she laughs in my face and walks off with the scarf still tied around her head and neck.

She grabs a cart, a trolley to us Brits, and I know now that she means business—this is going to be a shopping expedition. She loads everything into the cart from a pair of worn shoes to candle stick holders, and an old people's walker that doesn't work. After we've been there for two hours and I've given up on getting my drug test done, she walks to the check-out, standing there with her hands on her hips and she looks me in the eye.

"Now. So do I really want all this?"

I don't know how to respond and so I don't, but I do watch and wait.

"Well, this is broken, so I won't have that, and that's not going to match my colour scheme, so no, I won't bother."

I'm ready to spit.

"Wasn't that great?" she says. "I love coming here."

"D'you think the clinic will still be open?" I venture, almost too scared to ask.

"We have to find it first," she says, not answering my question.

I can't help her at all, for I have no knowledge of this area. But I'm grateful that she does and I try to praise her, but she blocks me, and so I sit in silence praying that the clinic will still be open.

She finds it and I'm relieved. I don't have to wait very long before a nurse in scrubs with long, straggly, bleached and permed hair that would be pulled up into a "bun" if she were a nurse in England due to the risk of spreading infection, leads me to a bathroom with a cistern that is shrouded with a thick chain and locked with a heavy padlock. I urinate after several minutes of straining, and of course they find nothing.

I feel more relaxed knowing that something vital has been achieved so that I can start work. I'm so thankful for Greta's help that I sit listening attentively as she drives and even try to play with her. Often people who've never played before don't know how to and need to be taught, and I suspect that Greta is one of those people.

She drives into town and heads for an Asian supermarket.

"I love these places," she says, and I have a sinking feeling come over me again. It's been hours since we left Ellen, and I'm worried about her. I also don't know how much more shopping I can stand as my feet are killing me. Since puberty my feet swell. It's ugly and painful, but I can't do anything about it as it's genetic. I only take my "water pills" when I'm sure there's a loo available.

There are no chairs in the Asian supermarket and the shopkeeper and his entire extended family notice my disinterest in their staple diet and imported Weetabix and Bird's Custard Powder that are marked up at extortionate prices. They watch me intently so I feel that I have no choice but to keep up with Greta and try to appear interested. We go up and down each aisle and she fills her basket with *bargains*, things she'll never use and spices that are too hot for Ellen.

She finally gets to the check-out and her packets of "buy one and get one free" turn out to be "buy two and get the third free," and her face begins to flush. I can see that she's doing some quick mental arithmetic and even in my brain-dead state I know she knows that she's been had. But rather than put some of the packets back on the shelf when the shopkeeper speaks in broken English and tells her that she's entitled to a free pack, she rushes back to select another. I wonder if she realises that she's just paid over the odds for her bargains; bargains paid for with her mother's money and ones that she'll never use. Did I mention that Greta doesn't work and relies solely on her mother's money?!

She seems to be able to just blow it off and gets into conversation with the man of the house about Indian videos and asks me what I'd like to see. Nothing. I hate sub-titled films as I have a hard enough time following any film let alone one that needs me to read within the shortest space of time—especially with my dyslexic brain. The worst thing I can think of is to sit and watch an amateur film with subtitles, but she's relentless and rents out two. I hope she doesn't want me to sit with her when she puts them on.

Finally we head off after she's promised the owner that she'll go to a film show next Wednesday. I pray that she doesn't want me to go with her, although if she asks me I know I'll end up going just to keep the peace. I know I need to work on my assertion skills.

I'm feeling anxious for it's been hours and hours since we left Ellen alone in the house with only a bottle of water and nothing for her to eat because she can't reach the fridge.

Greta drives down the road, the opposite way to the house, and I try really hard not to breathe out in exasperation but don't do very well. If she notices, she doesn't say anything. We are miles away from home now and I try to come to terms with the fact that this really is turning out to be a shopping marathon and maybe there's something I'm missing about her mother—perhaps Greta's got a carer coming in to see to Ellen. Maybe I'm worrying about nothing. Greta's certainly not worried, and so I try to make the best of it and still the anxiety that's flowing through me.

This next store has everything: it's weird, food in one corner and furniture in the other. She tries on hats and then shoes and I fight an image of one of the ugly sisters trying to stuff her foot into a glass slipper. "It fits," she says, grimacing. "Like it?"

"Hmm," I say, and she shoots me a look.

I wander away from her and come across a corner pine seating unit that would fit perfectly in her kitchen, that's if she'd get all the junk off the floor. I go to find her and act all excited, still trying my hardest to play with her. She follows.

"What d'you think?" I say, looking pleased with myself.

"Hmm," she echoes me, but I think her "Hmm" means something like, "Damn, I want to say something hateful but this is actually pretty good."

I leave her to it, knowing that if I go on about how suitable it will be for the room and how it will help Ellen to be able to sit up to table for a meal, she'll suddenly find reasons why it isn't suitable. My feet are killing me so I do something I've never done before—I sit in a reclining chair that's for sale and put my feet up. People walk past me and their little children stare at me. I say hello in my funny English accent and giggle when they search their mothers' faces to see if this weird lady is a safe stranger or not. I'm past caring when their mothers frown at me, and it seems a lifetime ago since I was amongst my friends at the hospital. All I want to do is go to bed.

Greta is brow beating the salesman over the bench unit, asking if he has another outside in the back, but he says, "No, it's the only one left." She is relentless.

"So you won't come down on the price but you expect me to dismantle this one and then put it back together again? I don't think so!" He squirms and I admire his resilience, and although he won't come down on the price (it's so cheap that she almost bites his hand off when he says that the price stands), he states that he will deliver it personally when he gets off work at 8 p.m. She winks at me having got what she wanted—hang his discomfort. I can see that she drives a hard bargain and the guy's just been had. His name is Keith, an all American good guy, working long hours for a minimum wage, and believing that the customer is always right.

I'm glad that's she's bought the thing, now perhaps we can go home, but no, she says that we have one more trip to make and that's to Best Buy to find a "thing" that networks the computer systems in her home. I feel manipulated, as I'm desperate to put my swollen feet up, but buying this gadget will enable me to be able to talk to Dessy on the Internet in my room, or so she says.

We go to Best Buy and I offer to go halves on the cost of it, when it's sorted out, as it's going to be for my benefit as well as hers and Ellen's. We stand in the queue for ages while she phones a Best Buy help-line to find out how much it will cost to have their technicians set up the computer network system. When they tell her $200 she says, "No, thank you."

"I'll do it myself rather than pay that," she says loudly, as we walk out of the shop.

Finally she drives home and I'm so relieved, although I know that the evening isn't over. Keith is coming in a minute with the pine corner unit and the floor is completely covered with everything that should belong in a garage. He won't even be able to get in the door, let alone set the unit where it's supposed to go if we don't get there quickly and clear it up.

I've spent ages wondering about the extent of the clutter on the kitchen floor. My house at home does resemble a builders' yard as Dessy and I try to renovate it, but if someone was going to come and stay, I would do my utmost to try and tidy it up as best I could. I'd be so humiliated to let them see our mess. If I had just half an hour I'd shove it all under the mat or in a cupboard, but if I had months, as Greta had before I arrived, I'd have it spick-and-span. So I have to ask myself as a psychologist, what's all this about, why would she do this? The only answer that makes any sense at all is that Greta wants to create the impression that she is so hard-done-by, and that she's in this all on her own. Then she can say, "Look what a hard life I have trying to do everything for my mother on my own."

But I don't buy it. It doesn't make any sense. Ask yourself as you read this, would you invite a total stranger into your house and leave it as a complete tip, not only cluttered, but filthy? Would you and if so, why? I'm messy, but I'd make an effort if I was expecting someone to visit or stay.

Once again I chase my thoughts away as I always do when the answers to my questions are too scary, and as we enter the front door, Greta goes straight into her mother's room and begins to shout.

"How did you get in bed? I've told you not to try and get yourself in and out of bed. That's how you broke your fucking leg."

I can hear Ellen trying to defend herself.

"I didn't get myself into bed; the fire department got me back into bed."

I feel my sanity slipping. My stomach's in shreds and anxiety chokes me. Greta explodes like a thing possessed.

"What?! You fucking stupid bitch. What did you go and do that for? What will the neighbours think? For Christ's sake, you can't be trusted. What am I to do? You can fucking well stay in bed from now on. Jesus! You have to ruin everything. Whenever I do anything nice that's for me, you have to go and ruin it, don't you?"

She storms out of Ellen's room and barges past me.

"Can you see what I have to deal with? She called the fucking fire department to put her back in bed."

I can hear Ellen calling out feebly. "I called my friend and said that you'd been gone for hours and I didn't know what to do. I was tired. I've been sitting in that wheelchair all day. She said to call the fire department."

Greta turns around and storms back into her room. "Well, that's fine, you won't be sitting in it any more when I go out; you'll stay in bed. You can't be trusted. You ruin everything."

"But I was tired and hungry," Ellen tries to say, but is silenced by her daughter's venom.

"*Shut up.* I'm not talking to you. You can go to hell. I hate you," and she walks out of the bedroom and passes me as I'm wringing my hands with more anxiety ripping through me than I can stand.

Greta shouts at me "…and you wonder why I hate her? She always does this, she ruins everything. I can never have any time to myself without her doing something like this. I fucking hate her."

She storms off down into the dungeon, and driven by extreme anxiety I begin to pick up the clutter from the kitchen floor so that when poor, hardworking Keith arrives he will have somewhere to put the seating unit.

I can't begin to say how I'm feeling. Somewhere deep within me and past my horror at her abusive behaviour, I recognise just how out of control and at the end of the road Greta is. Yet her behaviour is so abusive that it shadows my concern for her, and also some of my ability to be able to rationalise and work out what is *really* going on here.

My nerves are shot to pieces. We left Ellen for over seven hours with only a bottle of water and no food, to sit on her bony semi-clad body without being able to move. I feel very sick and very ashamed. I want to go and speak to Ellen but I don't, nor do I approach Greta for she is one frightening spectacle when she's angry. I busy myself with the mess on the kitchen floor and wonder how on earth Keith is going to get the bench seat in through such a tiny door.

I work until I can see the bottle green carpet underfoot. It's dark outside and I can hear Greta thrashing about down stairs, effing and blinding about how much she hates her mother, and my anxiety swells so much that I can barely breathe.

Suddenly two headlights swing into the drive and I breathe a ragged sigh of relief that at least someone else is going to be here, which will hopefully dispel some of the tension that grips the house. With a voice that's two notches higher than normal, I call down the stairs.

"Greta, I think Keith's here," as I manage to sweep the bottle green carpet with a weird shaped broom totally unlike any we have in England. Dust billows in the air and I start wheezing but I don't care. I can get my inhaler later. She ignores me as she appears in the doorway and says nothing about the vacant floor, but opens the door and smiles sweetly at Keith.

I can't help it, but an image of Kathy Bates flashes into my head, and as I hear Ellen calling for water from her invalid bed, starved and powerless, I think of the film *Misery*, and suddenly I'm more scared than ever. A flash of professional insight pops into my head: this is Borderline Personality Disorder type behaviour, and the insight does absolutely nothing to help my own state of mind.

I go outside and say hi to Keith and he suddenly seems like a saviour. I force a light tone of voice and say, "Y'know, this is so good of you to come out after a full day's work."

I know I've said the wrong thing and overstepped my status when Greta glares at me with a "mind your own God damned business" look written on her face, and I do just that.

Poor Keith tries to move the unit to the edge of his truck and my heart's in my mouth for I know what's going to happen next.

"Err, you need to be more careful," Greta dictates. "I've paid for that and you'll be paying for any damage."

I can't believe her attitude. He's been at work since 07.00, is hungry and wants to go home, yet here he is doing her a favour and she's giving him a hard time. I'm embarrassed.

The unit is at right angles and takes some manoeuvring. He's sweating and she's nagging: "Mind my car. Stop! No—not that way. Stop, come back. Back up." We all shuffle back towards Keith's truck and I feel puppet-like.

Keith tries to tell her politely how to do it. "Perhaps we could just..." but doesn't get to finish.

"No! Lift it up. Mind my fricking car, oh for God's sake. Celia, stop! Look what you're doing." I stop mid-way not knowing what she's referring to and realising there's nothing for her to refer to, but she does it anyway. She's only slightly less persecutory towards Keith and that's because she doesn't know him and wants him to do her a favour. I'm obviously already out of favour so she can treat me exactly as she pleases. It's scary that it's only taken three days for her to get to this stage of abuse, and the realisation lets me know that her pathology is extensive.

Human beings can normally project a social image for a lot longer than just three days. I'm not at all comforted by my flash of psychological insight and I wish that I didn't know so much. It would be great to be able to blame pre-menstrual tension for all of this but I know it's not that, it's something far more devastating and far more pervasive. I want to beg Keith to stay, to move in.

Once the unit's in the corner of the kitchen and Greta has rediscovered her sweet girlie giggle, I leave the room and go to see if Ellen's all right.

She looks awful: upset, dehydrated and wasting away. I wonder if her emaciation is through her degenerative disease or through daughter-induced starvation.

"I didn't know what to do," she beseeches.

"It's okay, babe," I say to her, and love her more every moment. "Try not to worry."

"But I didn't know what to do, you were gone for hours." do. do.

"I know, I know, I'm so sorry," and I mean it. I feel mortified and full of self-scorn, for I'd felt guilty and anxious all day, yet I hadn't said anything to Greta because let's face it, she terrifies me. I so want to do the right thing and make it up to Ellen. I feel dirty and used. It's quite one thing to go out and have a bit of free time away from a stressful situation. I think that's healthy because then you can come back refreshed and ready to start anew, but this feels different. It feels like a set-up—staying out forever, knowing that it will cause havoc, and then it will give Greta a reason to dump her hatred upon her mother. However, it backfired on her this time because she didn't reckon on Ellen calling the fire department to come and help her. I think that Greta was shocked at her mother's initiative and I also think that her violent reaction was beyond ordinary psychological game playing. I think she was overly defensive through fear when she realised her mother had taken the initiative and that she could be held accountable for her neglectful behaviour by an objective party. She'd been caught out and cornered.

I take Ellen's hand. "I'm so sorry," I say. "It'll be all right. Greta's found a really good corner seat unit, which means that we'll be able to have dinner together and chat."

Her face softens a little. "Well, that *will* be nice," she says.

"Guess what?" Greta says sweetly, as she walks towards Ellen's room. "Keith is going to fix the computer network for just thirty bucks. What a bargain. Best Buy wanted two hundred dollars."

I see that she's back to being Pollyanna, and I smile a hollow smile but notice that my head starts spinning.

"Are you hungry?" she asks Ellen, who nods. She seems afraid to say anything. The poor woman is starving. I mean, I'm hungry now and I had an all-you-can-eat Indian meal today.

Greta fiddles around in the kitchen and I ask her if she needs any help but she says, "No, I've got it." I hover not knowing what to do. She's bustling about and keeps on saying, "Yum, yum," licking dollops of food from her fingers, which disgusts me. She seems to be in a better mood so I ask her if I can leave Dessy a message on the computer, and I know my voice is full of apprehension. I know that going into the dungeon is to enter into her domain and she's pretty volatile right now, but I can't help it, I need to have contact with my man.

"Yes," she says, "I've already logged on."

By the time that I've finished leaving Dessy a message and venture back upstairs, it's as if I've stepped into an altered reality. Ellen's sitting in her wheelchair admiring the new seating unit and Greta is telling her that she'll have to raise the whole thing two inches to make it more user friendly. I stare at her and wonder why she'd want to make a simple and completed job more difficult.

# 4

I SLEEP BADLY AS FRIGHTENING dreams dart into my consciousness. It's hot and I kick off the sheet and toss about the bed trying to get comfortable. No matter which way I lie, my body's tense. It's probably less to do with the heat than the anxiety that constantly nibbles away at me, and the feeling of being powerless. If I accept my own feelings of powerlessness as being awful and sickening, then how much more must Ellen's be, for mine are nothing compared to hers. It's what stops me from sleeping soundly: if I recognise my own distress, I cannot ignore Ellen's.

I sleep in. I don't mean to but suddenly after tossing and turning all night, sleep claims me. When I awake I dart out of bed and gather my wash gear in the new blue plastic basket, my one dollar bargain from the pine corner-seat shop, and I head for the bathroom downstairs in the dungeon. Greta had said that I could use it and so I decide to take her at her word. I step gingerly down the steps, treading carefully over the clutter that litters each step. The dog imprisoned in its tiny cage cowers as I walk past him, and I'm impressed that he doesn't bark. Even the poor dog has learned to be silent so as not to incur Greta's wrath. I've never come across a dog like it, one that would stifle its instinctive behaviour so readily, and the significance of it creeps me out.

The door from the den to the downstairs bathroom is closed and I feel apprehensive about opening it. I tell myself not to be so silly, after all she did say that I could use her bathroom, and today I really don't feel like dealing with the bathing aid contraption in the upstairs bathroom and the stench of kitty litter.

I cautiously open the door and instantly wish I hadn't, for there to my right is Greta completely naked, her grossly obese body swaying from side to side like an Indian elephant hauling tree trunks as she waddles towards the bath.

I shut the door as quickly and as quietly as I can and almost run up the stairs back into the kitchen, praying that she hasn't heard me. I know that I've just invaded her personal space, and if she has any self-respect she should be really defensive about having been seen in all her nakedness. I know I would be. It's a bizarre moment, one that makes me want to scream, for there's a permanent image imprinted upon my mind of her sailing into the bathroom with parts of her body that are grossly deformed by gluttony. There's something else that troubles me when I have the misfortune to think of that image, for I can't imagine someone that big feeling comfortable enough to walk about in the nude. I realise that my thoughts may reflect my own inhibitions, those borne out of being dismayed at my own middle age spread and the inability to hold my stomach in after getting to the age of fifty.

I pray that she didn't hear me or realise that she's been seen without anything to cover the core of herself. As I shut my bedroom door and catch my breath, I think about what to do.

If I go back downstairs after just enough time has passed for her to take her shower, she could associate any sounds she may have heard with me having closed that door and having seen her.

If I wait a while, then should she have heard the click of the door, she might just ignore it as being a figment of her imagination.

I switch my laptop on and start to do some work on my PhD, and after an hour I remember that I need to take a shower and get ready.

It's been so long that she surely won't think I was at the doorway witnessing her nakedness, so I gather up my things again and open my door.

She's standing outside like a praying mantis and I can't tell from her face whether she knows or not, but then she barks at me, "Oh, you're not ready. I thought you'd be ready. You know, I've got a lot of things to do today. I can't wait around for you. I'm ready to go right now."

She tuts so loudly that I feel like a small child being reprimanded, but her attitude makes my heart soar. She sounds irritated, not shamed, so I deduce that she didn't see me witnessing all her naked glory. I can handle her irritation and so I chirp at her, "Oh believe me, I can be ready in just a few minutes."

I fly past her and dash down the stairs, say a throwaway "hello" to the caged dog, bypass the cat poop on the floor, and jump into the shower. It's bliss compared to the upstairs bathroom but I don't linger. I really am only a few minutes. It's always been one of my assets, getting ready quickly, with the end result being the same as someone who's spent all day getting ready.

"I'm ready," I call, but then she keeps me waiting. That's okay, I can cope with her passive-aggressiveness. She's nagging Ellen, telling her to behave for the carer who is coming to get her up and into her wheelchair today.

We're going to the car insurers and I feel an air of expectancy and excitement. Can it truly be that I'll soon be mobile and free to go where I please? I fend off a creeping fear that something will go wrong and that I'll be at her mercy forever more. She barely talks to me as we drive, and yet she bounds through the door of the insurance office and flirts unabashedly with the insurance broker, and is more jovial than I've seen her during these past four days. It makes me feel uneasy but I go with it and think: *Well, maybe she's just had a bad four days and now I'm going to see her play from her "Inner Child,"* but no, when we get back in the car her joviality evaporates.

I sit there trying to hold myself together and ignore her ominous silence and I pray that we get this red tape over with as soon as possible; then I'll be free to go out if it all gets too much to handle. It's so different in the States compared to England. You need a car here to go anywhere as everything is so spread out, but in England, because it's such a small country, everything is so much more compact. Not everyone has a car, in fact, only half my siblings and half my children can drive. Teenagers don't automatically learn to drive or expect a car while they are still at high school. We either walk places or use public transport. If I were at home feeling this uneasy and trapped, I could go for a walk and not be judged a "bag lady" or feel afraid of drive-by shootings.

As I contemplate what it will mean to me to have a car, I feel shame as I think about Ellen. She can't go anywhere when it all gets too much for her to handle.

"I can't hang around waiting in a line to get the tags," she says.

"Pardon?" Nothing she says makes any sense to me and I truly don't know what she means.

She looks at me and there it is again, "Duh."

"I said I can't hang around waiting in a line to get the tags."

I feel sick. I still don't know what she means but the look on her face and the tone of voice warns me not to say anything, and so I don't. Then something happens in the silence that's between us;

she seeks to bridge it, and I'm momentarily grateful.

"You know, it gets pretty crowded over there at Main Street. I guess we can give it a go and can always come back tomorrow or go somewhere else if it's busy."

I'm not sure what's just happened, so I say, "Okay," and try to work out what's going on as she drives. Is she trying to suss out just how far she can go with me? I mean, I'm an unknown quantity to her. It feels like she's playing games with me, to see how far she can go with me before I stand up for myself.

I've never been one to cope with confrontations and I'll do anything I can to avoid them, even play dead, which is what I'm doing now. I'm anxious and I feel like an expendable pawn in a game of chess. I don't recognise that my lack of boundaries feeds into her need to push and push until boundaries are placed around her. It's also too soon for me to know that when boundaries *are* placed around her, she'll turn with tiger ferocity to break through them. My withdrawal is the last thing she wants, for she can't enact this power-play if I'm not in the game, and so as I sit there in silence not knowing what to say, she engages with me again with her girlie giggle and pulls me back onto the chess board.

Her face breaks into that sickly smile, "It's Ozzy again. There's something weird going on here. I don't hear him forever and now every time I turn the radio on he's there. Too weird."

"Hum," I say, not knowing what's expected of me.

She turns into a derelict shopping precinct and pulls up. "Well, there are less people here than I thought there would be," she says, looking at the empty parking lot.

I have no idea where we are or what's happening, but I follow her as she waddles towards a building that reminds me a pawnshop. I truly have no idea what is going on, it's all so different to England, and not wanting to experience that scathing "Duh" again, I just follow her and watch and listen. It doesn't really help. She takes my bill of sale for the car, which doesn't look at all legal to me and tells the lady, who's holding a three-way conversation with someone in the back and trying to order her lunch on the phone, that she wants car tags. She raises her eyes to the heavens and shoots me a look, which is not lost on the clerk and yet again I'm embarrassed by her behaviour. She has to be the most passive-aggressive person I've ever met. The woman hands her a piece of paper and Greta walks away shouting over her shoulder, "I'll see you next door."

The clerk says, "Can I help you?" I say, "I hope so, Ma'am. I've never done this before and so I don't know what to do, can you help me?"

Not understanding me, she utters a puzzled, "Do what now?" Despite being unable to control her giggling at my British accent, she explains that before I can get my car tags, which turn out to be number plates, I have to pay my property tax, and it's her job to assess how much I owe. Oh! So that's what I'm doing. Why couldn't Greta tell me that? You know, just because someone doesn't know how to speak Russian it doesn't mean that they're stupid, it just means that they haven't learned it yet, and that's what's going on here. American culture is so vastly different to English culture that this is a steep learning curve for me. I'm not dumb just because I don't know about property tax or car tags, or because I'm confused by all the differences.

I thank her for being so patient and she smiles at me, barely able to constrain the giggle that seeps from her. "You're welcome," she says, as I walk away wondering what's next door.

I only have my bill of sale in my hand and nothing else, and everyone else in the building next door has a mound of papers in their hands. I sit next to Greta and she hands me a ticket with a number on it.

"Here, take this," she says, "then we won't be held up any more than we need to be."

People are filing in and all take a number from the little machine on the desk and I'm grateful that she had the presence of mind to take one for me. I say to her that I think she may have some of my papers that I'll need when I'm called up to the counter, for this is obviously where I'm to get my "tags," but she says, "No! I don't have your stuff."

I'm called up almost the same time as she is and we stand at the counter together, but separated by five feet.

"Bill of sale," the clerk snaps, "and your insurance documents."

I know that Greta has them because she took a wad of papers from me in the office next door so I have no choice but to go and confront her.

"I really think that you've got some of my papers. They need my insurance documents and I don't have them."

She knows as well as I do that neither of us has left anything in the car, so she's forced to look through her pile of papers.

"Well, I don't know how they got there," she says defiantly, handing me my documents.

I don't care enough to make a point and blow it off. I hand the insurance papers to the clerk and she tells me what I have to pay, and then she goes to the back and brings out a number plate: my tags. Why did it all have to be so much hard work? Why couldn't Greta just tell me what it was all about?

I write out the cheque and then Greta raises her voice and starts to make a fuss.

"Surely you can take a cheque. I mean, why can't you take a cheque? This is so embarrassing." She stands back from the counter, her frame huge and imposing. "Celia, is there any way that you can write a cheque for me or else I'll have to come down here again? It's five hundred and eighty dollars."

I gulp as I have very little in my account, so praying that there will be enough, I write her a cheque.

She thanks me and says that she'll give it back to me as soon as we get home. I tell her not to bother, as I owe her five hundred dollars for my rent, and she says "Fine."

She drives up the road sucking hard on a cigarette.

"You hungry?" she asks, and I wonder how I'm going to combat the feeling of guilt that's already creeping over me as I answer the call of my stomach whilst knowing that Ellen is lying in bed with nothing to eat, yet again. But I'm so grateful that I'm now legal to drive the car and to be free that I ignore my sense of doing what's right and seek to please her some more.

"Yes," I say.

She doesn't ask me what I'd like to eat this time but drives and pulls in to a ramshackle place, and I know that I'm about to indulge in a cultural experience. There's nobody in there—and if ever there is an indicator that a place is not up to scratch, it's an empty car park at lunch time in a country that seems to thrive on fast food and eating out.

I follow her inside, and compared to the feast at the all-you-can-eat Chinese restaurant, this is a famine. The food is lukewarm and there's very little choice. While Greta banters with the hostess, I sit and wonder about her insatiable desire to eat at all-you-can-eat restaurants, no matter how bad it is.

Greta seems in her element while I visit the counter and don't know what to choose. It's nasty and Greta seems affronted, and I wonder why. She's not the proprietor; she didn't cook it. It really *is* bad and I'm not surprised that we're the only ones in there. My mouth is burnt despite the food being cold and I can't help being cynical, thinking that the spices are extra hot to disguise the taste of "Local lost cat, answers to the name of Pussy—reward waiting."

We finally leave and go straight home and I'm so relieved that she's not going to go on a shopping spree again. I feel guilty when we walk through the door, my stomach full, even though it was awful, and there's Ellen sitting in her wheelchair with her bottle of water.

"Have you been out to eat?" she asks Greta.

"What of it?" she says, walking straight past her mother.

"I'm hungry," Ellen says, and my stomach knots with even more guilt.

"Well, get it yourself," Greta shouts at her.

She walks back into the living room where I'm standing not knowing what to do or say, and she puts her hands on her hips and cocks her head to one side.

"You know, Celia, this is what I get all the time, 'I'm hungry,'" she mimics, and turns to Ellen and shouts, "It's not my fault that you broke your fucking leg. You know, if you hadn't been trying to get out of bed by yourself when you were told not to, then it wouldn't have happened. So if you can't get around as well as you used to, then whose fault is that? Not mine. It's your fault," and she storms off into the kitchen.

"Can I get you something to eat?" I ask Ellen gently.

"Yes, please," she says shakily.

Greta appears in the doorway with thunder on her face.

"Oh, no, you don't. You can damn well wait until I'm ready. Celia, don't do this. She could have got something for herself if she'd been bothered. She can reach the fridge."

I feel swatted, and I don't know what to do, so I say, "I don't mind, really. If it'll help you, let me make her something to eat."

I've obviously missed Greta's point though, because she turns on me and hisses "I *said* no. I'll do it, and she can wait."

I shrug in a hopeless gesture but feel suppressed rage boil inside me and I go to my room to calm down. I strain my ears to hear what she's saying to Ellen, who's trying to stand up for herself, but all I can hear is Greta's raised voice telling her to shut up.

It's quiet after a while and so I venture out of my room to see if Ellen's all right. She's parked in front of the television sucking on her water bottle with a sandwich laid next to her on the small marble table and Greta is downstairs.

"Are you all right?" I ask quietly.

She nods and says, "Why, yes. I'm just fine. I have a nice sandwich." As she smiles at me I wonder how anybody can be so mean to this sweet woman. I feel very ashamed that she is so delighted with a meagre sandwich after we've just been out having our all-you-can-eat. I feel disgusted that Greta has used her mother's money to finance her greed, yet has given her a measly sandwich with stale bread that's been there all week.

"Where is she?" I whisper, and she nods towards the dungeon door through the kitchen. "She says that she's got to move some things about."

I had told Greta that I would help her move the furniture and so I wonder why she's gone ahead, trying to move it on her own. I go to the top of the stairs and there she is, half way up the stairs with the heaviest table you could imagine perched on a step, supported by her bulk.

"Christ, Greta. I said I'd help you move the table up the stairs," I speak out.

"Well, you weren't here, were you?"

This is sick and so I say, "You could have called me. You'll hurt yourself."

She's puffed out but still manages a "huh" and tells me that she's moved heavier things than this on her own. "I mean, who's here to help me. I have to do everything on my own," she bleats.

"But you don't have to do it on your own," I say. "I'll help you. Just ask."

I bend down and reach out my hand towards the table, and as soon as my fingers touch the table she begins to shriek, "Careful, careful."

I take my hand away as if I've just been burnt. I'm shocked.

She takes a deep breath and says in an even tone, "Celia, when you did that I nearly fell down the stairs. Do you hear me? You nearly pushed me down the stairs."

I'm dumbfounded. This is crazy; I merely reached out to touch the table, nothing more, certainly not enough to elicit such a tirade of hysteria. My head's spinning as I try to think. I can't just leave her here with it jammed against her and the walls, with all the clutter spilling down each step, so I take a deep breath and say as evenly as I can, "Greta, how would you like me to help you?"

"Take that end and lift it carefully, and remember I'm on the end of it."

I try and ignore her sarcasm and lift it in the way she wants me to. Why didn't she dismantle the thing? It would have been so much easier? As it wedges against the top of the staircase and the legs refuse to go around the doorway, she says, "Damn. I was hoping that I wouldn't have to take it apart. Okay, let's take it back downstairs again."

What? And have to go through this all over again? I don't think so. From where I'm standing it seems that if we just lift it a little to the side it'll slide round the corner, and I say so.

"No, it won't go," she insists.

"How about just trying it?" I heave the thing to the side as I say it before she can object and it slips round a treat.

I don't gloat and she's very tight-lipped as we lift it over towards the pine corner-seat unit.

"It looks great," I say, trying to jolly her along but she dampens my efforts by saying, "I knew it, nothing's ever easy, is it? I shall have to raise the seating unit up by two inches."

I'm getting the feeling that Greta's life-glass is half empty and not half full, as she seems to thrive on things being difficult, and if they're not difficult then by the time she's finished with them, they will be. The height of the seat is standard, just as the height of the table is also standard. I sit on the bench with my knees under the table and say, "It feels okay to me."

She shoots me a scathing look that says *and what would you know?* And says very slowly: "No! It needs to be built up two inches so that my mother can be at the right height."

I resist the urge to suggest measuring Ellen's wheelchair to see if it's the same height as the bench seat and then I think: *Why would she want to raise the seat by two inches since Ellen's going to be sitting in her wheelchair when she's up at the table? She won't be sitting on the bench*, but I say nothing because it's just not worth it.

I put the kettle on and ask her if she'd like a cup of English tea with milk, and she pulls a face. I laugh and tell her how good it is, and she says that she knows about English tea and, "No thank you very much."

She starts to clear up like a thing possessed and I'm wondering why. It seems incongruent to me, for if ever there was a time to clear up it would be before a stranger comes to your home for the first time, but as that didn't happen, I'm wondering why the urgency now.

"You have to go downstairs in a minute and stay out of sight because the financial advisor is coming and he doesn't know you're here."

So now it makes sense. Ellen's estate, most of which originated from her late husband, who apparently left her a lot of money, is being managed by a financial advisor. Since Ellen is now no longer able to get to the bank and manage her own affairs, Greta is in control of the cheque book and credit cards, and how she uses them is subject to the financial advisor's scrutiny. It's all beginning to make sense. She doesn't want him thinking that she does nothing all day except feed off her mother, hence the frantic scrambling to make the place seem tidier and as if she's doing a good job.

She ushers me down into the dungeon and I don't mind for it means that I can speak to Dessy without her hovering over me, and for once she doesn't get irate and huffy when I ask her to log on for me by putting in her password.

I'm down here for over two hours and use the opportunity to try and set up my own new user name so that I won't have to keep asking her to log me in under her name and endure her exasperation and the sense of having been manipulated as she chastises me. It all goes well and I'm pleased with myself until the system sends a new password to her email account, which of course is private, so I can't get it. I can't send it to mine either on my laptop as it's upstairs and that would mean showing myself to Chester, the financial advisor, and besides that, something is wrong with my laptop and I can't send emails from it anymore. At that time my computer literacy was so poor that it didn't occur to me I could access my email account on any other computer other than my own! Feeling snookered, I give up.

She comes down the stairs and the visit has obviously gone well.

"You can come up now," she says pleasantly. "Did you have a good visit with Dessy?"

"Yes, it was great, thanks."

"I'm just going to run to the store. D'you want to come?"

She's in a good mood and so I say yes, thinking that maybe the last five days have just been a hiccup and that this is the real her shining through. My naiveté amazes me as I keep trying to engage with her, even when my common sense tells me otherwise. I've always been the same; I'll keep going until the "nth," until it's so blatantly obvious to me that my efforts are completely wasted—but anyone in their right mind would have given up long before now.

She is very talkative. "Well, that told him. That'll keep him off my back for a bit longer."

"So it went well, then?" I say.

"Yes, he was impressed. He said that he didn't know how I managed, and I told him, 'You see all those cans over there with blue stickers, that's how we manage. I buy tins of food at knock down prices.' Yes, he was impressed, all right."

I listen, thinking that in the five days since I arrived I've only seen her use two of the tins that she'd bought at knock down prices. The rest of the time she'd been out for lunch while poor Ellen ate leftovers from the fridge. I wonder if the financial advisor had noticed just how much money Greta had spent through the weeks and if he knew not a cent of it had been spent on Ellen.

"You seem more relaxed," I say, encouraging her to talk.

"Well, at least now that'll keep that evil bitch off my back."

"Who's that?" There seems to be a lot of evil people in this woman's life.

"My mother's husband's sister. She's an evil bitch, as bad as her brother, always snooping and checking up. She's always talking to Chester, trying to spy. Still, at least he'll tell her I'm doing well, so that'll shut her up for a while."

I keep her talking, for although she's being mean about people, she's actually in a better frame of mind and that makes her easier to be around.

"I blame that creep of a husband for my mother's ill health," she says. "He was the most evil person I've ever met, he hated me and I hated him. He was a paraplegic, couldn't move from the neck down and my mother waited on him hand and foot to such an extent that her own health was shot to pieces. It's his fault that she's as bad as she is now, and yet I'm the one that's left to pick up the pieces. It was the best day of my life the day he died."

I say very little and let her ramble.

"She chose him over me, can you believe that? I think that's why I hate her. You should put your kids first."

"Do you see your birth father at all?"

She glances at me sideways and says sarcastically, "Hey, *Dr.* Banting, I know what you're up to. I don't want to talk about it."

"I'm sorry, I was just making conversation." I sit quietly until she yells out and turns the radio up again.

"There *is* something weird going on, that's Ozzy again. I love this music," and she turns it up even louder and starts bouncing in her seat as she drives home and sings along. She has a pretty voice and I tell her so, but she blows me off as she pulls up in the drive. I ask her if I might take my car for a drive around the block, even with a lawn-mover for a companion.

She snaps at me, "The battery's probably flat and I haven't got time to deal with all that now," and she leaves me standing on the steps as she marches into the house. So even though the car is now mine and I'm legal to drive it, I'm still thwarted and manipulated. But I say nothing and follow her into the house, where Ellen is delighted to see me.

I'm starting to love Ellen more and more, for her face holds a childlike wonder. Greta scathingly calls her Miss Pollyanna, as she sees the good in all things, but I think that it's just that Ellen's life-glass is half full as opposed to Greta's glass, which is half empty.

I chat with her for a while and say how the financial advisor had praised Greta's ability to shop around for bargains.

"You know it," she drawls. "She's always been one to spot a bargain. I don't know how she does it."

I keep quiet because I know how she does it. She spends all the time she should be spending taking care of Ellen, or even finding a job to help put money into the home, searching row upon row of shopping aisles for things that neither of them will ever use. I wonder just how much more impressed Chester would be with Ellen's finances if Greta only bought what they needed or used.

I try really hard to put my psychologist's hat on and look further, beyond the obvious pathology I see in Greta, and try to understand why she's the way she is towards her mother. It's hard, though, because her behaviours are so abusive and I feel such a sense of outrage at the injustice of it that it clouds some of my judgement. However, I recognise the hoarding as a scarcity issue, one that reflects a lack of sustenance or nourishment, not for the body—Greta takes plenty of that—but for the soul, and it's obvious that she is completely starved of love. Hoarding food is a psychological symptom of inner emptiness; it has very little to do with finding bargains or having enough food to be able to stay alive. Most of the food in their house will never be used and will be thrown away as it's well and truly past its sell-by date.

Greta was really irritated with me yesterday when I bought a drum of porridge oats, saying that she had loads at home. I didn't want to point out that the open pack was eighteen months past its sell-by date and had cobwebs over it.

The hoarding fulfils several psychological functions. It's initially related to scarcity, of inner emptiness, but the fact that it's food she's hoarding is more poignant and symbolic of needing nourishment: to be full and never empty. It says still more—this hoarding provides structure in her life, for she has imposed upon herself a life of drudgery and has set her life up to receive very few positive strokes (praise and appreciation). As her self-imposed exile from living in the real world and finding true intimacy with other people prevents her from receiving the strokes she needs to be emotionally healthy, shopping for bargains gives her a few strokes and validation.

I open a can of weak American beer and stand propped against the sink watching Greta make dinner, the first since I arrived, and I'm bemused by the cultural differences. I cook everyday at home and it's very rare that Dessy and I would go out for dinner, except maybe for a treat or to celebrate an occasion. Perhaps we English aren't as wealthy as Americans or maybe we were raised to accept that making dinner each evening is just something that has to be done. I remember back in 1990 when I first arrived in the States, being totally shocked to learn that people ate breakfast out rather than make their own. I couldn't believe it.

Greta seems to be in her element, and I remember that she emailed me once saying that she loved to cook. I cringe as I watch though, for she piles masses of brown sugar on top of canned sweet potatoes and then huge knobs of butter. I figured that she hasn't been smitten by Dr. Atkins. As I watch her, I think about her size and how it fits into her pathology. Being big is an easy way to keep others at bay, especially those who might want sex. It's a way of avoiding intimacy, and so the hoarding is not just a simple pathology, it's one that is multi-faceted and complicated. It's dishonest though, for all the time that Greta can appear to be so long suffering, always having to look for bargains to make ends meet, she can also say to Ellen and her financial advisor and relatives 'What would you do without me?" She can also play the psychological games of "Look how hard I tried for you," and "If it weren't for you," when really her self-imposed drudgery serves the purpose of allowing her to avoid being close to people and living her life. It also gives her a *legitimate* reason for failing to find a job to support herself, and validates the right she feels to spend her mother's money.

I wonder all over again as Greta shows me how to make a tin of sliced beans into a casserole, why she didn't marry the guy in England. I also wonder why she had failed to respond to me when I emailed her to ask her if she'd like me to try and retrieve the things she shipped over to England. She's told me several times since I arrived that she'd lost everything by sending her stuff to him and he refused to ship it back. Her failure to respond to my offer to approach her ex-fiancé gives me a flicker of insight that tells me it is part of the same "poor me" self-defeating behaviour I've witnessed since I arrived.

I don't challenge her though; what would be the point? Yet as I say "ahuh" and "really" while she chatters on, there's something going on inside of me that doesn't feel very healthy. I feel as if my integrity is gradually whittling away, and hence my ability to remain psychologically "safe" is being compromised. Leaving her grandiose sweeping statements unchallenged prevents me from interacting in an honest way with her, and interacting honestly has been my goal since embarking upon my psychotherapy training.

Standing here leaning against the sink being aware that I'm compromising my honesty makes me feel very bad. I'm treading on eggshells, and I've travelled this way before and swore that I'd never do it again, yet here I am doing it so readily. My supervisor, a wonderfully clever chartered clinical psychologist who I have so much respect for, once landed a profound question in my lap: "Celia, why do you allow yourself to be around borderline personality disordered people, and why do you stick around and allow them to hurt you?"

I worked the answer out. It's the answer to every therapeutic question and every therapeutic journey, "Because I want a different outcome," and once I allowed the answer to seep into the fabric of my being, I swore that I'd never travel this road again, yet here I am again.

It's dark outside, and with the smell of cooking wafting around the kitchen it feels more homely and comforting than I've experienced so far this week. I figure that if I can just be a little more tolerant and try to help her more, then everything will be all right. The beer is obviously getting to me and I'm in denial.

Greta orders me to go and tell Ellen that dinner is ready, and I'm instantly an obedient lapdog.

"Greta's made us a nice dinner," I gush.

"Oh, my, that *is* good," Ellen says, and struggles to turn her wheelchair around in her room so that she can wheel herself through the doorway.

I'm reminded of the premature babies I used to take care of, how they used more energy in the act of feeding than the calorific value the milk gave them, and so it seems the same with Ellen. She's so emaciated and has so little energy that to try and manoeuvre the bumps on the floor that separate each room will rob her of what little energy she has, so I go behind her and give her wheelchair a little shove. She looks so grateful, but then I'm caught.

"Celia, don't!" Greta bellows at me. "She has to do it herself."

I swallow hard and try not to cry. I was just beginning to feel a little closer to Greta while she cooked and I tried to make sense of her pathology with a compassionate eye, but now I feel crushed, with my supervisor's words echoing in my ears again: "Why do you allow people to hurt you?" I'm afraid though, because if I stand up for myself and for Ellen, will Greta hurt Ellen more by being even harder on her?

I don't find the courage to stand up for Ellen or to say that the bumps in the doorways stop her from being able to move the wheelchair easily, and that it exhausts her to try and scale them. I'm not even sure why they're there, but I assume they hide the edges of the flooring from one room to the next. I stand watching helplessly as Ellen struggles, and all of a sudden I've lost my appetite.

She takes forever to get over the bump in the kitchen doorway and then has to do a three-point-turn to get the wheelchair positioned correctly at the table. The whole time Greta is standing there with her hands on her hips watching her mother struggle, with the food on the table going cold. Once Ellen is situated, she ties a cloth around her neck and barks at her, "Eat!"

I feel tearful and suddenly it all seems too much for me. Greta's behaviour isn't that of someone who really wants to share her home with a lodger, and tearfully I ask them both if they really want me here.

Ellen looks panic stricken and says "yes" really quickly. Greta looks quizzical and says, "Why do you ask?"

So I pluck up the courage I don't feel and say, "Well, you just seem so angry at times and I wonder if it's because you don't really want me here." I know I'm not being really truthful but this is the best I can manage right now. It would have been more honest to say "I feel really uncomfortable when you speak so harshly to me. Is there a reason why you seem to be so angry with me?" But I can't find the courage to say that. I'm homesick and miss Dessy so badly, and everything seems so different and alien to me. I just sit at the table and cry.

Something is different in her countenance and I'm not sure what it is. Could it be that I've just challenged her in front of Ellen and she's feeling exposed, or is it something else?

Her face twists and that sickly smile is there again, with the girlie little voice. "I've had a lot on my mind just lately. You silly goose, of course we want you here. Eat up, have some more sweet potatoes."

I struggle to keep the sticky mess down as she piles more onto my plate, and I listen to her talking about what she's going to do to the house. She lifts the cushion up that she bought at Keith's shop, holding it against the wall.

I say, "It's a perfect match. You must have a good eye for colour. Mine's hopeless," and it is.

I'm feeling very sick, not only because my emotions are running riot and causing havoc inside me, but because the sweet potatoes really are disgusting. I can barely keep them down, but I know that I have to eat them, for to leave anything on my plate, Greta would see as a personal slight on her goodwill. Something nasty and silent settles over me and I know what it is. It is the beginnings of co-dependence, because if I leave the food Greta has made, not only will I suffer but Ellen will also. There's a heaviness weighing upon me. I swore that I'd never allow myself to slip into a co-dependent relationship again, yet here I am sliding out of control down into a pit where I'm being controlled because of my concern for another person.

"Oh, no you don't," Greta threatens, watching Ellen continually, and as the anxiety in my stomach knots even tighter, I wonder if Greta can be enjoying any of the food with her attention so focused on what her mother is doing.

I feel such compassion for Ellen, as she's aware that her spoon is missing her mouth and that food is dropping into her lap. I try to start a conversation so she will be less focused upon Greta's eagle eye, waiting to pounce. It does no good, though, for Greta talks over me and says, "No, no, no, no, no! You'll eat your meat first and have the sweet potatoes last. She really loves sweet things, you know," she adds scathingly, looking at me and trying to justify her bullying.

We sit there until Ellen has shaken her way through the whole plate, even though the food has been stone cold for ages. It sits heavily in my stomach along with a weighty dollop of anxiety and self-loathing.

Suddenly lights shine into the kitchen and Greta stands up.

"That's Keith, come to set up the network. He's late."

I'm so pleased to see him, and as she shows him downstairs, I scoot Ellen over the bump in the doorway and position her in front of the television, and she whispers, "Thank you." I squeeze her hand. She's so skinny that I don't want her to use all the calories she's just consumed trying to jerk her wheelchair over the bump in the floor for half an hour.

I go halfway down the stairs and ask Keith if he'd like a drink. He says "no," but he's the kind of guy that would say "no" out of politeness, and so I try to play with him, which dispels the tension hanging in the air.

"It's okay, I won't force you to have a cup of English tea with milk in it."

He looks confused and says that he'd like a soda.

Greta comes upstairs and smiles sweetly at me, saying, "The poor guy hasn't even been home yet; I'm going to make him up a tray."

"That'll be nice," I say, and I mean it. He's a good guy.

She's downstairs with him all evening and the fact that he's down there so long doesn't bode well, as he'd said that it would only take a little time to fix up. I stay out of the way and sit with Ellen, watching "Queer eye for the straight guy," and try not to react to Greta's periodic histrionic whispered updates.

After three hours Ellen is obviously ready to go to bed and so am I, for I have to get up early tomorrow to start orientating at work, but we both know that Greta is busy downstairs and I can't lift Ellen because my back won't allow me to. She says, "It's all right, I'll wheel myself into the bedroom and I'll knock three times on the floor; that's our signal, and then she'll come."

Maybe so, I thought, but in what mood, and at what cost?

Greta stomps up the stairs and I stay focused upon the television as best I can, while she hisses under her breath, "He's fucking well messed it up. Honestly, I could have done it better myself," and she walks past me and into Ellen's room. "You ready?" I hear her say and know that Ellen's landing into bed will not be a gentle one.

I'm ashamed of my selfish thoughts, *Oh, no, what else can happen to stop me from being in touch with Dessy and my family?* I've been praying that as soon as Keith sets up the network in the house, I would be free to talk to who I wanted when I wanted, yet listening to Greta cussing out poor long-suffering Keith, I fear that it's not going to happen. My heart sinks as I realise that I'm still at the mercy of her need to dominate and control everyone around her.

# 5

I STAY FOCUSED ON THE TELEVISION while Greta dumps her mother in bed and then comes back out into the lounge.

"What happened?" I venture. "Is he still here?" I never heard him leave and I'm concerned that he'll hear her foul mouth if he's still downstairs.

"No, he's gone. He obviously isn't as clever as he thinks he is," she says spitefully. "If he's fucked up my computer, he can pay for it."

I was going to ask her if she wants a beer but she walks away and disappears through the door in the kitchen down to the dungeon. I take myself to bed, disappointed that the network isn't fixed but as I try to console myself I think, what's the worst that could happen? I'll have to still use her computer to talk to Dessy and see his smiley face, even though I'll still have to suffer her crushing exasperation each time I ask her to log on for me. Of course she could help me set up a new user ID at this end and then I could be able to log on without troubling her, but why do I think that that would be just too easy?

I go to bed but sleep eludes me, because my mind is abuzz with feelings of abandonment and panic. I have astute antenna for things that are wrong and know instantly without words when something is amiss. It's uncanny and at times scary, but it's there and I can't ignore it.

I don't remember falling asleep but I awake to the sound of my alarm clock—despite my earplugs blocking out the world beyond my dreams of home—and to a sense of something unspeakable creeping ever nearer.

I have a short time to get ready and decide that I'm not really up for battling with the bath aid in the upstairs bathroom, and so I once again decide to creep downstairs past the silenced dog in the cage, to have a shower in the master bathroom. The dog is so quiet, and although I don't like dogs, I feel an affinity with this one, and whisper "Good dog," as I creep by. I open the door to the back of the house where the bathroom is on one side of a corridor, and Greta's bedroom is at the other end.

It's pitch black and I'm quiet, deathly quiet, as I feel my way to the bathroom, searching with my hands for the light switch. There are none in any of the normal places that English homes would have one, so I open the bathroom door in the pitch black and hear the imprisoned cat mew.

I'm anxious because by opening the door the cat could run out and then I'll be in trouble, so I open the door an inch or two and thrash my hand about trying to find the light switch. It's nowhere. I decide to step inside the bathroom, and as there are no windows, it really is inky black. I feel a sense of trepidation, as I know there are likely to be little mounds of kitty poop lying in the path from the door to the bath, like a field of landmines. Now that I'm in the bathroom I feel committed and try to tell myself that this isn't so weird; after all, this is how blind people have to take a shower every day. So I edge my way towards the bath praying with every tiny step that my toes won't encounter something soft and warm.

My toe is stubbed against the bath as I reach it before I'm ready to. I try to hang my two towels on the rail so that they don't fall on the floor where the kitty poop may be waiting. The thought of retrieving my towel from the floor and rubbing myself dry, smearing kitty poop all over me, is almost more than I can stand, so I try and wedge both my towels on the rail, but it's tight. There's a crash and both towels fall to the floor along with the rail.

I feel like an inept cat burglar being unable to sneak back out to shower upstairs, so I decide to just get on with it. I shower in the pitch-black and retrieve both towels from the floor, praying that they hold no surprises for me. They don't, and I'm lucky. I edge my way back out through the bathroom, hopefully along the same safe path to the door. The dimness outside the bathroom as I open the door is blinding.

I shut the door really quietly praying that Greta is still asleep, and yet anxious that when she walks into the bathroom the first thing she'll see will be the towel rail on the floor. I feel consumed with guilt but I try and contain it by telling myself that it's not broken, it just popped off its bracket, and had the light been on I could easily have fixed it myself. I also tell myself that if someone in my home had such an accident, I would be mortified should they feel anxious, and I would do anything I could to relieve their stress. "It will be all right. Don't fret, Celia," I tell myself.

I walk to work and suffer the same jeers by rednecks in huge trucks on their way to work. It's a little irritating: having a car and parting with the money for the insurance but not being able to use it because it *may* have a flat battery and a lawn mower seems to have taken root. I try to remain charitable, though, and tell myself that Greta is stressed, and if it takes her a few days to move the lawn mower, so be it, for in the greater order of things what does it matter? Still, I'm glad that it isn't raining.

As soon as I get in from orientating I go straight to the dungeon doorway and call down.

"Is it all right if I log on and speak to Dessy?" I ask, and she sighs and walks towards the computer.

"You know, that Keith is nowhere near as clever as he thinks he is," she says, as she stands over the computer and nods at me to sit down. "I managed to fix it in just two hours."

I'm impressed, and genuinely am in awe of anyone who can navigate their way around all this technology. It's a mystery to me and I deal with as little as I need to in order to get by. I want to give her a warm fuzzy, so I say "You're so clever," but she blanks me and starts to dictate what I need to do to get logged on. At the right time she puts in her password and instantly I can see that Dessy's online waiting to speak to me. I'm so relieved to know that he's there and my heart swells with love for him.

Greta's talking in my ear again as she always does when Dessy tries to talk to me, and I'm trying to speak to her at the same time, but it's hard.

She stands over me and has her hands on her hips and barks at me. "Someone's been sending an email to my account," her tone, an accusation, and I know that she knows I tried to set up a new account at this end so that Dessy doesn't have to at his end. I feel caught with my hand in the cookie jar and instantly try and set my voice even and make light of it, trying not to show any fear, but fear and intimidation is what I feel.

"Oh, that was me," I say too quickly. "I was trying to open a new account."

"You do *not* send things to my account," she spits, but as I sit there a small voice cries inside of me: *This is ridiculous*! I dare to speak up for myself.

"I was trying to be helpful so that I don't have to keep bothering you, and I couldn't come upstairs and ask you yesterday because Chester was here."

I know I've just deliberately manipulated her and her eyes narrow. I think that move was "checkmate" in our crazy game of emotional chess. She turns on her heels and her parting shot is: "Well, don't you be sending things to my account, that's all!"

She breathes a huge exasperated sigh and stomps off into the depths of the dungeon towards her room.

I talk to Dessy but can't say anything about how I really feel because I know she's listening, so I say one thing and write another. But knowing that Greta has been a technical supporter for this computer programme I cannot be sure that anything I write will be beyond her scrutiny. So I'm careful and don't really say what I feel or give any indication that things feel so wrong here that I'm scared for me, and even more scared for Ellen. Dessy is astute and writes, "I guess you can't say," with the laborious touch of a two-fingered typist. I love him and the closeness between us that needs so few words.

She's suddenly there again, behind me, and I say goodbye to Dessy, praying that she hasn't been spying over my shoulder and seen what he's written. I make my voice light.

"I must apologise for knocking the towel rail off its bracket this morning," I say, and she says, "Yes, I saw that," not "That's okay," or "What happened?"

I try to explain.

"I couldn't find the light switch and so I had to have a shower in the dark." I talk too fast. "It's quite an experience showering in the pitch black," I say, hoping that she will smile, but she doesn't, and orders me to follow her to the bathroom.

"The light switch is there," she says scathingly, pointing to a bare switch that has no cover around it and that's screwed to the inside of part of a dry wall. "I don't know how you could have missed it," she says with sarcasm dripping from her, and all I can say is, "No, I don't know how I could have missed it either."

"Can it be fixed?" I ask, knowing that it can but trying to appease her, and to let her know that I really do feel bad about knocking the towel rail down.

She walks away from me, saying, "Yes, when I can find time to look for the screw," and she silences me with her back and a huge long sigh as she says "*Another* thing for me to do."

I feel distraught and irritated. The screw doesn't need to be "looked for," it's on the floor, and I can easily mend the towel rail. But I feel more distraught than anything because her comments make me feel small and guilty. I feel like one of those poor dogs that Seligman electrocuted in his pursuit of researching "behaviour shaping" through "negative reinforcement and learned helplessness" back in the 1960s before ethics prevented such experiments. It seems that no matter what I do and which way I turn, she zaps me with her electric tongue, and I feel incredibly helpless and frightened.

I walk back upstairs and go into my bedroom, my heart heavy, and not even the sight of "Little Cely" lying on the bed helps me feel safe as I allow Greta's miasma to seep through me like murky, bone-chilling smog. I sit for ages on the bed turning away from the doll; I miss Dessy so badly even though I've just spoken to him and seen his beautiful smiling face. Then I lay down for what seems an inordinate amount of time and I hear Greta creep past my door to speak in hushed tones to Ellen, ordering her to stand up and come out for dinner.

She taps on my door and calls out, "We're about to eat, do you want to join us?"

I don't want to but I think that refusing will make things worse so I open the door and wear a brittle smile, and say, "Yes, that would be nice," even though I've lost my appetite. Ellen smiles her sweet smile and I can see she's grateful that I'm going to be joining them. After Greta has walked on ahead, I walk behind Ellen's wheelchair and chat to her about my day, keeping my voice light. As we reach the kitchen Greta is fiddling about at the stove and I know I can't help Ellen by giving her wheelchair a little nudge over the bump in the floor, so I step ahead of her and urge her on.

"Come on, Miss Ellie, you can do it," I say, playing with her. I hate myself for resorting to this rather than sticking up for her against Greta's bullying but I hope that it'll give her some extra fortitude. More importantly, I hope it'll show Greta a better way of interacting with her mother. I've only been here five days and yet I haven't heard her say one single thing nice to Ellen at all.

Ellen shakes her way over the bump and I'm triumphant for her. "Good job," I say, wanting to clap her on the back but I restrain, for she really is too frail. She smiles at me and giggles, and I love her sense of fun.

The table has only been there one day and already it's covered with junk. Why is that? It drives me crazy how some people, when they see a space can't leave it be, but have to fill it with something. As I think about the psychological issue of scarcity and emptiness I recognise the same drive—to fill emptiness or space. I shove as much junk into the corner of the table so that I can put my plate in front of me without it encroaching on Ellen's space.

"Those are chocolates," Ellen says, nodding to a long gold box of chocolates. "I love chocolate," she smiles as if we've just shared a secret.

"Me too, but it doesn't like me," I say, tapping my tummy, and Greta walks towards us with a dish, and says, "Food is made to be eaten; eat up, you can have chocolate later." I feel as if I'm three years old.

I know I have to eat everything on my plate or I'll be in trouble, so I do and it's horrible. I watch Ellen drop so much of it down her front and I try hard to stifle the thought that the floor is where this muck should be. But as I look at Ellen's bony frame and her hungry sunken cheeks, I feel a damp black cloud hover and slowly envelop me. I start to cry.

The change in Greta is profound and scary, as if another person suddenly joined us for dinner.

"Oh, dear, what's the matter?" she asks gently, but with fear in her eyes.

I blurt out that I've felt homesick today as it's my daughter's birthday, and although I gave her a present early before I left England, something she really wanted, today is the day that twenty-nine years ago in Adelaide, South Australia, I gave birth to her and didn't know if she was going to live. I don't tell them that, for to voice it will increase my crying to sobbing, and I can't afford to go there. I need to get a grip of myself or I'll never make it, and will want to get on the next plane home to the comfort of Dessy and the close proximity of my five beautiful grown-up children.

Ellen looks anguished and says, "Ah, the love of a mother," and Greta seems bigger if anything, and she says, "Oh, you silly goose, come here and have a hug."

I allow her to pat me on the back and somewhere deep inside me I recognise that my crying and vulnerability hooks something in her, which feels superficial to me and dangerous—co-dependent dangerous. I feel so annihilated after five days of uncertainty and persecution, not to mention witnessing oppression and abuse towards a frail and beautiful lady, that any kindness from her feels tainted and dirty. But I say nothing, grateful that for a few moments the dynamics in this house have changed.

Ellen takes forever to eat and she can't be enjoying it, but she has a look on her face that I can't quite make out: it's either gratefulness or fear, and I can't tell which. Judging by her frailty she must be starving hungry, and over the next three weeks I was to learn just how starved she actually was. There's fear in her face also, fear of being browbeaten to finish every morsel, as Greta lets us know how much time she's spent to make our dinner. I feel sickened. All she did was serve leftovers onto a plate and heat it up in the microwave, yet she adopts the persona of a co-dependent wife determined on making her husband pay for her domestic enslavement.

Ellen ploughs her way through it and although I long to go to my room, I daren't leave her there at the mercy of her daughter, for in some unspoken pact I know that my presence ensures Ellen's safety and a modicum of comfort. It's a huge burden to bear, particularly when my guilt for not doing the right thing is so overwhelming to me. I should kick this woman out of her mother's house and find some compassionate person to be a live-in carer.

Greta opens the gold box of chocolates and thrusts it in front of my face. "Here, have some," she says.

"Oh, no, thank you," I say, whilst she stuffs another into her mouth, and poor, shaking Ellen tries desperately to shovel the food from her plate into her mouth with grim determination; her eyes oscillate from Greta's bulging cheeks to the array of chocolate truffles stuffed under my ungrateful nose.

"Eat more," Greta orders, with her nostrils flaring as Ellen shakes most of her spoonful down her front, and I'm overwhelmed by Ellen's defeat and Greta's domination. I have no idea what to say or do as she continues to stuff the chocolates into her mouth in front of Ellen, who is desperate for one. It's cruel. I encourage

Ellen to finish so that she can have one but what I really want to do is yell at Greta, "*For heaven's sake give her a chocolate, let her enjoy herself and get some extra calories. How can you be so cruel as to plough your way through them when you know she wants one?*"

Finally Ellen's plate is cleared and she chooses a chocolate as if it's the last treasure on earth. The transformation on her face as it bursts on her tongue is exquisite to watch and I'm grateful that Greta, tired of bullying, has gone downstairs.

Ellen smacks her lips with the joyous wonder of a child opening a Christmas stocking. After listening for sounds on the stairs and watching for shadows in the doorway, I offer her the box again and tell her to have another. She's in heaven and begs that I should have one too, but I decline knowing that if I start I'll plough my way through the entire box, and so I abstain.

We visit—a strange phrase, so totally American. In England, "to visit" means to take oneself into the geographical proximity of another, but in America it merely means to chat with someone else; and so we "visit." Ellen is a delight and talks to me of her family and of her history. I'm fascinated when Americans talk about being a child in 1950's America, and share their precious memories of their grandparents, whose lives were harder than anyone's I know—particularly the lives of the grandparents of my black friends whose history is embedded in slavery.

We laugh, and although it takes her some time to get her words out, everything she says is a jewel and worth waiting for, and I love her more each minute. I figure that we're making too much noise, for Greta comes stomping up the stairs with a face like thunder.

"You're supposed to be in your bedroom by now," she snaps at Ellen.

She tries to stand up for herself and says, "Well, we were just visiting," but she starts to back away from the table. Dread starts gnawing at me when Greta stands over her mother as she embarks upon her laborious journey over the bump in the kitchen doorway, along the hall and over the bump in her bedroom doorway, before trying to do a three-point turn in a postage stamp sized space.

I sit at the table feeling sick and listen as Greta nags her to hurry up, saying loudly, "Don't you know that I haven't slept for days? Come on, move!"

I can't get past them as they're in the hallway and so I sit at the table and listen, feeling distraught, willing my thoughts away from this house. Once I hear sounds of Greta trying to move Ellen from the wheelchair to the bed, I go to my room and say goodnight as I shut my door.

"Hey," Greta calls. "Take this and charge it up." She hands me the phone.

"Oh, okay, goodnight, thanks for dinner, I appreciate it."

"Goodnight."

I listen to her warn Ellen, hissing, "Now, don't call me until to-morrow," and I hear her walk past my door.

My room seems very empty and I sit on the edge of the bed, my back towards "Little Cely," and deliberately so. I don't know how to take care of me right this minute. I long to hear my daughter's voice, to break free of all this and touch base with my child, so I call her.

It rings and rings; I look at the clock and I guess she's in bed. My heart is heavy and as the answer machine speaks to me in monotones, I launch into wishing her a happy birthday and then do as I normally do, sing happy birthday. I get as far as "Happy birthday to you, happy birthday to you, happy..." and my throat is so constricted that I can't go on, and I'm dismayed with myself. I've never been unable to sing happy birthday to my kids and I feel as if I've failed her, so I say I'm sorry, and that I love her to bits. When

I put the phone down, the distance between us is vast; she's asleep and happy with her man, and I sit on the edge of my bed, far from home, my back to my metaphoric soul.

I take my clothes off and get into bed, stuff my earplugs in hoping that they'll dampen the echoes of everything I've heard this past five days. I pull the sheet over my head, not because I'm cold—it's 80 degrees outside—but because I want it all to go away and to be alone with my breathing.

I cry myself to sleep.

I get up early and leave the house as soon as I've showered downstairs, and in the light, now that I know where the light switch is. The cat is in the corner and there are no unwanted warm packages on the floor so I dare to breathe in.

I walk to work again and wave at all the Redneck Billies that drive past honking their horns at me. Whatever!

It's a relief to see the people at work, to be around normality. I don't recognise it but gradually throughout the day their presence brings me back to a place where my stomach settles, and I laugh at the things we hear flying around the unit. "I can't be quiet; I've got talking in my mouth." Where else would I hear such things at work? My colleagues and patients are precious to me, and I giggle and feel warmth flow through me again.

After work a few of us go to a local bar and have a couple of beers and I feel the tension seep away; this is more like it. We laugh and banter, and after an hour my dear friend Vicki calls up some other friends and arranges for us to meet up for dinner. An hour later we're tucking into Greek food and as usual I'm amazed at how different the service is here in America. It's something Americans do really well, unlike us Brits. I ask for an extra bowl of black olives and they don't charge me extra. When the husbands go home, we girls wander around a clothing store and I tell myself that when it gets really cold I'm going to get a pair of thick fleecy pyjamas to keep me warm as I haven't got Dessy here to do it for me. My friend takes me home and it's nearly 2300. I've been out for hours. Today is the first day since I flew in six days ago that I feel a sense of normality and stability. Vicki waits outside the house while I fumble for my key, and I love her for it.

Moths flutter around the outside light aiming for my mouth as I quietly say goodnight and thanks. The door chimes throughout the house when I open it (and I'm to learn that whenever an external door is opened everyone knows about it) so my attempt at a silent entrance is in vain. I poke my head around Ellen's door and she's awake.

"Well, hello Celeste, did you have a good day?"

I suddenly feel really guilty, for I've been out having fun and she's had none. I've eaten and I can't be sure that she has, and I've had my soul lifted with laughter and caring, and I'm pretty sure that she hasn't.

"Is it okay to chat for a while or are you too tired?" I ask, with a grin upon my face that I can't squash.

"Oh, sure, it's good to hear about your day."

I dump my bag outside my door and lean against her chest of drawers as she looks at me with an excited air of expectancy. She says, "How was your day? What did you do?"

"Oh, Ellen, it was fun. You know this has to be the only job I've ever had where the things I hear are completely wacky. I heard things like "He's got his finger up his nose," and "I can't be quiet, I've got talking in my mouth." Now where else would you hear that? Not in some office that's for sure."

She giggles and we talk quietly so that Greta won't come upstairs and pour cold water on our girlie chats, which become a nightly ritual and one that both of us love. I tell her about my friends who I've known for seven years and who I love very much. I tell her about the food they cook at the hospital and how much I'm looking forward to Halloween because I'm going to dress up as a witch. Talking to her, I don't think I've ever seen that much wonderment in my children's faces when I wove exciting stories to occupy them on a rainy day, but for Ellen it is a lifeline, an extension to her world.

"Did you get up today?" I ask, "Did anyone come and call on you today?"

"No, she was busy downstairs." She falls silent and my enthusiasm melts away.

"What, you didn't have any carers come in today to help you wash and get you up?"

"No. Greta argued with them on the phone and so they never came. She says that a new one is going to come on Monday."

I have a sinking feeling in my stomach and a warning bell clanging loudly in my head. While I worked as a social worker in England, it was an accepted fact that those who abused and wished to avoid being detected by the authorities moved from one area to another repeatedly so that they slipped through the net. Those who deliberately argued with the services also did so in order to avoid being scrutinised. I ignore my instinct and my warning bells and say, "Well, that's good. Let's hope she's nice."

We talk some more and she tells me about her husband, the love of her life. She met him whilst living at an apartment complex and he was on a sun bed around the pool, accompanied by a full-time nurse, as he was a paraplegic. I try to hold my expression steady, listening to her describe her feelings about a man that she adored but that Greta had despised—the two images don't go together. At this point I'm faced with two choices, either the pathology belongs to Ellen or else it's Greta's. Ellen's face is full of love as she describes her man, and in her profound simplicity she drops, "Greta didn't get along with him," and I know that to be an understatement.

I was later to learn that Ellen's husband was so intimated and afraid of Greta that he slept with a loaded gun beside his bed. I'm glad I didn't know that then, but looking back perhaps it would have been safer for me to know it. Perhaps if we knew these things up front about the people we converse with on the Internet it would be a very good thing. But if I'd known about Greta I'd never have met Ellen, and knowing her has been a gift, something precious and rare.

"My kids didn't get along with my ex-husband; sometimes kids can feel jealous and pushed out," I say.

"Well," she gathers her thoughts, "he tried to get along with her but she couldn't get along with him. She really hated him."

I don't tell her that Greta's already made vile comments about him to me, so I nod my head and say, "Hmm."

"She hates me because she thinks that I chose him over her." I sip at a can of soda wondering how to respond. I know how devastating step-parent/child relationships can be and what it feels like to be in the middle of them. "But it wasn't like that. She's always been important to me, always, but I had a life as well," she says. I feel that she's looking for absolution.

"You know, it's okay to have a life of your own," I say, "for the relationship between mother and child is very different to the relationship between a man and a woman."

She looks grateful, but I didn't say it just to appease her, it's the truth. Yet as I think about my own life choices in the warmth of the still night air, I wince a little thinking that my children may still have remnants of anger left towards me for some of my life decisions.

I ask her if I can get her anything and she glances at her water bottle, which is almost empty and asks apologetically if I can refill it. I can do better than that. I'll get her a fresh cold one from the fridge, not some lukewarm top-up from the tap. She's too grateful and humbles me all over again as I pull the sheet over her that has slid to the ground, and squeeze her hand, saying, "Sleep tight, I'll see you in the morning."

I open my door and sit on my bed thinking that if I hadn't been there for our girlie chat, Ellen would have laid there all night without water and with no covers over her. I feel uneasy, really uneasy, but hide under my covers and focus upon the frivolity and freedom that the evening with my friends has given me.

# 6

The heat wakes me and my stirring frightens a cockroach as I sit up. I'm grossed out watching it dart across the wall and through the crack above the door, and I try to tell myself that it was a cricket. I gather up my wash things, open the door and poke my head into Ellen's room.

"Well, good morning," she says, with a smile that stays in my heart. She's leaning precariously towards the edge of the bed as she grapples with her reacher, trying to corral her water bottle that's fallen on the floor. It's too heavy and too awkward for her to grasp between the pincers, so I pick it up for her and notice her catheter bag full to the brim and backing up the tube.

"Why, thank you," she smiles. "I've been trying to get that all night." I feel bad that I didn't hear her as I had my earplugs in and hear nothing beyond my own breathing. I feel angry with Greta though, for her words echo around my head. "There's nowhere in this house that I can't hear my mother." As her room is directly beneath Ellen's, she would have heard the tapping of her reacher against the wooden floor all night but still didn't come to help her.

"Here, let me get you some fresh water," I say, "You must be thirsty."

"Yes, I am."

I take it back to her and then shower in the downstairs bathroom. As I come back up the stairs, Greta's in the kitchen and she makes me jump. I say "Hi," as brightly as I can and attempt to make small talk but she's obviously not interested, and grunts at me. There's something about the way she slams pots and pans about that begs me to speak to her, to ask what's the matter, and I figure that she wants my attention but doesn't know how to ask for it, so I give it anyway.

"You seem tired. Did you not sleep very well?"

"I never sleep very well."

"Can the doctor prescribe you anything?" I ask, but she looks at me scathingly.

"I can't afford to go to the doctor," she says slowly. "We don't have medical insurance, remember?"

I feel reprimanded again for my meagre efforts at trying to make her feel better or to give her the attention she so obviously needs. What can I say other than "Oh," but then I feel inadequate and stupid to have even asked the question. It feels like a set up to me so I attempt to stop myself from sliding down a slippery slope by recognising the 'moves' of a psychological game, and I'm grateful for my five years training in psychotherapy. I would feel more vulnerable than I already do without the little bag of tricks my training has given me in order to avoid psychological pitfalls such as this. But despite having had so much clinical training, my problem is that I don't recognise the games early enough before I get hooked in to them, but I'm working on it.

She's told me on several occasions that she's desperate to get back to work and I've no reason not to believe her, so I say quite innocently, "I know it must be hard right now, but now that I'm here you can go back to work, and then you'll have medical insurance and it'll be easier to get help from your doctor."

I think it seems a reasonable thing to say but the look on her face tells me that it isn't. I walk away dejected and go to my room and as I get dressed I can hear the clipped edge of Greta's voice in Ellen's room and the bathroom. She's emptied her catheter bag, and thank heavens for that, as there's no easier way to invite a urinary tract infection than back flow of urine from an overfilled catheter bag. I wonder if it's a requirement in America for home carers to learn basic nursing skills to prevent infection or bedsores, but it's not something I feel that I can ask her, although I know I should.

I make a bowl of porridge and ask Greta if I should make her mother some.

"No, the carer should be in shortly and it's her job to make her food."

"Oh, okay." She seems to want to talk now.

"We've had some terrible carers. We had one that just sat and talked to her and didn't do anything. Well, I got rid of her. Then there was another who was so stupid that if I didn't answer the door, she wouldn't come around to the back of the house and try the downstairs door, even though I'd told her to. I got rid of her, too. Oh, and then there was the woman who was quite happy to take my mother's money to be a companion but when I asked her to do some chores as well, she refused, so I got rid of her as well. I mean, if I've got to do the chores then *I* may as well have the money and not give it to someone else."

I don't quite know what to say. Is she describing the America care system in general or is this her experience of it, or is something else going on that she's missing by only viewing it from her point of view? I don't know.

"It seems that no matter who comes to help, they're no help, and I end up having to do it all on my own."

"That must be really hard," I say. I know that I'm appeasing her but I don't know what else to do, for I feel torn between recognising that Greta is obviously not coping with the situation, and between feeling a gut instinct that she is not telling me everything. I sense that she's manipulating the situation, possibly subconsciously (I hope) to fulfil her own pathological need. I daren't even think about her manipulating the situation consciously for that would be the hallmark of a very sick individual, and I'm too scared to even contemplate that.

"It's hard. Don't you realise that I gave up a life in England with my fiancé to come back and care for her? She doesn't think about me at all, only herself. She's always put herself first."

I'm starting to feel uncomfortable because I'm sure that Ellen can hear her and I don't want her to think that I'm a party to this, for I'm not.

"Tell me what happened," I say, trying to divert her from badmouthing her mother and trying to pull me across some invisible "taking sides" line that bolsters her and alienates me from Ellen.

"Well, I met him on the Internet and we talked for a while, you know, and then he asked me to come and stay for a while. I went and met his family, and showed them how to cook southern style." She laughs and I wonder how she'd manage cooking a roast with Yorkshire Pudding to die for like my Dessy can. "You English don't know how to make fried chicken and corn bread, nor biscuits and gravy."

"No, we probably don't," I say, *and you don't know how to use a knife and fork*, I think, glancing at the paper plates and plastic forks sticking out of the over filled trashcan.

"I think they really liked me," she says, smiling at her memories.

"How long were you there?"

"A month."

"Then what happened?"

"Well, I was only there for a month but when I got back we decided to marry, and I shipped everything I owned to England, said goodbye to my mother and went to start a new life."

"So then what happened?"

"She got sick so I had to come back," she said bitterly.

"What was that you emailed me about being stuck at Heathrow Airport?" I'm confused. I thought she'd come back because English immigration wouldn't let her in the country, that's what she'd emailed me. Which is it? Is it that immigration wouldn't let her in the country or is it that her mother called her back because she needed her to care for her?

"Oh, yes. What a fiasco! When I got to the airport the immigration people wouldn't let me in because I had a one-way ticket. They wanted to send me straight back on the next flight but I stood my ground and told them that I'd had a hell of a flight, so they let me sleep in a hotel overnight before sending me back."

"What did your fiancé say?" I ask, finding it hard to imagine myself being in the same situation and her answer doesn't help.

"Nothing, they couldn't get hold of him."

I frown. "But surely they'd have phoned him and he would have vouched for you. Surely he was there to meet you?" I question.

She shrugs, "That's the immigration system for you," she says. "Anyway, somewhere in England all my stuff is floating around. That pisses me off."

"Wouldn't he send it back?" I know I've already asked her this and she was evasive then as she is now.

"I emailed him once but never heard back from him. I guess he was pissed with me."

(She let slip a few weeks later that while going through the English immigration, she was dressed as a Muslin, and when she told me that, I could see why the immigration officials questioned her story, especially arriving with a one-way ticket and not being able to contact her boyfriend. Why would she do that, unless she wanted to sabotage herself?)

I don't bother asking her why she didn't invite her boyfriend to come to America as I've already asked her and don't really want to be landed with the same answer that has no exit point. What do you say to someone who will live with her fiancé in England but not in the US because he doesn't have a degree? To labour the point would take us to a self-righteous ballpark, a game I'm not prepared to play.

"Somewhere in England there is a two hundred dollar ball gown that I bought especially. Oh, it was beautiful. I loved that dress."

She shrugs and I wonder just where she thought she was going to wear it in England, surely not to the pubs that are on every corner.

My porridge is ready and as she's in the mood to talk, I sit at the table and let her carry on.

"So after the stupid immigration people wouldn't let me into England, I came back and that's when *she* decides to get sick and can't do without me, so I've been here ever since."

My mind is reeling with the tattered ends that don't tie up. I want to understand how all this feels to her because to understand may help me to interact with her in a better way. Although she is not someone who I would have gone out of my way to have as a friend, I hate to see her hurting and want to help her if I can. I hate to see anyone hurting and I've always had a need to help people cope with their pain, hence my profession, but to do so I need to understand their point of view, to step into their shoes and walk their walk. So I stifle my feelings and listen.

"Do you know what it's like being with her day in and day out? She's such a bitch." I know I wince. "She's constantly banging on the floor for me (I refrain from saying that I haven't noticed it since I've gotten here), and it gets old after a while."

I stuff my mouth with porridge covered with a takeaway sachet of breakfast syrup—I'd rather have English brown sugar.

"Then she deliberately makes things worse for herself by falling and breaking her leg."

I interrupt her as I wipe syrup from my chin in an attempt to halt the badmouthing I suspect is heading my way. "How *did* she break her leg?"

As this all begins to feel more and more pathological, I slip my invisible psychologist's hat on and analyse what she's saying and what I'm doing. I'm trying to manipulate her into staying in her Adult ego state, so I ask her concrete, matter-of-fact questions that invite her to shift into her "here and now" ability to think and be rational, but I'm yet to realise that her pathology is such that she cannot be objective, coherent or straight.

She raises her eyes to the heavens and says, "She was trying to move from the bed to her wheelchair and slipped. I told her that she shouldn't do that, but she wouldn't listen. No, she just carried on."

I listen to the anger in her voice while an image of Ellen trying to get into her chair because she's thirsty, hungry and has been left for hours upon end flashes into my head.

"She expects me to feel sorry for her, but I tell her, 'It's your fault that you're like this, not mine. *I* didn't try and move when I was told not to,' and all she does is whine and think I'm being mean to her."

I'm feeling nauseous because I'm sure Ellen can hear us, so I change the subject.

"Would it be possible for you to accompany me in the car around the block so that you can talk me through any little idiosyncrasies it has?"

"The lawn mower is still in there and I've already told you that I'm not putting it in my car, and with everything I have to do around here I haven't got time to take it back to the store," she states, as though the conversation is closed.

"That's okay, I don't mind having it as a passenger, if you don't mind being a backseat driver," I laugh, but she blanks me. Oh dear.

She stands up and makes for the dungeon. "I don't have time for that right now," she says, and I know I'm dismissed. I suppress the sigh that longs to escape from me and as I scrub my porridge bowl in the sink, I feel manipulated and think: *Well, rats! I'll just walk to work and wave to all the Redneck Billies as they drive past me. Whatever!*

My fists are clenched as I leave the house, and I mutter to myself as I walk past my car with its lawnmower passenger and start walking up the hill. It's a short day at work, I only have to attend a meeting, and as Vicki drives me home I tell her about how controlled I feel.

She puts it in a nutshell, "Tell her to give you your car or give you your cheques back." She has a way of saying things how they are.

She drops me off and tells me to be strong. I wave and go inside. Ellen is sitting in front of the television with a new bouffant hairstyle.

"You look nice," I say.

"Why, thank you. My carer came and did it for me."

"Is she nice?" I ask.

"Very. I hope she stays."

I tell her about my day. She's so thirsty for contact with the world outside her four walls. I tell her about my new colleague, Alex. "He's young, about my daughter's age, I guess, but has an old head on his shoulders, and is the kindest and the funniest man I've met in a long time. He has me in stitches and he's so sweet to the kids."

"Well, really," she says and Greta comes through the dungeon door and walks in on us, with a look that says: *What's this then, why aren't I included?*

"Come and join us," I say, smiling at her. "I'm just telling Ellen about my new friend."

"No, thank you," she says, and walks into my room without asking, then comes out with the phone in her hand and laughs at me. "You're supposed to put the phone face down to charge it, not face up. Duh!"

I think I'm supposed to feel humiliated but I laugh, saying how stupid I can be at times, and as her sails no longer have any wind in them, she pushes the phone into Ellen's lap and heads off back down into the dungeon. A fleeting image of the troll hiding under the bridge in the Three Little Billy Goats Gruff story pops into my mind. She made her entrance, said something unpleasant and disappeared into the depths again.

Ellen looks uneasy. "Go on," she says.

"Well, Alex is an amazing young man," I tell her. "He's living with an elderly man who is very frail, who is probably not going to last very long and he takes care of him. Alex told me that he sleeps on the couch next to Ben so that if he should wake during the night and need anything, he can get it for him. He said that Ben often coughs in the night and he couldn't bear to think of him being all alone if he was sleeping in the other room. Alex is an amazing human being."

"Well, yes he is," Ellen said wistfully. "That must be nice."

As usual she is profound with her punctuations and we fall silent, both pondering on what Alex's kindness means. He's not related to this man and yet shows him more love than any son could, but what is left unsaid between us is the comparison between Greta's lack of love or care towards her mother when she's Ellen's only child. The contrast is profound, especially when I think of the look in Alex's face when he talks of the old man, compared to the way Greta looks at her mother. Alex's eyes are full of love and Greta's eyes are cold, and as we sit there lost in our own thoughts, we're silent and there's a bad taste in my mouth.

She breaks the silence. "I looked after my husband," she says. "He was sick for a long time."

"That must have been hard," I say.

"Well, it was, but I didn't mind. He was a good man. Greta hated him." She falls silent and stares at the television, and says no more.

I go to my room to lie down for a while and think. It's been almost a week since I left England and so much has happened. My life in England seems a world away. Again I'm desperate to have Dessy in my ear and to see his smiling face, so I walk to the dungeon doorway and go a few steps down. I can see Greta's back as she sits at the computer in the far corner of the room and I know that she's chatting with her Internet "friends" so I won't be able to speak to Dessy. The loss feels intolerable, so I go back to Ellen and ask her if I can make a phone call.

"Oh, yes. Here…" as she grapples for the phone which has slid down between her thigh and the wheelchair, and she hands it to me shaking uncontrollably.

I go to my room and sit on the edge of my bed and call our house phone but an automatic voice says that I should try again at another time. I feel bereft and alone and try several times but don't get through. I go back to Ellen and hand her the phone and her eyes sparkle.

"Did you have a good visit?"

"No, I couldn't get through."

"Oh, no, that must be hard."

"Yes, it is. I miss him. He's a sweet guy; you'll meet him at Christmas. You'll love him."

"Well, I'm sure I will," she says, and I know she will.

I go back to my room and lie there staring at the fan going round and round and, try as I might, I feel miserable. I need to speak to my man. I can't wait until Greta sorts out the computer network in the house as she promised before I got here and has promised daily since I arrived. It will be a luxury to have a computer terminal in my room so that I can log on whenever I want to speak to Dessy and my children. I reproach myself and think: *Be patient, give it time, you've only been here six days. Come on! Rome wasn't built in a day.*

It gets dark outside and I'm feeling sleepy so I pull my sheet over my head and read my book until I drop off.

It's Saturday and I've been here a week. It's a strange feeling, for it seems ages but I know it isn't. I laze in my bed and read before dropping off again; it's a gift and one that I accept willingly. When I finally surface I poke my head around Ellen's door and she greets me as she always does with a: "Well, good morning, Celeste."

Her catheter bag is bursting and she has no water so I get her some and see to my shame that it's twelve thirty. I put the kettle on and pee over the mountain of kitty litter down the toilet. As I come out of the bathroom door I bump into Greta who grunts at me, and she goes into Ellen's room and begins to empty the catheter bag. I try not to slip down a path that leads to the conclusion that she only comes upstairs when she hears me get up and go into her mother's room. It's a thought that won't be chased away though, and I wonder how long Ellen would be left if I wasn't here and prompting Greta to attend to her mother by my presence.

I smile at her and say a forced, cheery "Good morning," and she barely speaks, other than to say, "It's my day off today; don't be calling me, right!"

I shut my door and think: *Day off, don't be calling me. What does that mean?* I wait until she's gone downstairs and I go into Ellen's room.

"Are you all right?" I ask. "Is someone going to come and get you dressed today, and get you up?"

"No, today's Saturday, no one comes, and I'm not allowed to ask Greta as she says it's her day off."

"What?"

I look at her lying awkwardly in the bed with a two-inch square of cake on a plate next to her and the water bottle I just brought her. Her pills are in a plastic contraption that has the days of the week on it and there are so many that they can barely fit in. I don't know what to do. I want to ask her if she wants to get up, to help her get dressed and come out into the living room, but she's so stiff and frail, and my back isn't up to shifting her from the bed to the wheelchair. I'm scared that I'll drop her to the floor and that would be disastrous as she's recovering from a broken leg. The one thing that was drummed into me during my nurse training was to be safe; safety is paramount, and for me to move her when I don't feel confident would not be right. I stand there looking at her, feeling helpless.

She rescues me. "I'm all right," she says.

"What can I get you?" I ask, wringing my hands.

"I'm fine. She got me a piece of cake."

"I'm going to work on my laptop for a while, and then I might watch some Lifetime movies," I tell her, not knowing what else to say, and having nowhere else to go without my car.

"Tell me what channel they're on and I'll watch them, too," she judders.

"Okay, will do, then we can watch them sort of together."

I flick through the TV channels and read the guide for her and she says a succession of "that sounds good" to several of the movies I read out. I change her water again and think how odd it is that she hasn't had a hot drink, and how alien it would be for me not to have a hot cup of tea periodically throughout the day. I ask her if she'd like one, but she says that coffee is her passion, and when I ask her if she'd like one she says that she better not. Greta appears in the hall like a malevolent phantom with something written on her face that tells me I've just been caught.

"My mother would love to drink coffee all day long if I let her, but that's not going to happen."

I go back into my room, the movies forgotten, with adrenaline flying through my body and I pound my keyboard even though most of my attention is lingering in Ellen's room and on Greta's muttering.

I get a lot done, such is my anger, and when I look at the clock I realise that I've been in my room for ages, so I check on Ellen. She's sleeping, and is still in bed in her nightclothes. There are crumbs on her plate, her tiny square of cake eaten but her water bottle is still full. Her catheter bag is dark yellow and nearly empty, and I know that she needs to drink more, let alone eat more.

She stirs as I withdraw my head from her doorway.

"I'm sorry, babe, I didn't mean to wake you," I say feeling terrible.

"Oh, you didn't, I wasn't asleep, just resting. It's boring really."

"Can I get you anything?" I ask.

"No, I've still got some water."

"Ellen, you need to drink more. Drink that up and I'll get you something else."

She reaches her hand out to grasp the bottle but knocks it to the floor and I swear I see fear flash across her face.

"It's okay, I'll get it," I say, bending down and retrieving it from where it has rolled under the bed. Is this why she hasn't drunk any, because she might knock it to the floor? Is the sight of a full bottle near at hand better than one lost under the bed? Why is Greta not here to help her and why is she so scared to ask for her help? I go out to the kitchen to fetch her some ice-cold water, and almost instantly Greta appears at the dungeon doorway.

"It's my day off today so we always have pizza. Do you want some?"

I refuse because I'm about to eat eggs and am conscious of my weight, although I'd far rather eat pizza. She walks away and I think I've offended her by refusing. I sit in my chair and put the television on, and do what I hate Dessy doing, and that's flicking through the channels. I find a movie full of drama, heartache, failed parenting and painful resolution—just the thing—and I go into Ellen's room and tell her to turn the channel over. She's full of expectancy and shakes her way to the controller and looks at me beseechingly.

"Shall *I*?" I ask, but as I take it from her and snap the channel onto the screen, Greta is right behind me telling me off again.

"She can do it herself, Celia. This is what she does. She'll have you running all over the place if you let her. She needs to do it herself."

I don't know what to do, so I say, "Do you want to have a beer with me and watch a slushy movie?"

She looks at me as if I'm simple and says, "It's my day off, Celia."

"Oh, okay," I say to her back as she heads towards the dungeon.

I glance at Ellen who looks scared, and I try to pacify the ripples of anxiety that spread through her room like the rings reaching ever outwards from a stone in a pond.

The pizza man arrives and Greta slaps a piece onto a paper plate and takes it to Ellen, saying, "Don't be calling me anymore."

How can she eat it? It's huge, floppy with its filling sliding everywhere and she's lying down in bed. I wait until Greta goes back downstairs and creep quietly into Ellen's room and slice the pizza into fingers for her to manage.

"Thank you," she whispers.

# 7

I WAKE UP IN A SWEAT TRYING to shake off a bad dream where Ellen is hanging off her bed with a piece of pizza snuffing out her breathing. I don't know where I am for a moment; the rhythm of the ceiling fan lulls me into thinking that I'm still asleep, or am I still on the plane? I orientate myself but still feel uneasy and I tell myself not to be so silly and I get up to make a cup of tea.

I poke my head into Ellen's room, which is fast becoming a ritual, and she smiles and dispels the image of having been suffocated by a triple meat and anchovy dinner. I change her water, it's the least I can do. I can't make a drink for myself and not for her, but I feel guilty that all she's having is cold water. A paper plate with the remains of the pizza sits on her bedside table and the dream springs into my mind again. In the cold light of day I think about what it could mean as I take it and dump it in the trash.

I've always been fascinated by the human brain and symbolism, and as I dunk my tea bag in my cup I search my head for clues. Often the brain will take words used in everyday language and replay them as images that have a surreal dimension to them. I'm left with the conclusion that it is my concern for Ellen eating lying down when her cough reflex is compromised that led me to dream about pizza killing her. It's not that the pizza was a bizarre facemask from Alien intent on killing its host, it's my concern that she may choke on pizza whilst being left in bed lying flat on her back that triggered my nightmare.

I put milk in my tea and wander back to her room.

"Are you going to get up today?" I ask.

"Oh, I hope so," she shakes.

"I hope so, too."

"What do you hope?" Greta asks from behind me. The image of the spider scaling a huge web springs into my mind again and she makes me jump.

"I hope it's going to cool down a bit," I say. "How are you?"

"Fine."

That's my cue to leave so I gather up my wash things and go downstairs to shower while she's upstairs. When I come back up the stairs feeling hot but clean, she's framed in the doorway.

Suddenly I'm desperate to get out of the house and so I say, "Is it okay if you come with me to show me how the car works? I don't care about the lawn mower."

She steps back to let me pass, and sighs. "Well, I've got a thousand and one things to do today and I haven't slept at all."

My stomach sinks and I don't know how to stop the irritation from flashing onto my face, so I walk past her and go to my room. Ten minutes later she taps on my door.

"We'll try the car now, okay?"

"Okay," I say, dropping everything and following her through the kitchen and out into the carport.

She pushes the keys into my hands and goes to her own car, which is blocking mine in, and backs it out. I sit in the car, it's filthy but I don't care—I can clean it. I turn the key but nothing happens.

My excitement is dashed in a heartbeat. There's nothing, just nothing, no cough or splutter, just nothing, and I can see her sitting in her car out on the road waiting. I feel stupid and childlike as I get out of the car and walk towards her with nothing on my tongue other than "I can't start it," not "It won't start."

She switches off her engine and sighs more loudly than ever, and snaps "Give me the keys," which I do, and half of me prays that it starts because I'm desperate to be free to go somewhere other than these four walls, but the other part of me is willing it not to start so she won't belittle me for being the incompetent fool she thinks I am.

The car does nothing and I don't know if I'm glad or plunged further into despair.

"Well, it worked the other day," she snapped. "I haven't got time for this now."

"Can't someone help with jump leads?" I ask, thinking that every time I've needed help because of a flat battery there's always someone who will lend a hand. She looks at me like I'm nothing, her head lolled to one side, with her hands in the air.

"Celia, how many times do I have to tell you that there is *no one* here to help me; I have to do everything myself."

Warning bells are beginning to sound off over and above the ringing of my own frustration. There is always someone to help. I know that many times I've asked complete strangers to help me start my car with jump leads. I don't believe that there's no one.

I remember once being so distressed in London the day my daughter left the country that I sat in my car for over two hours ignorant to the fact that my lights were still on. When I came round, the battery was completely dead so I had to bang on a resident's door to ask if he would use his jump leads to help me get my car going. Trust me to knock on the door of immigrants who couldn't speak a word of English, but even with our gesticulating we managed to understand each other and they came out to help.

My irritation eclipses my ability to be fully aware of the pathology of it all and I go back into the house defeated and angry.

The phone is still being charged (the right way) in my room and so I pick it up and call a friend that I rarely see because she's so busy with her young family.

"I'll be over in a minute," she says.

I get changed as quickly as I can, say goodbye to Ellen and wait down the road at the intersection. I'm fuming and so angry that I can't think straight. I feel used and controlled, yet all the time I question myself, asking whether I'm just having a bad reaction to this huge life change that's happening to me. I know I'm missing my man, and am not even daring to think of my children, but am I overreacting through anxiety at being in a stranger's home and wanting to do the right thing?

My friend pulls up and she gives me a big hug. Her baby in the back of her car has grown so much that he looks like a different child, and the sight of him brings me back down to earth. I coo at him and start to feel like my old self, for I really adore babies. We go to her house and I listen to how her life has been during the past year, and gradually normality seeps through me again. I feel more grounded and my anger has subsided.

She drives me home four hours later and I feel fortified as she gives me a pep talk about standing up for myself, echoing Vicki's sentiments about the car: either it's available or it isn't. She swings into our road and instantly I know something's changed. My car has been moved to the second driveway and my brain does a quick appraisal. I recognise that she had to push the car out of its parked space under the carport in order to be able to attach the jump leads from her car and she must also have taken the car for a long drive and taken back the lawn mower.

My friend and I look at each other and I say, "I'm free, I can't believe it."

We hug each other and I go inside. By the time I've opened my bedroom door Greta is standing behind me.

"The car is fine," she says, sweetly. "The battery had just run down."

My face softens and I look at her and wonder what's going on behind her eyes. There's a part of her that seems to want to please, yet it is fleeting, or is it only my ever-optimistic imagination? As soon as I think I've seen it, it's gone and there's an edge to her voice and her hand is on her hip.

I'm truly grateful and say so, and also marvel at her grim determination when she tells me yet again that there is no one here to help her, which I choose not to challenge, and that she did it all herself. The edge in her voice is multifaceted, there are echoes that praise her own stalwartness, that scorn my need for a man to do "men's work," and an ominous, "now you can pay in kind and be obligated to me and excuse my behaviour." There's also a deeply hidden "please need me" cry from somewhere. I'm so grateful that I'll agree to anything and put up with anything so I smile at her and say, "Thank you, I really appreciate it."

Ellen is sitting in her wheelchair parked in front of the television in her bedroom and she twists her head to greet me.

"I've just been to see my friends," I tell her and her eyes light up. She seems so starved of any life outside this house that anything I say opens up her world, and realising this I decide to make a point of telling her everything I can about my everyday life. It's noise to me but a lifeline to her.

"I met my friends years ago and helped to get them together," I say with some pride. "It seems rather odd to see them now, thirteen years later and with three beautiful children. I still remember her when we went to Memphis for the blues festival down Beale Street. We were walking along when suddenly I couldn't see her anywhere and I was in a bit of a panic, I can tell you, 'cause it was really crowded and it would have been easy to get lost, but then I heard her voice."

Ellen's eyes widened. "Where was she?"

"You'll never believe it," I grin at her.

"Where?"

"Up a tree."

"No!"

"Yes, she was up a tree, grinning at us like a Cheshire cat. That all seems so long ago; she was just a skinny kid. She's turned into a wonderful mother."

I hear Greta behind me and then she walks off. I get the feeling that she doesn't want to be around us yet doesn't want to miss anything either.

"Are you going to come out and sit with me?" I ask Ellen, and I lean backwards to peer around her bedroom door to make sure that Greta isn't in view, and quickly swing the wheelchair around and over the bump in the doorway. It will take Ellen forever to turn around in her tiny bedroom and then scale the bump on the floor; and as she wheels herself out into the living room we glance at each other like partners in crime.

I go ahead of her and switch the television on and Greta stands in the doorway, stating that she's got work to do and is going downstairs. As Ellen parks in the space next to the small marble table Greta states, "You can earn yourself $50 if you'll come and help clean up the den downstairs."

It's as if time stands still and I don't really know what to do or say as she stands there with her hands on her hip, a demand on her lips. I'm exhausted and have been all week, no doubt I'm still jetlagged, and I'm probably suffering from actually having let go of a year's worth of reckless commitments, for I feel like I've come to a grinding halt, physically and mentally. I don't relish the idea of cleaning all that filth, I will do it, but not right this minute. It's been like that for months, why now? Why right at this moment is there urgency in her voice to get me downstairs? I feel wretched by saying no. I hate saying no to people but I'm so washed out that I stick to my guns even though I feel like a heel.

Something doesn't feel quite right though. Why didn't she tidy the den before I came? Why would she ask for my help right this minute when Ellen and I were about to share an evening to which she's been invited but has refused to be a part of, and what is she doing promising to give her mother's money to me to do something that she should have done herself and I'd do for nothing?

"I'll help you for nothing tomorrow, but right now I'm just too tired," I say, as she walks away, obviously angry.

Two hours later Dessy filters into my mind and I'm desperate to speak to him but that means going to ask Greta if I can log on to the computer downstairs. I creep down five stairs and peer into the dungeon, driven by desperation, but I'm thwarted by the sight of her wearing headphones and sitting in front of the computer. Her back is a wall, a "don't you dare bother me" wall, so I creep back up the stairs and resign myself to not speaking to Dessy today. It feels awful.

I can't tell if Ellen is oblivious to what's going on or if she is desperate to hide it by making conversation and engaging me.

"Do you have pictures of your family?" she asks, and I retrieve my photographs from my bedroom that were taken at my beloved brother's wedding, three months ago. I point out who's who in the line of family members, and I'm reminded that my mother is the only person missing and yet is the kingpin in this dynasty before me. I drift to a place where my brothers and sister form four pieces of a jigsaw whose edges are as tight as can be and make a picture that is unique and disturbing.

I'm nudged from my musings by Greta, who's left the computer downstairs to see what we're doing.

"You're so lucky having brothers and sisters," she says, and I try to agree but she cuts me off. "There's only me. Perhaps if I had brothers and sisters I wouldn't be stuck here like this."

I want to tell her that although it presents an idyllic picture, having siblings isn't always easy and it comes with its own brand of agony, but it's not her intention to meet me in conversation but to use the arena to bewail her lot and discredit her mother. I feel sad. She still has her mother here, mine's in her grave, in hallowed ground, I know, but cold and snatched from us. My only comfort in the chilly notion of my mother being dead and buried is that she lies on top of her husband, and knowing what was between them and how often she cried, I feel a warped sense of satisfaction knowing that she rides triumphant on top of him. I don't feel like sharing all this with Greta though, for I can tell that she's not interested in exploring what it feels like to be a daughter, granddaughter, mother and a grandmother throughout the generations. What I feel is precious, even if it's painful, so I say nothing.

She hovers about in the kitchen.

I point out to Ellen my sons, my daughter and two granddaughters, who were at the wedding and in amongst the photos is one of my son, Luke, caught unawares, looking sullen. I say to Ellen, "That's Luke looking miserable."

Greta walks up behind me and says, "Let's have a look at the photo of Luke looking miserable."

Of course I show her. She grunts and walks off leaving me feeling angry. Why would she ignore all the good photos so that she could share in my family and get to know who they are, yet focus on a photo of Luke sitting outside a tent with a hangover, desperate for his morning cup of tea? Why?

Ellen seems enthralled as I point out who's who, and although I would have shared my precious family with Greta, I suddenly feel driven to keep them safe to my chest from an entity that can see no good in anything. I hate what I'm feeling but can't help it.

As she stands right behind me, I venture to ask her if I can log on and speak to Dessy, and hate the begging I hear in my voice: "I won't be long, I promise."

She shrugs and says, "If you want."

I follow her down the stairs and sit at her computer, feeling like a child that's just been given an unexpected treat, allowed to stay up after bedtime. I try to log on but need her password and I feel sick knowing that I'm going to have to ask her to help me yet again. She bangs around me, reaching across me, and I know that even though she's allowing me to come down here, I'm going to pay for it.

She sighs really loudly and punches in her password and I feel wretched but relieved as Dessy appears on the screen and I can hear him in my ear. She fades to the back of my mind, although her banging about gets louder. She's pulling boxes around the room, and when I laugh at something Dessy says she begins to grunt louder with the effort of moving things. She's very hard to ignore, especially when she resorts to pushing the Hoover around my feet, and I'm reminded of a comic farce, only this feels far from funny.

Suddenly I can't hear Dessy anymore, I can see him but I can't hear him, and I have no idea what to do. I feel knobbled, knowing that I'm going to have to ask Greta what to do, yet the act of asking means in psychological terms that I will reinforce her negative and attention-seeking behaviour. This is bad.

She stops the Hoover and says, "Do what now?" impatiently.

"I can't hear him anymore."

She plonks herself down on the sofa and starts telling me what to do, and all the time I can see Dessy's face frowning, when the top of his head isn't filling the screen as he tries to type with one finger. I feel awful. She barks orders at me. "Do this, do that, press this, delete that," and all the time Dessy's frowning and I miss his sweet smile.

I raise my hands in complete dismay. I have no idea what she's talking about and no idea what to do. I want to cry with frustration.

"It's something *he's* done," she says, and my stomach sinks further, knowing that Des is completely computer illiterate and may well have pressed any key at random when things weren't working, just to try them out.

She speaks fast and says words that mean nothing to me. Any other time I would have been in awe of her knowledge, but right now I'm eaten up with frustration and anxiety.

"He needs to…"

"He can't," I say. I'm not discounting my man, it's the truth, he just can't. I feel sick and my head is spinning.

"Look, Des can read, can't he?" she says, with scorn pouring from her, not waiting for me to answer. "Well, if he can read, he can fix it on his end."

I want to say that if it's hard for me to manage then it's virtually impossible for Des to do.

"Celia, don't baby him. He can do it."

I feel so angry; how dare she pass comment on something she knows nothing about. I feel like the seething inside me is hanging in the balance, as I want to agree to anything in order to be able to speak to him, yet my anger is so encompassing that I feel driven to silence her. The things that come from her mouth feel dirty, tainted with hatred and bitterness. My feelings are at the mercy of my adrenaline and I do what I always do when faced with extreme anger: I get tearful and try desperately to hold it back.

*Remember everything you know*, a small voice inside me says. *Come on, get into your Adult ego state and stay safe. You can cry later, now's not the time.*

I turn around in the chair and say, "Greta, Dessy cannot do it."

I feel bad saying it because I know that she's going to make judgements about my man, which will be unfounded.

"You know, I can't stand women who baby men," she says, pouring her stance on life over me, and I feel tainted. "That's why I choose to be alone. I couldn't put up with this kind of crap. Des can do this."

That's it! "Greta, Des has had two serious accidents in his life that have impacted upon his neurological networking system, and prevent the neuro-transmitters from working as efficiently as yours or mine."

I hate it that I'm having to tell her things about my man which aren't her business but she's so scathing that I have to explain why he's unlikely to be able to fix the computer.

Yes, he's had life altering accidents but he's able to function as well as the next man, although he needs a few minutes longer for his brain to get from A to B. I swore when I first met him that I would never finish his sentences for him, and although it's hard sometimes, being someone who always has something to say, I've kept to that promise. I have never known my husband to not find a lost word, and his endurance reminds me of the precious people that Oliver Sacks, a doctor who studies neurology and fascinating abnormalities of the brain, writes about. Although Dessy is as clever as the next man, there are things that he will find difficult, and fixing the computer is one of them.

As I attempt to keep my feelings in check and my voice even, I try really hard not to vent my anger that she should exert pressure on Dessy, or insinuate that he's stupid or that I'm molly-coddling him. My marriage and what's between us is our business and not hers, and even if we had a pathological co-dependant relationship it wouldn't be her business. The fact that we do not is still nothing to do with her.

I try to blind her with neural science and pray that she doesn't know as much as I do. She doesn't, she looks blank for a moment before her sugar sweetness creeps deftly across her face. She stands up and leans over me, pressing a few keys.

"There you go," she says sweetly, "all fixed."

I'm stunned, but so relieved to see Dessy's smiling face as we hear each other and blow kisses into the web cam once more that I fail to question how she could fix it so easily after giving me such a hard time and berating Dessy so badly saying that the problem was at his end. She turns the Hoover back on and as it whines loudly around me, I speak up but can't hear Dessy, so I steep myself in his kisses which are disjointed by the passing of cyber-time before giving up and going upstairs to be with Ellen.

An hour later, when it's almost time to go to bed, she puts a piece of cold pizza on the table and says to Ellen, "Come in here, I don't want to be cleaning up the mess you'll make if you eat in there."

Ellen leaves the film we're watching and tries a three-point turn to get herself facing in the right direction, and as I watch I feel wretched that I can't give her wheelchair a shove because Greta is watching her every move. She nags her to "hurry up, use those arms" in a tone that would have been more at home in boot camp.

She sits next to Ellen and although I've eaten with my friends and refuse a piece of stale pizza, I sit with them to give Ellen some moral support.

"You need your hair washed," Greta says unkindly, which Ellen doesn't take offence to, and I'm wondering if it's a cultural difference that I find offensive because she sounds so rude and persecutory. Yes, her hair may need washing but there are ways of saying it without making her feel ashamed. If she'd spoken to me that way, I know that I'd have felt shamed and humiliated. How about, "Would you like to borrow my strawberry kiwi shampoo? I'm sure you'd love it." Would that be so hard to do? My anxiety is such that I strive to make things better, so I start a conversation about how the carers manage to wash Ellen's hair, given that she is so frail and the bathroom so small. I fail to see the logistics of it all.

She starts to tell me but Greta shakes her head, saying, "She doesn't know. She's feeble minded. She hasn't got a clue what's going on now, let alone how the carer washes her hair."

I want to tell her to shut up because I want to listen to what Ellen has to say. I don't care if only a smidgen of what she says is coherent or the truth, I want to hear it. The irony is, though, that all of what Ellen says is coherent. Nonetheless, the conversation is over, with Ellen stifled and unheard, and I still don't know how the carer washes her hair.

There's heaviness in the air and I slip into a place where rescue is my name, and recount a time that tickled me when I had just finished my nurse training. Shutters appear in Ellen's eyes that silence Greta's words as she focuses upon me, urging me to break the tension hanging over the table and her cold piece of stale pizza.

"I was a nurse on an old people's ward and I came to love these people so much. One old lady was going to go out to dinner with her family and was really stressed because her hair wasn't done. My friend and I bent her over the bed backwards and poured water over her head to get rid of the shampoo. I planned to put some heated rollers in her hair once it had dried."

Greta has a strange look on her face, her lips tense and nostrils flaring but Ellen's eyes have a childlike rapture in them.

"Something happened. We had to rush an old lady from the dinner table to her bed as she'd just died with her fork on the way to her mouth, and so we didn't get time to fix this other lady's hair. I felt so bad because it was really important to her, and so because I didn't have enough time to sort it out before her family arrived, I enlisted their help as soon as they turned up. I plugged the heated rollers in and told them to come and tell me when they were hot enough, when the red spot had turned brown. Then I had to go and give a report to the next shift of nurses."

I'm giggling at the thought of it all and Ellen's face reflects her anticipation, but Greta turns towards the stack of cans with blue stickers on them and straightens the line, intent on letting me know that she's bored, yet not allowing herself to leave the table with the story unfinished. I'm reminded of a little Cub Scout with challenging behaviour in the care of my husband during Cub Scout meetings who was desperate to disrupt the group but whose attention had been captured, and who was caught between wanting to smash everything and listening intently.

"We were in report. Now, report in England is a very serious affair," I continue, trying not to laugh. "You don't interrupt it for anything. Well, I guess if the hospital is on fire you might, but then only if you're prepared to incur Matron's wrath. I'm sitting there feeling very junior, which I was, when there's a knock on the door and this relative pokes her head around the door and whispers, "The curlers are brown.""

I giggle at the thought.

Both Greta and Ellen look somewhat confused.

"It sounded like something out of a James Bond movie, a secret code, 'the curlers are brown,' and everyone in the nursing office looked confused, and even more so when I jumped up and ran out of the room."

"What happened?" Ellen asked, mesmerised.

"Well, I went to the day room and put the hot curlers in the old lady's hair and ten minutes later she looked like a princess and left with her family, a very happy lady. It just tickled me. It's one of those occasions when something seems surreal and sticks in your mind as being hilarious."

I can see that it doesn't appeal to Greta's sense of humour but Ellen smiles and says with her usual candour, "Well, she must have been very grateful to you," and while I think that she's missed the joke, her finger rests on the poignant point, as always.

"Anyway Ellen," I carry on, desperate to keep the conversation going, "you never did say how the carer manages to wash your hair."

Greta shoots me a look, which I choose to ignore. Ellen opens her mouth to answer but Greta silences her.

"It's easy," she says, turning around from the straightened cans. "The carers are useless. When she broke her leg I managed it easily, yet they say that they can't do it."

I'm having a hard time imagining how they would be able to manage it in the bathroom. I want to say that there's no room to swing a cat but the notion of cats in the bathroom instils images into my head that I'd rather not see.

"I guess there's not much room in the bathroom," I venture but am silenced by the scorn in her voice.

"There are other places, Celia. Duh. There's the kitchen sink."

I have a problem trying to imagine Ellen standing long enough to be able to lean over and go through the process of soaping and rinsing. She can barely stand.

"How did you manage when Ellen broke her leg?" I ask, interested, but trying to divert the conversation to a safer place.

Ellen shudders.

"It was easy; I just bent the wheelchair back and rested it on its handles."

"I was scared," Ellen says in a small voice.

"You were perfectly safe," Greta says, with biting sarcasm.

I try to picture the image of Ellen, frail and scared, tipped upside-down with her leg in a heavy plaster cast looming above her.

"I can see how that it would have been scary not having anything to grab hold of to make you feel safe," I placate. "I've seen many people in hospital be terrified when having to use hoists to get in and out of the bath because they felt unsafe at the time. It's quite natural."

Greta shoots daggers at me, and I'm silenced.

"No, that's not it," she says. "It's just the incompetence of the carers. If I can do it, so can they."

I think she just missed the point; she may have washed her mother's hair but she terrified her at the same time.

"The carers we've had have all been useless."

"Oh?" I say.

"I've told them time and time again that she is only 'minimal assist,' but they won't have it."

I frown, and she continues. "Minimal assist. That's all. I can move my mother easily, minimal assist, but no, they say that it takes two people to move her."

I'm thinking fast. I would say that Ellen needs two people to move her as she's very stiff and scared, which makes her awkward to move. Greta intrudes into my thoughts.

"All she needs is instruction as to how to move, and if they were to make her move, she can do it. That's what I do, I *make* her move and she's fine. Minimal assist!"

I placate again and say, "Well, perhaps the problem is that they try to move her using the one-person technique and she stiffens up and gets afraid, and so they assume that they need two people to move her. Perhaps they aren't aware of just how much she can do for herself."

I'm talking for the sake of it, trying to stem Greta's tirade and stick up for Ellen and the carers, who I'm sure have been sent away with fleas in their ears.

"No, she can move across from the bed to the wheelchair; all she has to do is follow directions. Minimal assist! These people are useless, that's all they are. I've had to get rid of loads of them, and so where does that leave me? Left with it all for me to do, that's what."

I sit there wishing that I hadn't asked how Ellen washed her hair. She looks down at her napkin, tries to pull it from her neck, and I assume that the conversation is closed. Her hair is matted at the back where she's in bed so long, and I wonder just how little time it would take for Greta to put some heated rollers in her hair and restore Ellen's femininity.

There is a picture hanging on the wall of Ellen when she was fifteen years younger and she was stunningly beautiful. Greta told me that it was a portrait done by a street artist in Florida. His talent sits in the room for all to see, for he has captured the sensuality of this broken woman before me, a woman as far removed from Greta as could possibly be imagined. A glimpse of insight flashes into my mind—as Ellen's beauty overshadowed Greta's dourness, so it fuels her hatred of her mother.

"Perhaps there's a lack of communication," I venture, trying to steer Greta towards rationality and compromise, but she talks over me.

"No, there's no lack of communication, these people just don't know what they're doing. They're just plain incompetent. She's minimal assist. They don't know how to do their job properly, that's all."

She has spoken and I know that there's no challenging her if I want to stay in one piece. Ellen pushes away from the table with her paper plate on her lap and heads towards the trashcan. I want to cry as I watch her wasted arms, and her nervous frame, bony and undernourished, trying to clean up after herself. Try as I might, I cannot see her as being "minimal assist." She is too frail, with too little power in her wasted muscles to be able to take her own weight and move with just a guiding hand from a "minimal assist" carer.

My anxiety is such that I can't think with my normal clarity. If I could I would recognise that Greta's scathing denigrations of her mother's carers serve to reinforce her own pathology. It's not her intention to communicate with the carers in order to find a way to support Ellen's occupational therapy within the limitations of her illness, but to justify her own existence in her mother's life and to validate the necessity to spend her mother's small fortune, left to Ellen by her deceased, wealthy husband, and love of her life.

# 8

I READ FOR AGES TRYING TO BLOT out the small voice deep within me that whispers a warning, and I turn my back on the doll, which is no longer the metaphoric core of me, but merely a doll. The small voice is also a reprimand that tells me that I've failed to use the doll in order to take care of myself emotionally. It's 0300 in the morning and I watch a cockroach scale the wall. I wonder if it's the same one I saw earlier or part of an extended family. I'm focused on where it's going, praying that it's not going to land on my bed and visit me in the night—that's if I should ever fall asleep. I call a friend who works nights, grateful that someone else is still up and we chat for a while and arrange a lunch date to eat sushi, his choice—I've never really been one to eat art forms. My room is lonely and I ignore the doll, conveniently forgetting what she represents. The ceiling fan rotates with rhythmic ease, slicing into my thoughts and through the sticky air.

I've been here just over a week and I've got my job and car sorted out, and I've paid my rent after begging Greta day after day to tell me how much she wanted. I guess we should have sorted that out before I arrived, but I figured that I would pay whatever she demanded because we were doing each other a favour and there's no price tag on that. At the start of the week she refused over and over to say how much she wanted, and it's added to my stress. I needed to know where I stood financially. After Chester called she finally gave me a figure, which I thought was a bit steep, and more than I would have to pay if I rented a studio apartment, but as we were out to help each other I let it go. I rationalised it away by thinking: *Well, I'll just work an extra few hours and that'll cover it.*

My mind is buzzing and I feel so far from home but I can't afford the luxury of feeling homesick, for Dessy's and my deal (him to finish decorating the house and me to pay off my tuition fees) spans an aeon of time and to feel homesick at this early stage would be disastrous. I can't begin to allow myself to think about it so I snuff out my feelings and with it my ability to be able to think really clearly, yet I'm left with a pervasive sense of things being profoundly wrong.

I finally fall asleep, yet too soon I awake. I cling to sleep as if it's my last friend, but one that betrays me. It's still dark outside but I can hear something through my earplugs that scares me. Ellen is hammering on the floor with her reacher calling, "Celeste, Celeste, there's someone at the door."

I'm instantly wide awake. It's dark outside. Where is Greta? If I can hear Ellen through my earplugs, it's impossible for Greta not to have heard her mother, yet she hasn't come to see what the matter is. I dive out of bed, startled, scared and concerned all in one. Ellen is trying to prop herself up and fear is alive on her face.

"Celeste, there's someone at the door."

Who can it possibly be? It's dark outside, in the middle of the night—only it isn't in the middle of the night, it's five thirty. A team of workmen have arrived to build a ramp in front of the house so that Ellen can wheel herself from the car to the house without having to scale the step.

I can't believe the sight before me. It's still dark but amidst cat-calling and bantering they start sawing and hammering, and lights punctuate the darkness up and down the road, as the noise pre-empts each household's alarm clock. Doesn't America have some sort of by-law against making noises at unsociable hours?

I go into Ellen's room and reassure her that it's only the ramp men.

"At this hour?"

"Yes, unbelievable, isn't it?" and I go back to my room.

Greta finally shows herself and I can hear her padding along the hall, saying, "Did she open the door to them?"

Who else would it be? She didn't bother coming up the stairs to answer the hammering on the door, and there's no way that she couldn't have heard it as she's already laboured the point that *there's nowhere in the house that she can't hear her mother.*

It feels immoral to be woken up at this hour in the morning, and I jam my earplugs into my ears and force myself to go back to sleep, which thankfully happens immediately.

I surface after 1100, and I guess that sleep has had its way with me, as it's possessed me for over eight hours, even though I stayed awake half the night. I'm ashamed of the hour and sidle into the upstairs bathroom, scale the kitty litter and the bath-aid to get ready quickly.

I make a cup of tea and try to behave as if I've been ready for hours.

"So the ramp men woke you up, eh?" Greta asks me, grinning.

It's good to see her smile and so my face reflects hers. "Yes, what an awful time to be woken up. I couldn't believe it; I didn't think anyone got up that early."

"I hear you," she says. "D'you fancy coming shopping? I've just got a couple of errands to do."

She's in a good mood and so I take the opportunity to try and bridge the gap between us, because I'm desperate to try.

"Yes, that'll be good."

We're gone within ten minutes and Ellen is left in bed awaiting the new carer, with strict instructions that she must not try and get out of the bed without the carer being there to "minimally assist" her.

Greta swings into the gas station at the end of the road.

"I didn't know this was here," I say, marvelling at how close it is to the house.

"Well, that's it, isn't it? If it's not here, then you don't need it," she says emphatically. "We've got a liquor store, garage, Wal-Mart, Walgreens, Shoe Express, Barnes and Noble and Blockbusters all within walking distance, so if it's not here you don't need it. D'you hear me?"

"Wow."

She pays with Ellen's credit card when she's finished filling her car with petrol, I mean gas, and a truck pulls in from the road and sits waiting to drive into our spot. But she sits there and plays with her purse, then her seatbelt, and then rummages through the glove box, whilst the truck still sits there in front of us. It's a Mexican standoff, one that came out of nowhere, with no rhyme or reason. *Move yourself*, I think, wondering what she can possible gain from stopping the driver from moving into our space. I pray that he's even tempered without a gun in his glove box. I say nothing and after an inordinate amount of time, the car at the next pump drives off and the truck takes that space. Neither she nor I say anything when she's suddenly animated and pulls away.

*What's that all about?* I wonder, but I'm not going to give her the satisfaction of challenging her passive-aggressive behaviour. I silently put it down to her scarcity issues, which suddenly seem more acute than I'd initially diagnosed. What could she possibly gain from being resistive at the gas station? The gas isn't hers, the space isn't hers, she's already got what she needs, yet because she could see that he wanted something, she wasn't going to let him have it. I was to learn later to my cost that this resistance ran through her every breath, as a fault line threatens a continent's stability.

She drives and seems happy. I ignore my feelings as I'm just grateful that she's in a better mood.

"They made a good job of the ramp," she says. "At last I won't have to wreck my back humping her wheelchair up and down the step."

"Yes, that would be bad. I know about bad backs," I say, not wanting to comment on the workmanship of the ramp. I was once married to a carpenter who was a perfectionist and who has ruined me for all time as I compare any workmanship to his. He would have slapped his head in despair, for the whole ramp is crooked. There are gaps between the joints and there are nails poking out waiting to snag your clothes. One of the uprights leans badly because they couldn't be bothered to cut a wedge off the decking already in place. I say nothing though, recognising that her standards are very different to mine and my ex-husband's. I guess that if it works, then that's good enough, but it doesn't sit well with me. All the time I can't help but think that she's bought it with Ellen's money, not her own, and I wonder if it had been her own hard-earned money would she so readily have accepted such shoddiness.

I change the subject.

"Dessy does a lot around the house. Did I tell you that he is a carpenter and built our wardrobes? They're pretty amazing. They span the width along two walls and let us put everything away and out of sight, and you know, I've got so much stuff it needs to be out of sight."

She virtually ignores me and doesn't say anything that would be considered good social skills, like "Oh, that's nice," or "You're lucky," but she does start moaning.

"Well, I've never known any man that's been willing to help me."

I think about poor overworked all-American boy Keith, and search for something to say.

"What about your dad?"

"What about him?"

"Do you have contact with him?"

"I used to. I've got several half brothers and sisters but they didn't want me around and I haven't seen them in years, so I guess they don't count."

I wonder how people don't count just because you haven't seen them in years. I haven't seen my mother in years—she's dead—but she counts.

We drive along in silence for a while until she coughs and clears her throat. "You know, I much prefer to have animals than people, they're so much less trouble."

I'm not sure what to say, as I don't do animals with their fur, exposed genitals and pooping on public ground. I don't need to say anything as she carries on as if she's in love, and I realise where her affinities lie.

"I've been wondering whether or not I should keep the dog."

"How long have you had it?"

She surprises me. "Two weeks. I got him from a rescue home."

So, although she is overwhelmed with having to put her life on hold and care for her mother, plus having two pooping cats, she adds to her responsibilities by getting a stray dog. Why? I want to tell her to take it back straight away so as to lessen her load but I don't, because it's obvious to me that she wants her load to be overbearing, to be an overt explanation for her exhaustion and distress. The pets are not pets in the normal sense of the word but are validation of her lot in life. They add to her debilitating stress that would be minimal if she only had her mother to care for, but add three dependent, liberally-pooping creatures into the equation and not even the most together of people would find it easy.

I want to ask her why she got the dog just days before I flew in, when she was battling with two antisocial cats which refused to be human and one of those she'd only just been given days earlier. She told me that she'd wanted only one cat but was told that they could not be separated and so she'd taken the two, yet now they're separated by upstairs and downstairs bathrooms.

As she explains it she sounds like an animal humanitarian, but I'm unable to see her in such a way; my psychologist's hat is back on my head. I wonder what her motivation is for seeking three more dependent creatures—all of which lack Ellen's toilet training—especially when she's got to cope with Ellen's increased dependency since breaking her leg. It doesn't make any sense to me but I can't trust my judgement because I just don't do animals, and I think that my clear cut thinking is due to my detachment towards pets, rather than the pathology that I later come to recognise.

"I just don't know if I should keep him, or not," she says.

I'm jolted from my musings. "Well, it's a big responsibility, especially if he's not house-trained."

I hope to persuade her, for any attention directed towards the animals is attention deflected away from Ellen, and I know that she needs all she can get.

"Perhaps now isn't the time," I venture. "And having had him for so short a time means that you won't have bonded."

I've said the wrong thing.

"I love that dog," she says, with an accusation firing from her, her demeanour telling me that she'll keep the dog no matter what. I hold in a sigh as I think of the reduced amount of attention Ellen will get from now on.

"I think I'll take dog training classes," she announces.

"Oh?"

"Yeah, they're weekly for about eight weeks on the weekend."

"Well, if you've decided to keep him then that sounds like a good idea," I say, hating myself for being such a lapdog.

"Yes, that's what I'll do, take dog classes."

I try hard not to think about dog jokes, and remind myself that I'm in America now and perhaps the jokes and quips about dogs don't mean the same here as they do in England. I'm lost; I have nothing else to say so I look out of the window.

She takes me back to the Chinese all-you-can-eat restaurant and this time she orders me to follow her. She leads me to the Japanese grill and I copy her by placing raw food onto a plate then take it to a circular hot plate where a Chinese young man dumps my selection onto a space on the grill and I watch it steam and cook before me. I'm dumbfounded and enthralled. I've never seen anything like it. It's wonderful. Not only am I going to get a "stir-fry" meal of my choice that'll be hot and fresh, but I get to be entertained as well. This could only happen in America and we Brits have a lot to learn about service.

I feel like a kid at Christmas waiting with hungry anticipation as the young man tosses and folds water and soy sauce over my food, and within minutes it's ready.

We sit at the table and everything is forgotten as I tuck into this bounty; the lack of conversation means nothing to me as I crunch hot crisp broccoli and bean shoots in my mouth. This has to be a gastronomic heaven for I'm completely consumed by taste. I want to feel shame but this is just too exquisite, and I curse the limits of my girth for I don't want it ever to end. I choose fresh vegetables and lean meat, each mouthful is a feast but I try to keep my face straight when I look at Greta's plate. It's loaded with fried chicken and fish, fried cheese, fried rice and noodles and pastries. I can't imagine how anyone, when faced with all this exquisitely healthy and delicious food, would choose fillers with minimal taste.

My psychologist's hat slips unwittingly onto my head again and I curse the fact that it does it automatically when my instinct tells me that something's wrong. It's that scarcity thing again. When an individual is empty inside, eating isn't about enjoyment or the pleasure of tasting or experiencing the joy of "alive" food, healthy food. It's about filling the emptiness with foods that fill, that distend the stomach and hurts, so that the pain reminds the person that they're alive, but only just.

I don't know what to say. "How's your pastry?" I don't think so, although that's exactly what I *do* say and she grunts at me, revealing the standard response of someone who can never be filled by food: "It's crap. I don't know why I bother," she says, stuffing the whole cake in her mouth.

I want to go back to the buffet and taste more, knowing instinctively how it feels to be an alcoholic or a drug addict. Although I don't need it, the longing's there and I have to have more. I'm not in control of myself and fill my plate with more water chestnuts, broccoli and steamed chicken. I guess it could be worse because Greta heads for the dessert table and picks up several brightly coloured cakes and smiles at me, saying "Now, *these* are good."

We sit and grin at each other and I feel the same sense of satisfaction as a mud wrestler sitting steeped in mud, satiated and replete, exhausted and dying for a nap.

We head for Kroger's and she says, "You must remind me to..." and I don't hear the rest of what she's saying as I try to play with her by saying, "My memory is terrible, don't rely on me, I have a hard enough time remembering my own stuff." She looks put out.

As she pulls into the car park I say, "Don't forget whatever it is that you wanted me to remind you about," and she shoots me a scathing look. I follow her to the automatic door and say again, "Now, don't forget whatever it is you have to remember," and she walks off ahead of me to search through the shelves of reduced items with blue stickers on them.

I catch up with her at the check-out and help her carry to the car the bags that are loaded with obscure contents in bent tins to add to the collection she already has at home.

She wedges herself into the seat and slams the car door.

"For Christ's sake, Celia, you didn't remind me to get any cash back. Now I won't be able to buy my mother a milkshake."

I'm stunned. I didn't even hear her say what it was that she needed to be reminded about, but despite that, I'd reminded her twice since we'd arrived at Kroger's. I try to blow it off by being light-hearted.

"Come on, Greta," I smile, "I said it twice and that's without knowing what it was that you needed to remember, and with my awful memory."

She's not amused and snaps, "But I needed reminding at the check-out, not as we went into the store. Oh, well, she'll have to go without, that's all."

I feel as if she's trying to hook me into another psychological game-play, a sequence that follows the lines of "If it weren't for you," or "Now, see what you made me do," and it feels dirty. As much as I feel intimidated by her, I stick up for myself.

"I'll buy her a milkshake, there's no problem."

She drives in silence and pulls into McDonald's drive-through.

"Hand me my bag," she snaps.

I hand it to her and then reach for my purse to find some change.

"Forget it," she says coldly. "I've got a twenty dollar bill here."

I'm dumbstruck and wonder what's just happened, and sit in silence as she drives home, my fresh vegetables churning inside me.

Ellen is up and sitting in her wheelchair watching television and her face lights up as I walk in the door. I feel cheered.

"Well, hello, Celeste, did you have a good shop?"

"Yes," I lie, "Greta got you your milkshake. Your hair looks nice; did the carer wash it for you?"

"Don't start her off again," Greta hisses in my ear as she pushes past us and dumps the milkshake on the kitchen table.

I don't know what to do, because by the time Ellen manages to wheel herself to the table the thick shake will be thin and ruined, but if I go and give it to Ellen while she's sitting in the living room watching television that'll be wrong. I don't think I can handle Greta's sarcasm right now, so I excuse myself and go to my room and stare at the fan going round and round before I drift off.

I awake and go to the bathroom and there's kitty litter scattered all over the sink and vanity unit where the cat has leapt from the floor to the toilet seat via the basin and back again. I don't want to touch anything but I need to go to the bathroom so I have to lift the seat up, remove the kitty litter tray and balance it on the trash can, replace the seat, and then reverse the procedure. I hate cleaning my teeth in the basin as I cannot be sure that kitty germs aren't everywhere and jumping onto my toothbrush. I'm scared to take my contact lenses out in the bathroom, too, for one of the easiest ways of contracting germs is through the eyes. I know my nostrils are flaring every time I have to go in there.

Ellen is still sitting in her wheelchair in front of the television and I join her.

"I love this show," she says, and I can see from the terrible acting that it's a soap opera. Okay, so America is better at service than England, but the acting in our soap operas is much better.

"I don't get to watch many soaps," I tell her, "and Dessy hates them. Mind you he knows all the characters and everything they're getting up to."

We giggle.

"Well, I never used to watch them," she says, "but now I don't have much else to do."

"I only really watch one at home, Eastenders."

"Oh?" she says, bemused and curious. "I haven't heard of it."

"It's about people who live in the East End of London, and some say that it's depressing but I think it's a pretty good reflection of real life and they address some pretty serious social issues. It's clever, really."

"Don't you know it," she says wisely.

"My girls watch every soap there is. They're slaves to them."

"I wish I wasn't," she says sadly.

"Shall we see if there's something else on?" I ask, picking up the television guide.

"That would be nice, I can't see too well."

We watch Discovery Health channel and gasp as we watch a baby being born, our knees tightly clamped together.

"I'm so glad that I didn't have any nursing knowledge before I had my babies," I say, shuddering. "I might not have had any. Did you have to spend part of your nurse training in obstetrics? We did, and it terrified me."

"You know it," she says. "I hated it, too. I didn't have a good experience and it stayed with me for a long time."

"What happened?"

"We had to follow a patient through labour and delivery and I was with this young woman whose baby was born prematurely—at about twenty-eight weeks. When it was born they just left it, thinking that it would die, and I had to sit with it until it did."

"How awful."

"It was gasping like a fish out of water and I couldn't do anything to help it. It was a little girl. It upset me for ages and put me off working in obstetrics."

The phone rings and Ellen reaches out to answer it.

"Hello, hello, who? Hello," and puts it down again.

"I know what you mean," I say, suddenly very serious and wanting to cry. "I used to work in a neonatal intensive care unit when one of my daughters had a baby whose birth was mishandled. The baby's father and I kept a vigil throughout the night watching him gasp for air until he died. It's had a profound effect upon me. It's actually something that never leaves me."

"How awful," she says, and there's empathy in her eyes and the bond between us seems to grow stronger.

We hear Greta thumping up the stairs and we both stop talking. She marches over to me and thrusts the hands-free phone into my hand.

"It's for you. I don't know who it is but she's fucking rude, whoever she is."

I'm shocked and take the phone. I speak into it but there's no one there.

"Who was it?" I ask, nonplussed.

"Someone called Rita, I think. Whoever it was, she was fucking rude."

She storms out of the room and disappears down into the dungeon.

Ellen looks scared and I feel sick. My friend Rita is a beautiful human being and wouldn't be rude to anyone.

I raise my eyes to the heavens in front of Ellen, which feels daring but she mirrors me and shakes her head. I go down the stairs and call Greta. She stands in front of me and resembles an outraged rhinoceros.

"I don't appreciate having your friends call this house and being so fucking rude," she states, with her hands on her hips.

"What did she say?" I'm confused. Perhaps it wasn't Rita.

"I told her that you were upstairs and she said, 'Who are these people?' Fucking rude! I told her that she'd been talking to my mother who's an invalid and she shouldn't be so fucking rude."

I feel sick. Rita's a sweet and wonderful person, who knows more about pain than anyone I know. I don't know what to do, so I go back upstairs with Ellen.

The phone rings again and Ellen answers it.

"It's for you, someone called Rita."

I grab the phone from her and croon into it, "Rita, how are you?"

It's been eighteen months since I spent time with my dear friend and I long to see her, and I know that she longs to see me, too.

"Oh, Celia, I think I may have offended the lady that answered the phone." I can't stop the old theatre joke, *That's no lady* popping into my head. She speaks quickly. "I was on the freeway using my cell phone when this car came out of nowhere and pulled in front of me, and I said out loud, 'Who are these people?' and then the woman started saying that I'd been speaking to her invalid mother. She sounded really angry. I'm so sorry if I caused any offence."

"Rita, there's nothing wrong, okay. I can't wait to see you. When can we meet?"

A few minutes later after saying goodbye and explaining to Ellen what had happened, I go to my room to stifle the anger I feel. What is wrong with Greta that she should instantly assume that the words "Who are these people?" are a derogatory slight upon herself and her mother? How did she get to that conclusion so readily without any other explanation presenting itself as being plausible? She instantly stomped up the stairs to berate my friend to me, to make it uncomfortable for her to call me again on that number (which after that time she never did again) and to silence me with her outrage. It makes no sense that *she* should feel affronted that her mother may have been slighted yet she slights her all the time. What is that? I'm too angry to work it out, and with my friend's honour at stake, and not my own, I feel able to tackle her. I hear her talking to Ellen in the lounge, so I leave the safety of my room to say my piece.

"Greta, my friend Rita would never speak badly of anyone or rudely to anyone."

She starts to look defensive and takes a deep breath to shout me down but I get in there first.

"She phoned back because she felt that she'd offended you." I ignore the satisfied look on her face and carry on. "She was calling on her cell phone while driving along the freeway when a car cut in front of her, and she said 'Who are these people?' meaning those in the car. She would never be rude to anyone, ever," I say, daring her to tackle me.

She blows me off and says, "How embarrassing," as she leaves the room and goes downstairs.

I feel impotent, and I guess that's what I'm meant to feel. I turn to Ellen who is cringing and she shakes her head.

"Well, she sounded very nice to me. I didn't think she was rude."

Bless dear Ellen.

I sit beside her and tell her Rita's story, about how her son was found with his head shot off in their bathroom, how it couldn't have been suicide, and how he'd been plagued by rival gangs in high school and that the police would do nothing to open an investigation into his death. She had said during the months after, when we'd sat up night after night at work and she'd sobbed and I'd felt guilty that my sons were still alive, that the police weren't interested in "just another young nigger's death." I wince at the thought, as I know I did when she voiced it, and deep within me I knew it to be true. What could I say to her? Nothing that made any difference. Through my impotence grew a fierce protectiveness towards her, which would stand no slight from anyone towards her. And that means Greta, even formidable Greta.

Yet all she could say when she'd been shown that she got it so terribly wrong was, "How embarrassing." I want to spit. The anger that I smother when an injustice is done to myself bubbles up, threatening to engulf me when I think of the injustice done to someone I love, someone who's known so much pain, who can endure no more.

I struggle with my emotions and am dismayed to feel hatred towards Greta. I keep on trying to wear my psychologist's hat to attempt to understand her behaviour, but it's getting harder and harder all the time to excuse or explain her attitude and caustic tongue with the psychological theory I know, and with the compassion in my heart. There are some things that are just not right. Everything is starting to feel out of control and as I try to sleep that night, it dawns on me that it's me that's beginning to feel out of control. I'm scared, and I don't know how to make it right, and the doll is right across the bed facing the wall. I curl up in a foetal position and face the opposite way.

# 9

----

IT'S A LONG HAUL FOR ME TO attempt to restore any positive feelings towards Greta after she's character assassinated my dear friend without compunction or shame, yet I know that I have to tread that road. I can't live here with her and allow my feelings to degenerate to a place where open contempt can emanate from me. In scrambling back to that no-man's land I lose some of my integrity and feel as if I'm acting whenever I'm around her. I don't know if she realises. Ellen seems more anxious, or maybe she's always been this anxious, but I'm aware of it only as my own anxiety grows. As I attempt to placate, I over compensate and still try to understand why Greta is the way she is.

The nature versus nurture debate is still out for deliberation, and I'm acutely aware that pathology isn't only in the genes but is a complex interplay between genes and the raising of a child. What has happened to make Greta turn out to be so devoid of love? When I think like this I'm able to contact the compassionate side of myself, and so I keep trying to befriend her, to reach out to her, in the hopes that she'll reach out to me and grow.

Later that evening after Ellen's in bed, I ask Greta to share a beer with me and she does. I prompt her to talk about what would make her happy. She tells me that she has an Asian or Middle Eastern part-time boyfriend that she "met" on the Internet, who she sees very occasionally as he lives interstate. I'm glad for her. We all need to be loved and to feel special. She reveals that she chats to several men on the Internet, as having just one would bore her, and this way she can switch them off when they become irritating. I find it difficult to stay positive, for my suspicions that she's a person who is either scared of intimacy or incapable of it are confirmed. The Internet is a fertiliser-grow-bag for transient shallow "fix it for the moment" relationships.

I'm reminded of a lonely time in my life when I answered an ad in a newspaper and thought I was in a "relationship" with this guy. I quickly learned that he steeped himself in the masses of strokes he got by all the lonely women who replied to him, yet gave virtually nothing in return. It wasn't a real relationship but a parasitic symbiosis and I ran as fast as I could. Being lonely was preferable to being in such a situation, but I can see that for those who are incapable of true intimacy there is an appeal for Internet or advertisement "dating." There's a bad taste in my mouth yet again.

"The man I had before said that I had no heart," Greta said in her girlie "please like me" voice. "And I said, 'What, after I've given you so much,' I mean, how can that be?"

I frown, not really knowing what to say. I'm dumbfounded a lot these days.

"I mean, I've given everything, and I mean *everything* to the men in my life. Well, they can go to hell."

"Don't you think that we all have a good heart?" I ask, trying to encourage her to talk more, as talking promotes growth, and growth is sustenance for the soul.

"Pah, not everyone," she says, finishing up her beer.

"Have another," I urge and go to the fridge to retrieve two more cans.

As I hand her one I say, "I think there's goodness in everyone, but sometimes that goodness gets squashed or buried by the things that happen to them in life."

She looks at me as if I'm stupid or a member of a snake-worshipping cult.

"Not everyone!"

"Who?"

"Her husband," she says. "You know he was evil, just evil. I despised him. How could she choose him over me?"

There is a retort perched on my tongue that's all but ready to launch itself into the space between us that says, "So what, get over it, get a life, you're thirty-six years old," but I nod with my therapist's hat on.

"You obviously didn't like him much," I say slowly.

She lets rip. "You should have met him, he couldn't move from the neck down, how sick is that?"

I want to say that a marriage is not only about squelchy, slushy bits coming together, it's about caring and the meeting of minds, and of humour and playing. I'm reminded of my Dessy and a pang of homesickness flashes through me.

"Could there have been something else between them?" I ask, hoping that she'll cotton on.

She doesn't, and launches into a tirade, "Oh, yeah, there was something else between them, she was his unpaid servant. She waited on him hand and foot."

I hate what she's doing, for I'm sure that Ellen will hear her, as she doesn't bother to lower her voice.

"She's so fucking stupid that she'd go with anybody, she's so co-dependent that she had to have a boyfriend no matter who it was, and he happened to be the one who was there at the time."

No matter how I try I can't see Ellen being like that, especially towards a man who couldn't move from the neck downwards. It seems to me that the marriage they had, which spanned many years, was a marriage of minds, of humour and of indulging in the same chicken soup made with two fresh, trusting, loving souls. That's the sort of soup that nourishes you until you die. I know, though, that she doesn't get it. She's never partaken of such a soup nor had such a relationship, and so it's not part of her vocabulary. I feel sad for her, yet alert and defensive.

I begin to wonder whether her anger isn't borne out of frustration that she could no longer manipulate her mother while her husband was there, and when faced with the consuming love between them she had to trash it to justify the lack of it in her life.

"It was the best day of my life the day he died," she says. "I only wish he'd died in pain; the bastard deserved to."

She's a loose cannon, but I listen even though what she says appals me. I want to help her and hope that by venting she'll find some peace.

The beer has got to us and the nibbles prevail. I hate it when this happens, for my mouth and teeth have a mind of their own that has nothing to do with sensibility or nutrition. She darts out into the kitchen and begins to throw things into a bowl, and I stand next to her watching and chatting, hoping that this is going to be a turning point where we can form some kind of friendship so that we can live together harmoniously. I reframe my denial into something more palatable.

She mashes avocados and my mouth is watering as she tips in mounds of garlic powder. She dips a nacho into the mixture and puts it in her mouth, pulling a face and says, "It needs more taste," so she pours in even more garlic. "Try it," she demands, and I dip a cracker into the green mixture, and flavour bursts onto my taste buds.

We go back to the lounge and she puts the bowl of dip between us, scooping great dollops into her mouth. I dip one chip to her three, lightly, because the flavour is so strong. Although I have the munchies I hope my face doesn't display the same desperation and emotional starvation that's on her face. This is just a tempting snack to me but there's something more vital about her face and consumption that scares me. It scares the "child" in me, and scares the adult in me too, for this "child" is starving, abandoned and out of control.

I can't eat anymore, even though she urges me to match her nacho for nacho, but I'm done and she looks affronted.

"It was great. Thanks for making it and showing me how to," I say, meaning it.

She grunts and takes the bowl and wraps it in plastic wrap telling me that I'll have to eat it up tomorrow, as it'll go off, before leaving abruptly through the dungeon door. I guess the evening's over so I go to bed.

I feel sick when I wake up, for my breath is gagging me, and the taste in my mouth from half a bottle of garlic powder is almost worse than the ripe kitty packages that welcome me every morning. Today I stifle an overwhelming urge to vomit. Somewhere deep in the recesses of my mind I wonder if I have scarcity issues too, for it seems that I'm unable to vomit and release all that's mine by mastication rights.

I've got to go to orientation at the hospital and I'm sickened by the thought that I will greet all my old friends, and some new ones, with such terrible breath, which I know will be with me for days.

I try to talk the whole day with my hand in front of my mouth but I'm sure they notice, although they're generous and say nothing. Perhaps they assume my garlic breath is a characteristic of English people, a cultural norm. I hope not.

That evening when Greta presses me to take the leftover dip to work saying, "You must take this to work; you know it'll only get wasted if you don't," I struggle to find an excuse that won't offend her. I could *never* take it to work, not only because if they thought that I'd made it they would rubbish my prowess as a cook, but I could be had up for trying to poison my colleagues.

It's there every time I open the fridge door, and poor Ellen is dealt a deadly hand each day when it's all she's given to eat in Greta's pursuit to get rid of the foul mess. When I look back I reproach myself for not scooping it all into a bowl and dumping it in the trash at work, but telling Greta that I gave it to my work mates who were very grateful. Why didn't I do that? Sometimes I can be so stupid.

Greta seems desperate to provide, almost like a feeder, but is unable to give without demanding something in return, something that appears vital to her emotional survival. Her need is all consuming and feels suffocating, which initiates a resistance to give her anything for fear of being emotionally stripped naked, forced to a place where there's no way back. I'm enlightened as a psychologist but scared as a human being. Again an image of a massive spider pops into my mind, where Ellen is being sucked dry and I'm being fattened up.

That night after I've scrubbed and scrubbed my teeth and tongue so hard that they're sore, I set my alarm as I have to go to a training workshop to learn how to de-escalate violent behaviour. It's run by my old friend Simon, who is part of the institution and every child's idea of a perfect father. He's adorable and I know that we're going to have a great day.

I leave the house in the dark and it's windy. It feels good to me and reminds me of home, English weather, weather to dampen down the hot flushes I'm having. As I open the car door a small green reptile jumps into the car, and I'm so surprised and spooked that I'm reluctant to get into the car and shut myself in with it. I tell myself that I'm dreaming and that it was just a leaf. I don't have time to hunt for it or I'll be late, so I slam the door loudly hoping that it will have found its way out, and pray that it doesn't land in my lap as I drive up the road. My imagination blossoms and I imagine the headlines in the local newspaper: "English nurse dies in a road accident. Witnesses identify a guilty green frog hopping from the scene."

As I wait at the traffic lights I feel a children's story coming on and I'm excited. I've been writing stories for my grandchildren for years and this will make a perfect story, exaggerated a little of course, in the name of artist's licence.

I have such fun during the day with Simon and Alex, my new friend, who has to renew his annual training. We end up throwing each other to the floor, gently, not knowing how we'll be able to do this to 200-pound aggressive patients, but we do it anyway and at the end of the day we're certified for another year.

I feel in high spirits when I go home and stop off in Ellen's room to tell her about being thrown to the ground and giggling with my friends.

"Oh, my," she says. "It sounds such fun."

"It was. They're such wonderful people. I wish you could meet them," I say wistfully.

"Now, wouldn't that be nice," she says.

"What would be nice?" Greta intrudes, and I marvel at her ability to just appear out of nowhere. It must be the bell on the door that rings whenever any external door opens that tells her

I'm home. She knows I'll be chatting to Ellen and telling her about my day in order that she doesn't feel so isolated. I'm not sure if her appearance is to dampen Ellen's excitement or whether she seeks to be included.

"I was just telling Ellen about my day." I start to tell Greta but she just walks away, so I guess her appearance isn't because she wants to be included.

I tell Ellen about the training blow by blow and she's enthralled and tells me about when she worked as a psychiatric nurse. We speak the same language and understand the joy and trauma of working in such a field. Eventually I excuse myself and go to my room to write a story for my grandchildren.

I can't help the feeling of excitement that spreads through me as soon as I put pen to paper—it happens every time.

An hour later I join Ellen in front of the television in the lounge, and with a satisfied smile beaming across my face, I tell her that I've just finished my story.

"Oh, my," she says. "Can I hear it?"

Greta miraculously appears through the dungeon doorway again and Ellen calls to her. "Celeste has written a story."

Greta grunts and stays in the kitchen, banging and crashing about, although she's within earshot.

"Are you ready?" I say to Ellen, and she nods excitedly like a precious child.

"A Funny Thing Happened Today"

*Very early this morning I rushed out of the house, fearing that I was going to be late for a meeting. It was very windy and all the leaves that had fallen during the night were blowing all over the street. It was barely light and I fumbled for my keys to open the car door so that I could see by the light inside the car.*

As I opened the door a gust of wind swirled the leaves around my legs and the light shone on a little bright green leaf that shot into the car. It happened in a flash and I stood there stunned, not really believing what I'd seen. I thought it was a leaf but my eyes told me that it was a bright green frog.

"Don't be so silly," I told myself and wished that Granddad was here to help me. "Now, come on," I said sternly. "It was a leaf and to prove it, all I have to do is to look down by the pedals and there it will be."

But it wasn't there.

A shiver ran down my back. I looked under the seat and it was nowhere to be seen and I even lifted up the carpet, but it wasn't there. The wind howled around the car and as I searched for the leaf, I told myself that the wind must have blown it back out of the car.

I was going to be late for my meeting if I didn't hurry, so I threw my bag into the car and drove to work.

"Oh, there you are," my boss said, looking at her watch impatiently. "We thought you weren't coming. Everyone's waiting."

I followed her into a large room full of people waiting for me to talk to them, and feeling flustered, I dumped my bag on the table in front of us and began to talk. I talked and talked, as Granddad says I can, and gradually I became aware of my boss beside me making little coughing noises.

"Do you need a glass of water?" I asked her quietly, but she shook her head and had a strange look on her face.

"As I was saying," I continued, talking to anyone that would listen, but then I became aware of a gentle giggling and sniggering rippling through the room, and so I stopped, which was hard, as you know how Nana likes to talk a lot!

Before long everyone in the room was howling with laughter and pointing at my boss, whose face wore a horrified expression. My *mouth dropped open, for there in her hair was a little bright green frog, the little bright green frog. My eyes had not deceived me—the thing that had shot into my car was not a leaf but a little frog, and he had traveled in my bag into the meeting. My eyes had been right after all.*

*Do you think that the little bright green frog had jumped into the car when I opened the door or was he already living in the car? I know I saw him shoot across the carpet, but I can't be sure that my eyes saw him jump from the ground into the car, and he knew exactly where to hide so that I couldn't find him.*

Her eyes are wide with wonderment, and I'm pleased that she likes it but disturbed that such a simple children's story should hold so much pleasure for her. I'm forced to acknowledge that this poor woman does not have anywhere near enough stimulation in her life.

Greta places a paper plate on the kitchen table with chips, a gherkin and a large dollop of the guacamole mess that I swear I can smell from where I'm sitting, and her tone of voice is clipped when she speaks to me.

"There's plenty here if you want to eat. It'll only go to waste if you don't eat it."

I try to tell her that I ate at the hospital, which is true, I did, but it was hours ago and I am hungry, still there's no way that I can eat anymore garlic-infested dip. She mutters and I see her disappear down into the dungeon with a paper plate piled high with several pieces of reheated pizza. I wait until she's safely ensconced downstairs before I open a can of fat-free turkey chilli and my favourite: spinach. It seems an unusual combination but better than sloppy green smelly stuff. I hurt as I watch Ellen attempt to dip her chips into the mess and get it into her mouth without spilling it down her front. I'm forced to acknowledge that she must be starving to even try and eat that stuff. I feel very bad.

"Can I get you something else?" I ask her quietly, as the dungeon door is open.

She shakes and says, "No, not a thing. I best eat it."

I swear she's embarrassed. I'm not; I'm just mortified. How could Greta serve her mother an inedible dip with chips while she filled her own plate with pizza, albeit filler food, but food that was at least tasty and edible? I make a decision that if I can't force Greta to feed her mother properly then I'll supplement her diet by bringing treats home for her; at least that'll increase her calorie intake and will please her.

I had a habit at home of buying a "garage treat" every time I filled my car with petrol, I mean gas, for whoever was at the end of my destination. It's a fun thing to do and I make up my mind that I will fill some of the emptiness in Ellen's life by bringing home little surprises for her.

I get the munchies, and nibble my way through a bag of baby carrots, and Ellen says, "I need to be eating good things like that. You know, she shouldn't be giving me that stuff, it's not good. I should be eating the same kind of food that you eat. You have vegetables, meat and proper food. That's what I should be having."

"Yes, you should."

I offer her a couple of baby carrots but she declines, saying that they are too hard.

"One of my favourite things is spinach," I say. "I could eat it anywhere and at any time."

"I wish I could," she says.

Greta appears again and I get the feeling that her purpose in life is to snuff out any conversation that may incriminate her. Her appearance is uncanny, for as soon as anything is said that could cast her in a negative light, she appears, an omnipotent, threatening presence. Ellen and I fall silent and after Greta throws her paper plate into the trashcan, she goes back downstairs, and Ellen and I watch TV.

It's getting late and my anxiety is growing; surely Greta will come and put her mother to bed soon.

Ellen says, "Don't worry, we have a sign. I have to knock three times on the floor and she'll come upstairs."

She bangs three times on the floor to illustrate what she means and almost immediately Greta's there, her face like thunder, standing over her with her hands on her hips and a face that would sour milk.

"You know that you don't call me until you're by your bedside and ready to get into bed."

She walks off and disappears into the dungeon and leaves Ellen to wheel herself into her bedroom. I feel my chilli churn in my stomach with anger and anxiety, so to relieve poor Ellen, and myself, I push her over the bumps on the floor and leave her in her bedroom. She knocks three times on her bedroom floor and I hear Greta bounding up the stairs, so I dive into my bedroom and shut the door quickly. Her voice comes through the wall demanding to know how she got into her room so fast.

"How did you get in here so quickly? I only left you a moment ago. Did she help you? She better not have done."

Ellen joins me in a silent resistance against oppression.

"No, I wheeled myself. I'm ready to go to bed," she says emphatically.

I'm sure Greta doesn't believe her but she starts ordering her mother to stand, lock her knees. "Don't do that, you stupid bitch. Pay attention. Oh, for Christ's sake!"

I wait behind my door, listening. These walls are paper-thin and I can hear everything that's going on in the next room.

"Well, just so long as she didn't help you get into your room," I hear Greta say. "Don't you be getting her to do everything for you. D'you hear me?"

I wait a while and do what I've become accustomed to doing, and that is to creep out of my room as soon as I think Greta's gone in order to check that Ellen is all right.

"Are you all right?" I whisper, scared that Greta may suddenly pounce upon me, as she has an uncanny knack of appearing as soon as I leave my room.

"Oh, yes, I'm just fine," she says, happy to see me. "I loved your story."

"Thanks for saying. It's just a bit of fun for my grandchildren. It keeps me connected to them."

"No, it was beautiful," she says, and I love her for her generosity. I tuck her in and go to bed.

I refuse a friend's invitation to dinner the next day because it's the day of the Indian amateur film and I know Greta wants to go. I figure that if I go with her, she may be more amenable. I fill the car up with petrol on the way home from work and buy Ellen a chocolate bar as a treat.

Ellen's sitting in her wheelchair in her room and her eyes light up as I hand her the chocolate bar and pull the wrapper half way down so that she can get to it. She's like a starved child, and I'm humbled.

I fiddle about in my room and hear Greta talking in hushed tones to Ellen in the next room and my stomach twists with anxiety. I hear her walk past my door and so I open the door and follow her into the kitchen.

"Are you still going to the Indian movie?"

She turns around to face me and there's "something" alive in her expression. "I don't have time for that," she says, and a part of me is relieved that I don't have to endure watching something I don't want to see. Yet another part of me is irritated that I've given up a dinner date to consider her, but mostly I'm anxious at the animosity in her face.

"Did you give my mother chocolate?" she demands.

I flinch. "Yes," ricocheting back to being reprimanded as a small child by my teacher after being as good as I possibly could be yet knowing my effort still wasn't enough to stem the criticism of a bully.

"Well, I hope she eats all her dinner, that's all I can say," she bites at me as she heads for the dungeon doorway with me thoroughly chastised.

I speak quickly. "I thought you wanted to go to the Indian movie? I'll come with you if you want me to." I know that I sound as if I'm begging, which feels bizarre because I don't want to go. My simpering humiliates me but I quickly ignore it.

"I've got a blinding headache and I haven't felt well all day, and besides, Keith is coming round tonight to fix one more thing on the computer."

I don't know what to say because I thought she'd said that it was fixed and that he was a moron and not as clever as he thought he was. I obviously haven't been paying attention.

"Oh," I say, and turn the television on. I sit there with the images flashing in front of me yet not taking them in. My thoughts are buzzing. Why would she be so antagonised by me buying a bar of chocolate for Ellen? Of course Ellen will eat her dinner. She makes Ellen wait so long for any food that even if she'd eaten copious amounts of chocolate, she'd still be hungry for her dinner. Why would she be dead set on going to the Indian movie, yet when she has the opportunity to go, she refuses?

Keith breaks into my thoughts by pulling into the drive, so I go and call down into the dungeon to let Greta know that he's here. She stomps up the stairs and pushes past me, and summons from somewhere her sugar-sweet voice to tell him that she's been waiting for him. She then attempts to make him feel bad for keeping her waiting, saying that she was supposed to be going to an Indian movie night, but now she's missed it.

"Hi, Keith," I say as he walks past me. "Can I get you something to drink?"

She shoots me a scathing "butt out" look, which I can't ignore, so silenced, I go back in front of the television and flick channels.

They're downstairs in the dungeon for ages and Ellen wheels herself out to join me and we sit there glued to a movie about ungrateful children and long-suffering women.

She looks at me and says, "Well, I don't know, but can you smell something bad?"

I sniff and pray it isn't her, and then pray even harder that it isn't me. I get up to investigate and walk through the hall towards our bedrooms. The smell gets more pungent and I feel sick, but follow my nose. I'm so grateful that the light's on and I haven't stepped in it. There on the carpet runner is a pile of ripe kitty poop. I guess the cat's voted with its backside on Greta's final attempt to relinquish its innate bathroom habits by opening up the hole in the kitty litter tray so much that it leaves nothing for it to dig into. Greta has removed most of the litter tray so that it has to stand on the toilet seat, squat and aim for the water below. But the cat is just being a cat and having nowhere to dig and shovel, it's found the nearest thing to the texture of kitty litter pile: carpet pile.

I'm so grossed out and fed up with coping with solidified kitty litter and kitty residue down the toilet that I cease to accommodate it any longer, so I walk away from the stinking mess and without compunction I call down the stairs.

"The cat has just left a pile of poop on the carpet." I can hear an impatient edge in my voice.

There's a subtle lying down of swords somewhere in my voice as well, and I walk away from the dungeon doorway, not caring that she may be exasperated or even embarrassed in front of Keith by her cat's resistance to learn good bathroom manners. There's something inside me that's reached a limit, and stinking cat poop lying in wait to be spread around the house by my feet or Ellen's wheelchair has driven me to that point. It's time for her to realise that a cat is a cat and not a human being. Ellen glances at me as we hear Greta stomp up the stairs and I can feel her anxiety through my own.

"I like this programme," I say, as we hear Greta sighing loudly in the hall trying to scoop up the kitty protest. I have a crazy image of the cat carrying a banner that says "Let me be a cat, not a human—bring on the dirt box," as we talk loudly.

"Yes, I like it too."

"Did you see it last week?"

"Yes. It's one of my favourites."

"Yes, it's one of my favourites, too."

"Can you get this in England?"

"Yes."

I listen and hear Greta go into the bathroom and flush the toilet and Ellen and I look at each other, a narration unspoken.

She walks into the lounge and slices through our anxiety with a barbed slight: "You know, it only had to be placed in the toilet." She doesn't wait for a reply, but picks up the disgraced cat and disappears into the dungeon where Keith awaits.

I feel mean but there's a positive outcome for me, although not for the cats, and although I have no affinity with furry animals,

I fear for those cats that have let Greta down so badly by refusing to adopt the bathroom habits of humans. I never saw them again. I can't be sure what happened to them. I only know that the kitty litter tray was removed from the upstairs bathroom, along with the bath aid. I saw this as my cue to use the upstairs bathroom only, and I wasn't welcome to use the downstairs one.

I wondered whether the cat was in disgrace along with its mate, and banished to the downstairs bathroom where it could learn the error of its ways, or if something else happened to them. All I know is that I never saw them again. I'm ashamed to say that their departure was a relief to me, for I no longer had to scale the kitty litter and its gifts waiting for me each morning in the pursuit of my own ablutions. Although I don't *do* fur and spontaneous defecation, I prayed that they were all right.

# *10*

I'VE BEEN HERE TWO WEEKS AND I've settled into work as if I've been there forever, and I love it. I wish it wasn't the weekend—I just want to be at work.

I get up lazily and go into the kitchen to make a cup of tea, wondering what I'm going to do all day. I can hear Greta banging about downstairs and I call down to her.

"Hi, are you okay?"

She appears at the bottom of the stairs, stuffed into a pair of leggings and a sloppy sweater, looking harassed.

"Do you need any help?" I ask, trying to head off the irritation I can see on her face.

"Yes, I could use some help," she pants, so I go downstairs.

"What're you doing?"

"I want to make my bedroom into a sort of study and so I'm moving my computer into my room."

I'm surprised and look around, coughing, as the dust has been stirred up where she's been shifting stuff around. I get the feeling she's trying to be pleasant but that it's an awful effort, because her expression oscillates between a sweet smile to biting sarcasm, and my stomach twists with anxiety.

"You can take *that* computer up to your room," she says, nodding to a second computer resting on the floor, covered in dust.

"Oh, okay, thanks."

I struggle up the stairs with it, feeling scared that I might drop it, as I'm not used to carrying heavy things. I know that I'm a betrayal for all female kind, but I believe that when there are men around, they can do this stuff and I'll do the stuff that women do on Venus. I'm panting by the time I get to the top of the stairs and I start wheezing. That's another reason why my man does all this sort of stuff: I'm asthmatic.

I stagger to my room, resting the computer on the desk and suck on my inhaler, waiting for my heart and breathing to slow.

After an hour there's a computer in my room and a computer in the study next to my room which is supposed to be for Ellen to use, and then we start on shifting Greta's computer from the downstairs den into her room, which is in the depths of the dungeon. I try really hard to ignore her biting comments about how I'm not lifting it properly or far enough, and I put on my best "Please Others" face and pretend to be someone else.

I compliment her on how well the desk fits in her room and how cosy it'll be, but she blanks me and then I'm dismissed.

I put the kettle on and go back to making my cup of tea to wash the dust out of my throat and then I go to chat with Ellen.

"Have you had anything to eat today?" I ask.

"No."

"Can I get you something? You must surely be hungry?"

She whispers, "You could pass me some of that chocolate you brought me from England. It's over there, in that drawer. She put it in there."

I hand her the box of chocolate shells, which is still nearly full, and I try and stifle the irritation I feel that Greta should put Ellen's chocolate where it's impossible for her to reach it.

"Can I get you something proper to eat?" I say, full of concern. I mean, if I'm starving hungry then I know she just has to be.

"I'll just eat some of these," she whispers, her voice beseeching me to be quiet. "She always gets pizza on Saturdays so I'll eat some of that later."

"But that's hours away," I say, a frown on my face.

"I'll be all right. You could get me some water if you don't mind."

This is not right. I hunt around the kitchen and find a raspberry strudel cake with a reduced sticker on it: it being out of date by five days. There's no mould on it and I imagine that it has sufficient preserving agents in it to stop it from going off, so I cut her two pieces and put them on a paper plate.

"Here, have this in case you're hungry later. I'm just going out. I won't be long. I'm going to buy a web cam so that I can see Dessy when I log on to the computer upstairs. See you later."

I walk out to the car and it feels strange to be free to do what I want on a day off. I feel strangely single and miss my Dessy because I'm not single and am totally committed to my man. It leaves me feeling kind of empty. I decide that retail therapy is in order, so I go to K-Mart. Greta has already told me that they have the cheapest web cams, and by chance they are the retailer that sells the jeans I like, and I need a pair.

I quicken my step and ignore the small voice inside me saying: *Control yourself, Celia, you're here to save money, not spend it.* I haven't been paid yet so I have to manage on a budget.

It's amazing how easy it is to silence that voice, to shift my reason to a place where everything fits as I want it to. Freud called it "defence mechanisms," cognitive justifications to defend against emotional distress or anxiety. I leave my small voice and conscience in the parking lot, battling over the rights and wrongs of buying something for myself, while I grab a cart and rush to the jeans section. I find my size, amazingly so, and tell myself that "it's meant to be." They wouldn't be there if I wasn't meant to have them, and all restraint leaves me. I pack my body into them and stretch this way and that looking in the mirror, thinking that they were made just for me. I buy two pairs and then I find the web cam, and Greta's right, they are cheap. I feel smug as I line up at the check-out. Yes, I will have a good day, thank you Ma'am, and I can't wait to get home to put my jeans on. I'm in heaven.

I'm also in heaven when I stop off at Burger King and drive through, such an American thing to do, to order a double whopper. It's too good to eat in the car so I decide to take it home to eat later. My mouth is watering and I know they're bigger and better than the imitations that English Burger King's offer at home. I'm feeling greedy and my small voice has long since deserted me, and is probably still standing there arguing with my conscience in the K-Mark parking lot.

I stop off at Kroger's and buy some more beer, as you can't buy it here in the States on a Sunday—a bizarre practice that reminds me that although this is supposed to be the most powerful nation in the world, some of their practises belong to the Middle Ages!

I'm reminded of a dinner party I once held years ago on a Sunday, and as I was slow in organising the catering, I left it until the morning of the "do" to go shopping for food and wine. I was never more embarrassed than when I was refused the wine at the check-out and had to ring round to all my guests and ask them to bring their own. I've never made that mistake again.

I pick up a Kit Kat for Ellen and remind myself to tell her that they are very different in England; she'll be enthralled.

Her face is a picture when I give it to her.

"For me?"

"Of course," I say, opening it for her.

"The Kit Kats we have in England are a very different shape. I once took loads of these home for the cub-scouts in my husband's pack. They couldn't believe that they came in different shapes. Then they brought out the chunky version. Oh my God, that's to die for."

"You don't say," she nods, her mouth full and in such chocolate heaven that she doesn't care that splinters of chocolate are hanging on her chin. Who would?

"Do you ever have a hot drink—tea, hot chocolate?" I ask, knowing how good chocolate is with a hot drink.

"Well, not often, not as often as I'd like. She won't let me have coffee." Her eyes glaze over. "I love coffee but she says it's bad for me."

"Well, she's probably right," I concede. "Most things that are good are bad for us," thinking of beer, cheese on toast (grilled cheese) and cake. "Still you could have decaffeinated coffee and that wouldn't be so bad, would it?"

"That's what she says I have to have, but I still don't get any."

I make a mental note to ask Greta if I can give Ellen a cup of decaffeinated coffee, not only so that she can have what she likes but so that she can have a hot drink. It seems completely alien to me that she drinks only cold water. I'd die without my hot cups of tea, but then I'm English and I'm not sure if drinking cold water is an American cultural norm; it certainly isn't in England. The first time I went to an American restaurant I was shocked when the waitress brought us glasses of iced water. It just doesn't happen in England. Weird!

"I bought some jeans," I gush.

"Oh my!"

"I'm just going to put them on. Oh God, I'm excited," I enthuse, as if Father Christmas has just whispered a secret in my ear.

"You know it," she says, biting off another mouthful of chocolate.

I look at her as I'm about to dart off to put my jeans on and I love her so much. We're children together, blessed with the gift of play.

"Won't be a minute."

I pull the jeans on and I feel as if I've come home.

"DaDuh!" I say, twirling in front of her.

"Wonderful," she shudders.

I feel like a child, and nothing can strip me of my excitement, or so I think.

Greta appears in Ellen's doorway.

"What's all the noise?"

"Hey, Greta, you were right, the web cam was cheap at K-Mart, and I bought myself a pair of jeans. I love jeans and have been waiting for ages to get a pair."

I know I'm being pathetic, but I can't help it. I'm easily pleased. Sunshine will do it, or a rainbow, a mouthful of chocolate, babies' smiles, swallows diving, a robin's footprints in the snow, fruit hanging from trees; those are the things that are priceless to me. Diamond rings, ball gowns and fast, flashy cars are extraneous to me. Buying a pair of jeans seems decadent to me, and I'm so excited that I can't stifle it.

"Cool jeans," she says, and I appreciate it.

"Thanks," I say. I smile at her. It's a nice thing to say, and again I tell myself that maybe I'm wrong and that the last two weeks must have been stressful for her having a stranger in the house, and perhaps that's why she's been off. Maybe this is the real her in front of me, and so I try to engage her.

"I'm a bit fat for jeans, I know, but I love them so much. When I was a kid "teddy boys" were all the rage, and I so wanted a pair of jeans and a pair of baseball boots, but my mother wouldn't let me have either, saying they were only for boys, so I guess it's stuck with me all this time, for I just love wearing jeans."

She raises one eyebrow and I'm again reminded of an identity kit game, as her eyebrow looks so mobile that it belongs somewhere else other than on her face.

"Mothers!" she says, and in an instance my exuberance is snuffed out, and I know that we haven't communicated in the slightest, despite my hopefulness. I stand there with my mouth open, not knowing what to say and have the urge to strip myself of my jeans and don a tweed skirt and a twin set. How did she get to the exclaimed "Mothers!" said in such a derogatory tone, when I was enthusing about fulfilling one's desires by wearing the latest fifties' fashions?

I'm stumped and I glance at Ellen. She knows that I'm cast adrift in an ocean of castration, where joy and fun are shipwrecked and drowned beneath the waves of resentment.

Ellen doesn't know what to say, nor do I.

Greta speaks and she transports the conversation to a place where she's in charge.

"Did you get the web cam and microphone?"

I'm kick-started into joining her wavelength, and suddenly animated, I repeat myself, saying "Yes, you were right, it was really cheap. Thanks for the advice."

I swear she grows a few inches; she certainly looks smug.

"Well, go and get it then," she orders and I do as I'm told, happy that she's going to help me so that I can contact Dessy at will.

I'm in awe of her knowledge of computers. I know that we all have our own fields of expertise but that doesn't detract from the fact that I'm in awe of people who know things that are alien to me. I virtually skip to my room and bring out my purchases.

"That's the same one I got," she says, and I feel comforted. Good, at least I did that bit right.

She goes into my room and switches on the computer. I walk in behind her and stand there alive with anticipation.

She says "Oh no!" loudly, and I look over her shoulder to see what's the matter, although I don't know how I'm supposed to react. The monitor has a wild dance flickering across the screen.

"Well, it's never done *that* before," she says, and I'm aware of a sinking feeling in my stomach that robs me of my jubilation. As I stand there behind her, I hate the fact that I'm not at all surprised, or that somewhere deep within me I expected this. She shrugs, and I sense the same pathological payoff to the psychological games entitled *"Look how hard I've tried,"* and *"Look how hard I've worked for you."* I feel helpless and childlike as I whine in my head: *But it's not working and you said that you can fix it!*

I do a remarkable job of re-framing it all, *for* if the computer in my room is duff then there's always the one in the study, which is meant for Ellen to use. So I say, "Well, it doesn't matter so long as the computer in the study works. After all, Ellen and I can share one."

She huffs at me and I feel chastised and wretched—the excitement of my new jeans long gone. I'm silenced by her saying, "Look, I'm tired. I didn't sleep last night. I don't have time for this, okay? You're eating into my day off and I'm not doing anymore, all right?"

I feel like a heel. I've always hated to ask for anything, so I've already over stepped my mark and I backtrack, big time.

"I really appreciate that you've made a computer available for me and for Ellen upstairs, thank you. It's okay. Why don't you go and rest."

I've said the wrong thing.

"How can I rest when she constantly bangs on the floor for me? She's been doing it all day. I can't rest; there *is* no rest for me."

I hear my mother's voice and I'm scared deep within the core of me, "*There's no rest for the wicked.*" It doesn't occur to me then that my brain is showing me the way, that the symbolism I postulate about all the time as a psychologist is telling me something. She's tired, continually tired. There's no rest for the wicked and wickedness rests upon her.

I feel like wringing my hands with helplessness and resign myself to another day of not seeing or speaking to Dessy. I really do feel wretched.

I take a walk up to my friend's house, desperate to talk my feelings out with someone who'll anchor me back to sanity, but she's just on her way out so I walk back down the road.

While I was out Greta has got Ellen into her wheelchair and she's parked in front of the television so we spend the whole day watching slushy movies. I can't sit there all day and do nothing, so I knit.

It's that time of year again when I knit a little footballer doll for my daughter to commemorate the death of my grandson, Jordan. Ellen's eyes are wide with wonder as he suddenly takes shape with black boots, blue and white striped socks, white shorts and a blue sweatshirt.

"Well, would you look at that," she says.

Periodically Greta comes upstairs and casts an eye over his progress. She comments about how inane the movie is, but we don't care for we're having fun "visiting" all day.

I slide into bed feeling vaguely ashamed of myself for having watched eight hours of television, a thing I never ever do, but justify my slothfulness by a sense of satisfaction that the doll is almost finished. I just have to do his arms, ears, boot tags, and think about how to do his hair. The hair is what makes them unique. I've done David Seaman's dark ponytail (England's famous goal keeper), David Beckham's Mohican, and my grandson's grandfather's balding grey strands. Each one has a number on his chest to remind us of that dreadful day when the doctor pushed his thumb into Jordan's fragile skull trying to push him back up into the birth canal, then ruptured his liver trying to get him out by caesarean section. My daughter has a line of the little footballers propped on a shelf each with a different hair style, and she says that they give her a modicum of comfort when thinking about her lost little prince.

I awake feeling desperate to talk to and see Dessy and I wonder how I'm going to tackle Greta to see if she'll set up the computer in the study for me to use. I'm already resigned to the fact that the one in my room is a dud and the one downstairs is now out of bounds, being in her bedroom and not in the den, but hopefully the one in the study will be okay. I don't have to approach her, because once I remove my earplugs I can hear her next door in the study.

I get up and say brightly, "How's it going?"

She's in a foul mood and my heart sinks. "That's the best I can do. You can see and hear him but he can't see you."

"Oh, why?" I ask, confused.

It feels like a reasonable question but the look on her face tells me that I've said something I shouldn't. I guess I've dared to challenge her. She's so sarcastic that I feel flayed alive. "I've already told you *that* when I was trying to fix it last week, when I tried to download my web-cam software, it wiped out the sound. I've already told you, so why are you asking?"

She stands up and starts to walk out of the room.

"If you try and download the web-cam you bought yesterday and it wipes out the sound, don't come asking me to fix it because I'm not going to do it, and you'll have to pay someone to come and put it right."

She's gone and I'm left with my thoughts reeling and anger coursing through my body. Again I feel helpless and controlled; for she knows that I don't know how to do any of this. Her threat leaves me unable to even try my new camera. Perhaps something is wrong with hers, why won't she try and download mine? I don't get it, and I think I'm not supposed to.

I log on but I can't tell Dessy about it all as she'll hear me so I type it out for him and I spend most of our time together looking at his bald patch while he leans forward to read the screen. I can hear him and see him so it's easier for me than it is for him. The sight of him hurts and gladdens my heart at the same time, and I type "Blow me a kiss" and "Smile," which he does obligingly.

"What's happened?" Dessy says through the computer. "Why can't you use the computer that works?"

I have to type it all. Yes, why indeed? What was the purpose of taking the only computer that works properly and moving it into her room, where it would be impossible for me to use, as she'd promised me I could before I came to America? Why did she have to move it from the den? I understand that she wanted to make a private "bed-sit," a space of her own in the house, but the whole of downstairs is her domain anyway. Ellen can't get down there, and I would only log on for one hour each day before going to work, a time when she would rarely be on the computer. It would have been so much less trouble to have left the computer where it was.

She kept saying to me during my first week here, "Celia, you live here now, you can go anywhere in the house except my room. You *live* here," and I had thought her so generous. But the reality of it is that the one thing I need to keep me from going crazy with homesickness she removes from me like a dog in a manger, and replaces it with something that will keep me constantly at the mercy of her. Greta has found the perfect way to control me, as she knows that I'm desperate to see my man and my kids, and in my I.T. ignorance I *have* to ask her to help me. She calls my bluff about trying to do anything for myself, knowing that I won't have the money to pay for any repairs if the faulty computer subsequently develops symptoms, which it inevitably will. I feel completely knobbled, and so cornered that I'm desperate to sob, but I do what I'm good at and hold all my pain in.

"You're breaking up," Dessy says, meaning one thing but two things to me, and then I can't hear him and he can't hear me. I log out and on again and we make contact again. "What happened?" he types laboriously.

"I don't know," I say, "maybe it's got something to do with Greta being logged on to the same programme downstairs. I don't know; it's all beyond me."

It happens again, and then again, and Dessy gets fed up and logs off for good. I'm so irritated and the whole thing feels crooked. It's already obvious to me that Greta needs to be in control and manipulates people and situations around her to justify her inactivity and withdrawal from the world, but even recognising that, it feels more sinister. There's spitefulness about her, a sense of "If I can't have closeness in my life, you can't either." It's as if I can only have contact with my family through her, and she has to be instrumental in it, as if she's the pivotal axis in the lives of those around her.

I muse through my anger. Is it a need to be in control or to be needed, to gain strokes and recognition, or is she driven to destroy anything good around her in order to maintain her barren existence? If it's the latter, what would be her motive to remain in such a joyless situation, and then it dawns on me—it's her hatred of her mother that is her main driving force. All the time she has no joy in her life and stays only semi-alive, she can blame her mother and say, "It's because of you that I have no life." How better to hurt someone than to have them totally reliant upon you and to constantly let them know that they are the cause of your pain, isolation and failure? I'm sickened by my insight and curse my knowledge.

I do what my mother used to do when she was upset or at a loss as to what to do: I make a cup of tea. I put the television on and try to find the news channel, as I'm desperate to hear of the world outside these four walls. I feel cast adrift from the rest of the world. It doesn't tell me much though, because American news is mainly about America and the rest of the world seems to be ancillary.

I start knitting the doll's arms and swallow back tears as I think about my grandson lying alone in his grave, on top of a windy hill that overlooks the town I grew up in. An hour later Greta walks past me without speaking and goes into Ellen's bedroom, and I hear the poor woman cry out beneath instructions to "Lock your knees. Stop it. Put your hand there, no, not there. For Christ's sake listen to me. What did I just tell you?"

Moments later Greta storms through the living room and disappears out of sight. I get up and move so that I can watch Ellen wheel herself out to the lounge to be with me. I feel such love and compassion for her as she struggles to push the wheelchair forward. I'm ashamed to say that I feel so scared and intimidated by Greta, should she creep back up and catch me, that I don't go to Ellen's aid to get her over the bump in her doorway but let her use her wasted arms to wheel herself towards me. In that moment I truly hate myself.

Greta is prowling, obviously unsettled, and within minutes she's back in the kitchen pacing between the counter and the doorway.

"She always takes this long. You'd think that no one's spent hours giving her occupational therapy (OT), wouldn't you?"

I don't know what to say. I feel caught. I feel that she wants me to side with her, to acknowledge how hard her life is, but although I can see that she's not coping, I can't sit there and "join forces" with her against this defenceless woman. All sense of decency would stop me from doing that, even if Ellen were a bitter and twisted woman that defied any human being to find good in her.

I feel as if I'm being forced to sit astride a pair of scales, justice scales from the Old Bailey in London, and choose where my allegiance lies. How do I make a choice when it's obvious that I would choose goodness and sweetness against such antipathy and hatred? Yet the choice is not so simple when the one full of antipathy and hatred has all the power; power to keep her mother alive and power to give me a roof over my head. I hear my mother's voice in my head: "Do the right thing," and right this minute I long for my mother and no one else.

Greta's banging and clattering in the kitchen, and Ellen cringes and shoots me a look that says: "Please be okay with this and don't worry, this is how she is," and I shrug, wearing a bleak smile. I want to dispel her shame and to reassure her at the same time, yet I'm sure that my face is giving me away as it always does.

Compelled by anxiety, I leave Ellen in front of the television and go into the kitchen where Greta is opening a can of processed ham, the sort that only very poor people in England would eat.

I don't want to eat it and yet I know that I'm going to have to because something tells me that part of Greta's worth is tied up in cooking and rationing out food and favours.

"What can I do to help?" I ask.

"Nothing."

"Shall I set the table?"

"If you want."

I set about trying to make myself busy but succeed in irritating her because I have to ask where everything is. I'm trying not to wring my hands.

"D'you want a beer?" I ask, dismayed that in times of stress it seems to be the only thing I resort to.

To my surprise she says yes, and so I crack one open for her and dare to hope. I try to engage her in conversation and I know that I'm creeping. I hate myself for doing it and feel the slippery slope of co-dependence calling to me.

I try to be empathic. "It's obvious to me that you've got an awful lot on your plate; do you get enough sleep?"

Her face appears to soften and suddenly it all feels a little safer, so I dare to carry on.

"It's really important to get enough sleep, you know; no one can cope without enough sleep."

"I sleep really badly," she says. The whole of her face changes as if she's become someone else.

"You know, when I was Matron of a four-hundred-year-old school in England, the one thing I used to harp on to the kids who suffered with exam stress was that without sleep everything seems so much worse."

She virtually ignores me and opens a can of cut green beans that are a funny colour even for canned beans, and pours them into a saucepan, and then starts to make powdered mashed potatoes.

What happened to peeling and mashing potatoes like my Dessy insists on doing?

"Well, that's just fine if you can get any sleep, but with her constantly wanting me throughout the day, the only time I get for myself is at night."

I say "hmm," feeling silenced, not really knowing what to say. I understand her need for time for herself, everyone needs that, so I steer the conversation towards the computer software that allows her to speak to, and see people, around the world.

"I guess that's when you chat to your Internet friends. It's good that you have that medium to reach out to others."

She puts a huge dollop of butter in the powdered potatoes and I'm already thinking about my waistline and arteries. She smiles at me.

"You know, I love to cook," and she hooks up a glob of potato on her finger and pops it in her mouth. She smacks her lips. "Hmm, it needs more butter," she says, hacking off another chunk and dropping it into the mixture.

"It's okay, but it's hardly real though, is it?" she says, getting back to what we were saying.

"Do you still act as a mediator?"

"No, I gave that up. It was crazy. I couldn't be bothered with it all."

I want to ask her how she makes her money then, as I was under the impression that she worked as a consultant for the owners of the software, helping users to sort out their technical difficulties and then by monitoring the users in chat-rooms.

"Too many people think that they're the bosses," she says, slopping potato onto three plates.

"So you just chat on-line now then?"

"Oh, I do more than just chat. There's a game that I'm involved in with people all round the world and sometimes I play it all night. It's pretty cool."

I'm feeling a bit confused. If she stays up all night playing some Internet game, then should I be feeling sorry for her when she feels tired and unable to cope? I banish the thought and say, "Oh, it's all beyond me."

"Sit up to table," she barks at Ellen, while I open the fridge and take out two more beers and put them on the table.

"Ellen, what would you like to drink?" I ask.

She stops wheeling herself and shakes, "Oh, I'm all right. I've got my water."

"Are you sure? There's some juice in the fridge."

"Yes, thanks, I'm fine."

She gets stuck on the bump between the two rooms again and once again I feel knobbled, because I know that I can't give her wheelchair a nudge while Greta's in the room, and so I watch with anxiety gnawing at me while she trembles and tries over and over, her jaw set with concentration. All the time Greta is sighing behind me with predestined exasperation. How much easier Greta could make her own life and Ellen's if she would help her mother, yet that's not what drives her. This isn't about making her or her mother happier; it's about humiliating Ellen, and procuring sympathy from me for the awful situation Greta has found herself in, and to offer condolences and veneration for her martyrdom. I feel so sick and not in the slightest bit interested in eating.

Once Ellen makes it over the bump on the floor, it takes her forever to make the three-point turn in order to park herself at the table. When she's finally there Greta puts a tea towel, that serves as a napkin, on the table and orders her to put it on, and then she plonks a paper plate in front of her. I'm feeling really nauseous, as Ellen can't even raise her hands to the back of her neck to place the tea towel around her let alone tie it, so I go to help her but Greta says "No!" almost before I've lifted my backside off the pine bench.

"Oh no you don't, Celia. This is part of her OT," she states. "Her physiotherapist has given her exercises to do and this will help her achieve them."

I'm silenced, but I sit there thinking of all the patients I've nursed over the years whose mobility has been compromised, and the idea of therapy was to strike a balance between what a person can do and striving to reach achievable goals. This doesn't feel at all like that, though. This feels like the goal is set way beyond her reach. In fact, as I sit here watching the poor woman struggle and fail, I'm struck with the idea that the goal is nothing more than humiliation and an excuse to offload anger and hatred. Nausea is my constant companion.

Ellen struggles and I gulp my beer down in an attempt to do something with my hands, which are desperate to wring themselves, and Greta stands over Ellen whilst she shakes and pats the tea towel to her chest, for that's as far as it's going to go. Greta walks away to the counter to pick up her own plate.

Ellen looks over at me and sees me downing my beer.

"I think I *will* have a juice," she says.

Greta explodes and I feel blasted to kingdom come.

"See! As soon as I fix myself a tray she wants something so mine gets cold. She does it every time. I can't have anything for myself without her ruining it."

She's instantly beside herself and as the beer seeps through me and loosens my tongue, my need to placate her and rescue poor Ellen, who looks stunned and frightened, overcomes my own trepidation.

"Come and sit down. Surely there can be a compromise. Ellen

can wait for her juice. She didn't mean that she wants it right now. You're standing behind her; she can't see that you're just about to pick up your meal and sit down."

"Celia, you don't know anything. She does this all the time. As soon I try to get myself something to eat she starts and mine gets cold, and I'm sick of it."

She picks up her plate and stomps off down the stairs into the dungeon.

I stand up feeling utterly sick and tie the tea towel around Ellen's neck to reduce the humiliation I know she has to be feeling, and I ask her if she'd like some juice with her dinner.

"No, I'd better not," she says fearfully.

"Listen, Ellen, if you want some juice you can have some juice. It really isn't a problem and it's no trouble," and it isn't.

I pour her juice from the fridge and grab another beer. I'm not coping, I know I'm not. This feels sick, sick and totally pathological.

I push Ellen's wheelchair in so that her stomach is touching the table, knowing that such a small action will prevent her from dropping most of her food on the floor, and suffering the consequences. It's such a small thing to do yet the simple manoeuvre allows Ellen to succeed and maintain what little dignity she has left. She's so embarrassed as she eats and it pains me. I afford her as much dignity and self respect as I can by ignoring the food dropped down her front and talk to her about her history. I listen to her describing the gems in her life between each spoonful of dinner that zigzags across the space in front of her to her open mouth, an expectant chasm that is often left unfulfilled and shocked as the plastic spoon hits the side of her lip, its contents cascading down her front.

My feelings are in turmoil. I feel set up. That's what this feels like. This unpleasantness could so easily have been avoided. *I* could have made the dinner rather than Greta feeling compelled to cook, Ellen could have been helped to the table, which would have prevented all the food from being cold, either I or Greta could have tied her tea towel around her to avoid spills down her clothes and messing the floor, and I could have got her juice or she could have waited. As I ponder on these things I'm sure that unpleasantness and trauma is Greta's goal, and Ellen and I have just been conned.

I shove my thoughts away because they're too painful and too scary. Somewhere deep down I know that I've walked into a hornet's nest and it feels extremely unsafe. I feel scared, so I pack my feelings away and force myself to think of Ellen and how she must be feeling.

We "visit." She tells me about her childhood, how she was considered the favourite, although she couldn't see it herself, and how she loved her mother, but was a little scared of her father, and I tell her about my parents, but leave out the pain.

She finally finishes the food on her plate, which is stone cold, and I suggest that we go and watch some more television. I glance behind me to check that Greta isn't prowling about, and I push Ellen over the bump in the doorway. She looks up at me and whispers "Thanks" and the bond between us grows stronger.

I know that I would never disempower anyone by doing things for them when they are capable of doing it for themselves, but this isn't about disempowering, it's about saving someone from humiliation and persecution. It's about recognising what Ellen can do for herself and what she can't. I've underestimated Greta though, and the severity of the game she's playing, for she knows exactly what Ellen can and can't do. So if I stick up for Ellen and say that she's done what Greta demands of her in order to protect her, she'll know I'm lying.

The balance of power and the dynamics between us is changing and I'm beginning to feel really frightened. Once again the image of a giant spider lurking, biding its time and watching me struggle, becoming more and more ensnared in its web, becomes ever more vivid and infiltrates my dreams each night.

# 11

I GO TO BED, FEELING BAD that I've left Ellen sitting in front of the television but not knowing what to do, I sit on the edge of my bed with the bean casserole churning in my stomach, and I try to read my book. It's only moments later when I hear Greta wheel Ellen into her room and I crane my ears to hear what she says as she dumps the poor woman into bed, but her voice is so low that it's muffled and I can't hear anything. I hear Greta padding past my door, a sound that will be indelibly etched into my brain for all time, and I turn my light off, praying for sleep to dampen the disquiet in my head and the agitation in my stomach.

I toss and turn but finally fall asleep until I'm awoken by hushed mutterings that filter through the muffled sounds of my own breathing. I snatch out my earplugs, instantly alert.

"What else do you want?" I hear Greta ask her mother, and almost instantly she says, "No, I'm not doing that. The carer can get you that since that's her job. If they don't do what they're supposed to do that's not my fault," and I hear Greta walk past my door.

I'm so glad it's Monday. I can get out of the house and go to work. I have Vicki, Dwayne and Alex there to sustain me, and in the absence of my Dessy I value them more than I can say. Every evening I have a story to tell them of the latest horrid thing Greta has done to her mother and how afraid I am, and Dwayne, in his quiet and unobtrusive way, says that I need to find somewhere else to live. I don't listen to him though, because I'm scared. I feel so alone and long to go home to the comfort of my man who would make everything turn out okay. But he's thousands of miles away and I have to sort this mess out myself, only I'm too scared to know what to do.

Each evening I grab a "sanity hug" from Alex, who I decide in an instant that I want as a son-in-law, and curse that I don't have more daughters. He sustains me and amazes me. He's only thirty-two yet has the shoulders of someone much older. I have the strangest feeling when I'm around him that he's a natural with wounded souls.

I jump up and open my door, peering around to see if Greta's gone, and when I think I've heard her go downstairs I poke my head into Ellen's room.

"Hi, babe, is everything all right?"

"Why, yes."

"Can I get you anything?"

"Some water would be good."

I take her old water bottle, which is again lying empty on the floor and leave it in the kitchen sink before going to the fridge to get her a cool bottle of water. I can feel anger racing through my veins again. Is this what Greta said that the carer should do: fetch her some water? I'm ashamed that it's midday and that I haven't stirred before now, but my shame is usurped by anger and the realisation that Ellen has been without water since last night, yet when she's asked for some, Greta has refused and also used the opportunity to denigrate the carers.

I take the bottle to Ellen and she sucks thirstily on the straw. My heart is heavy.

There's a knock on the door and Ellen looks scared.

"I'll get it," I say, and walk through the lounge and open the front door, even though I'm still in my nightshirt.

"Hello, I'm Tracy, I'm Miss Ellen's new carer."

"Oh, come in. I'm the lodger."

"My, it's cold outside," she says. "They said the weather was going to change and they weren't wrong."

She seems a nice lady, one whose concern is about empowering people and leaving them with dignity. No sooner have I let her in than Greta appears in the doorway.

"You need to fix my mother some food and clean her room. Oh, and don't forget you need to change her bed linen," she orders.

"Ma'am, I'm only allocated an hour but I'll try and do as much as I can, okay?"

I go back into my room and after only ten minutes Greta raps on my door and asks me if I want to go shopping with her. I'm still trying to befriend her, so despite not wanting to be anywhere near her I agree to go. I've got time before work.

She pokes her head around Ellen's door and asks her if there's anything she'd like and Ellen asks for a vanilla milkshake. Bless her, she has such humble tastes.

It happens again, Greta doesn't need anything from the shops and as soon as we drive up the road she suggests going to the Chinese restaurant, so I agree, partly because I'm hungry and partly because I need to placate her. In my naiveté I believe that if I can only befriend her and make her happy, then she'll be nicer to Ellen. Looking back I see that I'm a naïve fool and nothing I can do will change this woman or have a positive impact upon her hatred for her mother. I'm in a league that is way beyond me and I'm too stupid or too full of my own importance to see it.

We're full to the brim with exquisite food, and I mean full. As we stand there waiting to pay, I can't help the thoughts from popping into my head again that she is dining on her mother's money. Greta does nothing to earn any money herself, or to pay her own way. Yet she spends her mother's money, not as if it were her own—she'd be more careful if it were her own hard-earned money—but as if it were going out of fashion. I'm sickened by the heaviness in my stomach but also by the heaviness in my heart.

She drives towards home and I remind her to get Ellen's vanilla milkshake.

"Yeah, right," she says, and turns the wheel but misses the turning for McDonald's and pulls into TCBY, which is right next door.

"This isn't Maccy-Dees," I say trying to play with her, but she's in no mood to play.

"Oh, this'll do her. She likes TCBY."

I don't really know what to say because it's likely that she does like TCBY, but she asked for a McDonald's vanilla milkshake and that's what she should have.

I feel a bit sick and have no idea what move to make in this new pathological game of human-relationship chess. I use my fail-safe strategy: when all else fails, play.

"Oh, come on, it's only next door, we've just eaten a feast, we have to take her what she wants."

She huffs and puffs and shoots me a look that could wither my soul, but from somewhere I gather some fortitude.

"Come on," I play. "It's only next door, you don't even have to get back onto the main road; it's in the same parking lot."

"She'll be all right with a frozen yoghurt," she says, in a tone of voice that says: *If you know what's good for you, you'll shut-up*, but she double-backs and pulls into the drive-in at McDonald's and I feel some sense of relief. To me it seems immoral that Greta should eat to her heart's content at her mother's expense while Ellen has so little, and whatever she does want is denied through disdain or her daughter's "I can't be bothered" attitude.

She speaks into the drive-through microphone: "I'll have a happy meal to go," she says.

"With a vanilla milkshake," I prompt.

She shoots me a vile look, which I'm able to ignore this time.

"Make that a vanilla milkshake," she adds with some venom, daring me to say anything else. I don't, for my goal is to get Ellen's needs met, and although I hate confrontations, the means to an end justifies my discomfort and Greta's irritation.

I wait until she hands me the bag and pulls away before speaking. "At home you get a toy with a Happy Meal. Is it the same here?"

"Yep."

"That'll be fun," I say with a giggle in my voice, hoping to lighten the atmosphere that hangs heavily in the car.

"It'll just end up in a box with all the other free gifts. She's got a box full of them," she says, dousing my enthusiasm. There's that scarcity thing again. It seems that whatever she's forced to get for her mother, she'll make sure that Ellen isn't allowed to enjoy it. It's like the stacks of bent cans of food, all with blue stickers on them, bought to elicit praise for Greta's thriftiness but left on the shelf uneaten; their purpose is not for enjoyment.

She dumps the Happy Meal bag on the kitchen table and shouts at Ellen to "Come and get it," and goes straight downstairs without putting the food out so that Ellen *can* get it. I fetch a paper plate and start to put the food out, but by the time Ellen reaches the kitchen and I've scooted her up to the table to save time, her food is stone cold and congealed. I can't leave her all alone, so I sit with her and tell her that in the box is a gift. Her eyes light up.

Remembering my first night here when Greta opened the cellophane on the chocolate shells I brought Ellen, I rip the plastic surrounding the small plastic doll. "Oh," I say. "It looks like it's part of a set. Cool. We'll get you all of them by the time we've finished getting you your vanilla shakes."

She's so easily pleased and says, "Oh my, isn't she beautiful," as she looks at the doll. This trinket isn't going to just end up in a box. She can at least look at it even if she doesn't want to fiddle with it, so I stand it in front of her so that she can see it while she tries to lift the cold food to her mouth. She picks up the milkshake as if it's incredibly heavy, which it probably is to her, and tries to move it towards her mouth, but the plastic dome lid is so high that it almost obscures the straw, so after she fails to connect her mouth to it time and time again, I take the lid off and hold it steady so that she can suck the milkshake up into her mouth. My only concern is for her to consume as many calories as she can before the effort of eating or sucking beats her and she gives up defeated.

I hear Greta stomping up the dungeon stairs and I can tell from the look on her face as she fills the doorway, with an accusation resting on her lips, that she's not happy.

"Haven't you finished that yet?" she snaps. "It's time you went back to bed." It's only 1400; does this mean that Ellen's day is over?

I suddenly feel really panicky, because I've thrown the dome lid away and if Ellen is in bed there's no way that she'll be able to drink from the paper beaker without spilling it everywhere. It's a catch twenty-two situation; she won't spill it if the lid is on but she won't be able to drink it because the straw is too short and without the lid she'll be able to reach the straw, but if she's in bed she'll spill it all over herself. I make a quick decision. Both Ellen and I are going to be in trouble if she takes the drink back to her room, so as there's only an inch left in the bottom of the cup, I snatch it up and run water into it before dumping the cup in the trash.

Greta says, "Right, get your stuff, you're going back to bed," but seeing me rinse out the cup, she says sarcastically, "Well, I guess you don't get to take your shake to your room."

My stomach is in shreds, and to hide the feeling of having been caught with my hand in the cookie jar for throwing the lid away, I become a bit brazen, and speak up.

"She's finished it and I'm just rinsing out the cup so that it doesn't attract bugs in the trash and mess up the bin."

Greta can't answer for there's nothing smart to say, and she storms off pushing Ellen into her room. It's the first time I've seen her help Ellen over the bumps—shame it has to be in reaction to feeling angry with me. I swear that her anger is a response to the girliness she hears between Ellen and myself. It seems that the closer I get to Ellen, the worse she is to both of us. It appears that I have crossed a line and it feels very dangerous, yet I ignore it because it's too scary and too painful to contemplate.

I'm so thankful to get to work. Alex instantly puts his arms around me and gives me my "sanity hug," and makes me giggle by asking how Godzilla is. I'm amazed that in the short time I've known him just how instrumental he's become in anchoring me down to reality when my head starts spinning. His presence is a stark reminder of what's right, and with each day that passes his wit and support are a gift, a priceless benevolent gift.

He has me in stitches at his tactics to restore order amongst fifteen wild prepubescent boys all intent on fighting and calling "your mother" at each other (an American insult—I had to ask what it meant!). He walks up and down the hall describing the most succulent pizza imaginable, and little by little each child stops insulting each other's heritage and groans.

"Stop it, Mr. Alex, you're making me hungry," they groan and he winks at me and moans in ecstasy as he relives the taste of cheese stuff-crusted pizza. I can barely contain myself as the giggles bubble from me and melt away the strain that had wrapped itself so tightly around me since I arrived in the States.

"Miss Celia, you know how stuffed crust is, dripping in cheese, with sausage and pepperoni dotted all over it?"

"I just love juicy black olives," I say, joining in.

"Don't, Miss Celia. Stop it, Mr Alex."

"Now, listen up," Alex says, and every head turns his way, the hall is so quiet that you can hear a pin drop. "Show me good, safe and respectful behaviour today and this evening I will buy you guys the pizza I've just described."

The kids line up quietly with their lips tightly jammed together, and when one little boy jabs his neighbour in the ribs and threatens to punch him, Alex takes a sharp breath in through his nose and says very loudly, "Ah, the smell of pepperoni and sausage stuffed crust pizza," and silence settles instantly upon the hall again. He is as true as his word and treats the children and staff alike to pizza, refusing any contribution to help pay for it.

He leaves at 2200 to go home to take care of Ben, and I know that he can't be sure of how much sleep he'll get. I'm left feeling moved by his care of others, and as he heads for the elevator, the nurses' station suddenly feels empty. Dwayne and I talk about him after he's gone and wonder at his generosity and caring. He is an asset to us, the hospital and every child that has the fortune to be in his care. We know that he's gone home to resume his care of Ben, who has slept throughout the day whilst Alex has been at work and who will be awake throughout most of the night needing assistance, which Alex will readily give. Dwayne and I vow to keep an eye on him.

The final hour after Alex has gone seems to drag; the sparkle's disappeared, with us aching from laughing so much from his continual clever quips.

I have so much to tell Ellen and giggle to myself as I drive home. Not only does Alex sustain the staff and children at the hospital, his wit and generosity reach those beyond his confines. I know Ellen will love him.

I shiver as I drive home and notice the first covering of frost since I arrived. It's almost midnight as I let myself in, cursing the fly-screen, and the bleeper that lets everyone know that I'm home, and the moths dive-bombing the outside light that try to get into my mouth. I snap the door shut and creep to my room. It's late and I don't want to wake Ellen if she's already asleep.

"Why hello, Celeste. Did you have a good day?" she calls, and I know that she's been waiting for me to get home. Has she been in bed, uncovered, since Greta forced her to go to bed nearly ten hours ago? I shake the thought away and although it remains niggling at my conscience, I try to ignore it and choose instead to pass on the sustenance that Alex has given me. I walk into her room ready to tell her about Alex's novel way of keeping control of fifteen feisty, damaged children, and his love and generosity, but cold silences me.

It's freezing outside and yet both Ellen's windows are wide open. Since I arrived it's been hot and stifling, yet Greta's never seen fit to open the windows, but now that the weather has changed to freezing temperatures they're suddenly opened. Not only that, but the ceiling fan is whizzing around at full speed, reducing the temperature in the room, directly above poor shivering Ellen.

"Babe, aren't you cold in here?" I ask astounded.

"Yes, I am. She opened the windows earlier and put the fan on."

"Don't you worry, I'll shut them," which I manage with some effort for they seem to be stiff and are obviously not used to being opened. The phrase "There's more than one way to kill a cat" pops into my mind and I try desperately to banish it, as my relationship with Ellen is not close enough yet for me to speak my mind about her daughter. I mean, we mothers are defensive about our children, no matter how bad they may be, and although our friendship is growing by the hour, I can't be sure how she would take it if I voice my feelings about Greta's treatment of her. I look at her, completely uncovered and unable to draw the one blanket she has up over herself, and I wonder what would happen had I not been here to help her. She would have been left since two o' clock until sometime the following day with the windows wide open and the ceiling fan turned up to its fastest, blasting frigid cold air directly onto a frail, infirm lady who could not pull her blanket up properly, and who had no water or food.

After tucking her in and vowing to make her some bed-socks, for her feet are purple, I decide to tell her about Alex. She's delighted and I'm humbled. It's nothing for me to tell her about my day and the precious people in it, and yet it's everything to her— her lifeline to the world outside these four oppressive walls.

The room is suddenly quiet as the ceiling fan grinds to a halt. I tell Ellen about the pizza and the way Alex is around wounded children, and she punctuates me with "Oh my, he sounds very special," and I agree that he is. I tell her about Dwayne too, for although he's quieter than Alex, he's so full; full to the brim with righteousness, tough caring, yet compassion with strength. He gives a precious gift to these children, a gift called boundaries. Between the three of us we make a perfect therapeutic family for these children.

"It sounds wonderful," she shakes, and I tuck her up so that she's warm enough to sleep.

"It is," I tell her, and I know that she knows, since she was a psychiatric nurse too when she was able to work. I smile at her because she looks as snug as a bug in a rug, and I know that we understand each other.

"Are you warm enough?" I ask.

"Oh, yes, I'm fine, don't you be a worrying about me," she answers as if her needs are completely insignificant.

I go to bed torn between reliving Alex's priceless impersonation of a pizza boffin and Ellen's acceptance of her deprivation. Sleep evades me and I struggle to know what to do. My own denial forces me down a path that insists that I do something to help both Ellen and Greta, for both suffer, although Ellen's suffering is easier to see than Greta's, as Greta forces everyone away. It is my psychology and psychotherapy training that forces me to acknowledge the depth of pain that Greta must feel, even if she refuses to acknowledge it, and how she benefits from her position of self-imposed martyrdom.

I wake up the next day to the sound of someone banging on the front door and voices outside my bedroom door. It's the occupational therapy lady and I can hear from Greta's tone of voice that she's angry, so I stay out of the way until the woman has gone.

I venture out of my room to make a cup of tea, and Ellen is already sitting in her wheelchair at the kitchen table whilst Greta is slamming dishes about.

"Morning," I say as brightly as possible but she grunts at me. I put the kettle on and she turns on me.

"You need to turn that kettle round the other way or else the steam will ruin all my packets of sauce mix."

I apologise and instantly turn the kettle to face away from the shelf above it, and stifle the thought that it didn't matter if they were ruined, they were all past their sell-by dates and she had no intention of ever using them anyway. Why can't she ask nicely? Why does everything that comes out of her mouth have a barb attached to it? I try to ignore it and put a teabag into my cup before sitting next to Ellen.

I pat her hand and she peers over the rim of her glasses and smiles at me, and I can tell that she's relieved that I'm there at the table with her.

"How did you get on with your OT, Ellen?" I ask, aware that Greta has stiffened.

Ellen opens her mouth to start speaking but is silenced by Greta and closes her mouth again, smiling sadly.

"The fricking woman's crap," Greta explodes. "You know she had the nerve to tell me that I've got to buy her an electric wheelchair. No way. I'm not having her tearing up the furniture with one of those things. She can't even use the one she's got properly without smashing into things; she'll be lethal with one that's motorised."

She slops a paper plate down in front of Ellen and I wonder how much longer that stale cake will last.

"It's okay for her to come in here and demand what I should do; she doesn't have to try and find the money for these things." I fight off the thought that flashes into my head that she doesn't have to find it either—Ellen's financial advisor does. "The woman's useless. What my mother needs is to build up her muscles by moving manually. She's lazy enough as it is; a motorised wheelchair will make her even lazier. Anyway, what's the point of spending all that money when we don't know how long she's got left to live?"

I can't believe that she can talk this way in front of Ellen, as if she's not in the room. I'm embarrassed and so is Ellen. I squeeze her hand and tell her that we'll have to feed her up, and she smiles gratefully at me whilst Greta looks at me as if I'm filth.

I leave the kitchen feeling totally helpless. I'm becoming sure that my presence and gentle attitude towards Ellen is making Greta treat her worse, so with my stomach in shreds I go to log on, determined to talk to Dessy.

He's there and he's breaking up but at least I can see him, and the sight of him makes me want to weep. He suddenly leaves the screen and goes downstairs, and it feels so weird watching things go on in my own home four thousand miles away, while I'm somewhere else. Dessy comes back and parks himself in front of the web-cam and I shriek, for his son and fiancée are standing behind him grinning at me. I'm so over the moon and we chit-chat with part of me being filled with wonder at modern technology and the other filled with awful homesickness.

The homesickness wins as they are suddenly dashed from my view and I have no idea what's happened. I try so desperately to avoid slipping into conclusions that may or may not be appropriate. Greta can hear me laughing with Dessy and she's gone downstairs to be on her computer. She has management access to this programme and suddenly my family has disappeared from view and they cannot hear me. We sign off in exasperation and it's all I can do to remain calm and grounded. At least I know that Dessy is all right as his son and fiancée are with him, but I feel alone, silenced, knobbled and very far from home. I can't understand what is going on with the computer or why it should be okay one minute and not the next. I feel a sense of anger tinged with helplessness; anger that Greta has moved the one computer that works properly into her room for her use only, and helpless because she has taken away the one medium I have to stay connected to my family. I try really hard not to make unfounded assumptions, but I don't trust her.

Suddenly she's standing behind me and asks how Des is. I tell her that the sound broke down and then the picture went, but she shrugs and turns away saying that she can't do anything about it because she's too busy.

"I just don't have time for this," she tuts, and rolls her eyes with her hands on her hips before walking out of the room. I try to ignore the sensation that she's merely come upstairs to gloat and to offload her irritation on me, but I can't help it. She'd gone downstairs after I'd left the kitchen to log on to speak to Dessy in the study and then after the programme was working it suddenly goes off and she's stood behind me, her tongue preloaded and my humiliation complete.

I'm relieved to get to work, and the nurse working with me sits and listens patiently as I tell her how mean Greta is to Ellen and to me. I feel ashamed of myself as I talk, because I've always been a forceful person. I've just finished working as a probation officer and nobody gets past me, but as I tell the nurse everything, I know that I sound like a prize wimp.

"You need to find yourself somewhere else to live," she says, and I nod but don't let the notion in for the thought of leaving Ellen appals me. I know that she's not my responsibility and that she's lived in these circumstances for several years, but now that I know about it, I don't know if I can live with myself if I just walk away and leave her in such dire circumstances simply because it makes me feel uncomfortable. I have to be honest too, I'm scared of living on my own since I've only done it once before. It was scary to me then at seventeen, and although I'm grown up now and very capable, I'm scared that if I'm alone my homesickness will be intolerable. I hear what my colleague says but don't really listen.

It's the same the next day and the next, where I offload the latest spitefulness that Greta has done towards Ellen and block my colleagues' advice that I should find somewhere else to live. I tell them how Greta badgers the physiotherapist telling him that Ellen is "minimal assist" and that he should work her harder, but watching him trying to get Ellen to take a step using a walker is nerve racking. She's too frail to do it and can barely lock her legs (one of which has just been broken) or take her weight, let alone move one foot in front of the other. He's told her that she needs continual physiotherapy and that she's unlikely to ever walk again. Greta is furious and fires him on the spot for his incompetence.

I tell them that the head physiotherapist came round to the house saying that he had an appointment with Greta and Ellen as he had to "sign her off," but Greta took Ellen out and missed the appointment. My face is red with shame when I tell my nurse colleagues that Greta insists that Ellen's catheter bag remains in situ because she's "damned if she's going to clean up the mess when she wets all over herself." They remind me of the risk of urinary tract infections, which in Ellen's malnourished state could kill her.

Alex looks at me and puts me straight.

"You know, here in America it's the law that you have to report abuse, and if you don't and it comes out later that you knew it was going on but you hadn't done anything about it, especially being a professional person, you'd be charged with a felon yourself."

I know I looked shocked and I want him to be quiet and go away. This isn't what I want to hear because it suddenly has nothing to do with my anxiety at living on my own and coping with my homesickness, it's solely about doing the right thing by Ellen.

"He's right," the other nurse says. "It's your duty as a professional to inform the authorities of any abuse you witness; you have to call it in. If you don't, you could lose your licence and you'd never be allowed to work again."

I feel sick and cornered. I'm not ready for this and am relieved when one of the children kicks off and the conversation ends, but it's only a temporary distraction, and my dilemma hangs over me throughout the shift and as I drive home.

Greta is up, and as my own denial clouds my judgement, I tell myself that both these women need help and perhaps I can do something to help them both. I ignore all the warning bells clanging loudly in my head, and as Greta makes for the dungeon stairs I call her.

"Greta, I've been thinking. It would be really nice if we had a lunch date once a week as I've been so busy lately that I feel that we haven't really had any time to talk. What do you think?"

I tell myself that perhaps she's so moody and resentful because my full and stimulating life shows up the barrenness of her own.

Her face lights up and I think I'm right.

"That would be great," she says.

"Good," I smile, stifling neon thoughts that say: *Crisis averted, perhaps you won't have to report anyone or find somewhere else to live.* "Shall we go tomorrow? It's Friday, and it'll be a nice way to end my week."

She smiles sweetly at me in the same girlie way as when I'd first seen her on the Internet, and as she heads for the dungeon door she says, "Oh, by the way, I spent hours sorting out the computer for you. It should be okay, now."

"Oh, thanks. What was wrong?"

"Oh, it's too complicated to explain it to you," and I feel that she's just blown me off.

A bucket of cold water flows over me and it all feels incongruent again, but I try my hardest to ignore my instincts and tell myself that I'm just too sensitive and that homesickness must be having more of an effect on me than I'm aware of. But deep down I know that I'm lying to myself.

# 12

IT'S FRIDAY AND TOMORROW I'll have been here three weeks. It seems ages since I left my man and an aeon until he comes out for Christmas. I don't even want to think about it for it seems insurmountable, so I steer my thoughts away to safer ground and head for the computer. Greta said that she'd fixed it, so I sit with anticipation waiting to see my man, but immediately I can tell that something's wrong and he's breaking up, then he disappears altogether. I try really hard to control the anger I'm feeling. What is this? She makes a point of saying that it's fixed and there's nothing wrong with it, yet within hours it's not working. Instinct tells me that when I tell her it's not working again, she's going to say something catty and denigrating towards either my or Dessy's lack of computer literacy.

As I fester with frustration and powerlessness I can't shake off the thought that if she'd left the one computer which worked perfectly in the communal den, then neither of us would be stressed and it wouldn't be an issue. Plus of course, if she had just the one computer that she had perfected, she wouldn't have had to spend her mother's money frivolously on buying two more computers in order to set up a network. She walks past the study and I pluck up the courage to tell her what I suspect she already knows: "It's not working."

"I'll have to get to it later," she says, as she goes to empty Ellen's bursting catheter bag. "If we're going out I won't have time to fix it now," she calls from the bathroom, and as I stifle a sigh I can hear Greta humping Ellen into her wheelchair.

I'm between a rock and a hard place and I feel so manipulated. I'd much rather stay home and talk to Dessy on the Internet but I can't do that until Greta's in a good mood with me, and she'll be in a bad mood with me if we don't go out to lunch. So I leave the neutered computer, feeling neutered myself, and am resigned to giving her my time in the hopes that if she's satisfied with my efforts to befriend her, she'll be more willing to work her magic with the computer. I feel as if I'm selling my soul to the devil and I hate what I'm becoming.

We say goodbye to Ellen and I ask her what she'd like us to bring home for her, and she says "a Happy Meal." I ramble on about the free gift adding a new doll to the one she already has, which is propped in front of her bed for her to look at.

I get into the passenger seat and resign myself to a few hours' ordeal—that's what it feels like—but I quickly tell myself that I have a choice. I can allow myself to feel despair by Greta's need to control, or I can go out and try to enjoy myself, which may make a difference to her and could improve the situation. I'm forever an optimist and looking back I see the folly of my ways, although now I understand them.

She drives and I mentally work out just how long this ordeal will take, but she cheats me by driving the back route, saying "Oh, look, garage sales. I just love garage sales," and she screeches to a halt and reverses so that she can enter a sub division. To my dismay there are adverts stuck to poles along the road that show the way to two garage sales, and as she milks my presence, I become resigned to handing over my time. I mean, what does it cost me, nothing I can't afford as a human being? I tell myself that all life is an experience, and as I've never actually been to a garage sale before, this will be part of my education.

We pull up and as we're here, I make the best of it and walk towards the home, whose garage is open like a gaping mouth showing everything it had for breakfast, dinner and tea. I'm embarrassed as Greta ferrets amongst the molars looking for titbits to feed off, but under the scrutiny of the owners I remember my manners and try to cope with my feelings. I don't quite manage to shake off the feeling of intruding into someone else's life and picking the bones as vultures would over a kill.

The elderly couple opening their home hear my accent and are enthralled, calling their son to come and talk to me. "He's just spent several months in England," they say. I feel better; this is turning out to be a sweet experience, not because I can pilfer their bargains but because I can talk to sweet, honest people from a different culture. Their hospitality is a gift and we *visit*. Greta does no such thing and is intent on finding a bargain as she sifts through these beautiful people's things.

The difference between Greta's issues of scarcity and these sweet folks' generosity of giving and letting go is glaringly obvious before me. Their son tells me that he had been camping, and we talk about camping with the cub-scouts and trekking, and he leads me to a box of dried Soya instant ground beef. "They're okay," he says. "Not exactly the Peabody Hotel cuisine, but passable as stew, and they're only 10 cents a packet."

Greta comes up behind me and grabs a handful, whispering, "They'll be all right for *her*."

I hear the owners recount their tales of camping and how good the packets of Soya, were so I think: *Well, I'm here to earn money and economise so if they're that good I'll have some too.* So my first garage sale purchase is six packets of Soya meat. I was later to find out that they were awful and yet poor Ellen was forced to eat that or nothing, despite Greta having a freezer full of cheap chicken.

We leave and I wave to the sweet owners of the garage and feel privileged to have met them. They wave back and I know that my accent and tales shared with their son will please them long after the garage door is pulled down.

Greta pulls up in front of our favourite Chinese all-you-can-eat restaurant and I'm relieved that she chose it. I present my jovial façade but feel as if I'm going to the dentist without anaesthetic, and follow her into the smoking area. I don't smoke and she doesn't ask me if it's okay for me, but then we're not here for me.

God is with me though, for as I sit down my seat knocks into the one behind me and I turn to apologise, and there is my colleague from work. She cracks out laughing and we hug. I introduce her to Greta and pray that my friend doesn't say something like, "Oh, so *you're* her, are you?" but of course she doesn't, and she introduces me to her friend. I don't think I've ever been more pleased to see anyone, even though Greta and I stay at our table and my friend at hers, just her presence helps me.

My mother taught me good social skills so I start to make conversation to find out more about what makes Greta tick. I want to know, because even now I still want to help her, so I ask about her hopes and dreams.

Her mouth is full of food but she says through the churning mass, "I always wanted to be a nurse but as soon as I told *her*, she went and trained as a nurse herself and fucking well pissed on my parade."

I try to keep her talking but don't have the guts to ask her why her mother's nurse training would prevent her from undertaking the training herself, for truth isn't on the menu today, so I ask her what she'd like to do now. She says that she'd like to go to college and do something in computers so that she can work from home and not have to deal with the human race.

My friend scrapes her chair back and leans over to kiss my cheek, telling me not to tell the children at the hospital that she was "pigging out" today, and we laugh. Greta's lips are pursed with disapproval. After they've gone and I have nothing else to ask, I follow one of my basic instincts, and that is to devour pudding... chocolate pudding, so I leave her and shake a dollop into a bowl and savour the orgasmic delight that bursts upon my tongue. I feel like Nigella Lawson licking her fingers.

I look up and she has a plate piled high with all kinds of cakes and pastries and a bowl brimming with all kinds of pudding. Something changes in her face as she misses her mouth and a dollop of pudding drops on her chest, on her sparkling best top. It's a look that I'm not too sure how to interpret. I shake away my own embarrassment as being a relic of my mother's rigid table manners—a dollop of pudding down one's front would have been the height of sloppiness—but my mother's not here and maybe this will make her feel more human and closer if we can laugh about it. Not a bit of it. She pulls a face, one that says: *Don't even go there,* and without even glancing to see if anyone's noticed, she scoops the dollop up with a napkin as demurely as she can, but something is on her face that is unpleasant and unfathomable.

What is it? "Don't make fun of me or you'll be sorry," or "Don't even *comment* or you'll be sorry." I don't know how to make it right for her as she doesn't seem to be able to make light of it, as I can. I mean, I'm always throwing food over myself and one of my favourite sayings is that "A meal isn't really satisfying unless you can wear it, too!" I have no idea how to react, so I go to the pudding counter and help myself to some more. I'm comfort eating.

Americans' concept of "pudding" is called something quite different at home in England: "blancmange," and a pudding in England refers to any dessert. I giggle as I dollop the chocolate pudding into a bowl and think of a co-worker, a seasoned southerner here in the US, who was incredulous when I tried to explain that a "Spotted Dick" was a type of steamed raisin and suet dessert back home. We'd hooted with laughter one evening when he said that he could never go to England because if someone came up to him and asked if he wanted some Spotted Dick he'd have to go to the penitentiary because he'd just *have* to kill them.

I sit back down trying to stifle a giggle and wonder if I should I tell Greta what's tickled me but the look on her face silences me, so I plough my way through my second bowl of chocolate pudding.

"Are you done?" she asks, and I nod as she gets up, and even after having eaten a huge quantity of food she goes to the cake counter and demands that she should be able to take two cakes *to go*.

I'm embarrassed by the expression on the young, skinny Chinese waitress's face, and wonder what she must be thinking, having come from another culture where eating in such vast quantities would be unlikely.

Greta makes a scene, demanding something to put the cakes in and I stand there wishing the floor would swallow me up, yet watching the non-verbal communication of the staff around me. She stands in a silent game of people-chess, hands on her hips, with "Duh" on her face as she asks again for a napkin to go. When she gets one she picks out two small cakes and wraps them up. I'm embarrassed. How can these people make any money out of all-you-can-eat?

I feel like a robber. I should pay twice what they've charged me as the value is so good, but here Greta is taking a *"to go"* package. She could have at least given them a dollar for the cakes, but she's very brazen and obviously thinks it's okay to act this way. Perhaps I'm too English and am used to not having anything for nothing. I don't know.

"Thank you," she says at the receptionist, whose nostrils are flaring in disgust. "My invalid mother will really enjoy these."

She drives home, and although Ellen has asked for a Happy Meal and is always desperate for a vanilla milkshake, Greta *forgets* to go to McDonald's, and as she pulls up outside the house she acts all goofy.

"Oh, I've forgotten her burger and shake. Oh well, never mind, I've got her some dessert."

I can't believe it. We're stuffed to the gills and she can't even remember her starving mother, and even if she had forgotten her, she could quickly nip back down the road, it's only two minutes away at the most, but she doesn't and as she gets out of the car she yells. She's dropped her purse.

"Oh, no, I dropped my credit cards," she grins at me with her pseudo girlie smile, and says, "There are twenty-four of them."

I say nothing but I'm incredulous. That's an immoral amount of credit cards that are all charged to her mother's account. I don't know whether to help her retrieve them or hurry into the house because I'm worried that we've left Ellen alone too long, having gone to the garage sale instead of just going to lunch. It seems that to give Greta an inch, she can't just accept that, she has to take a mile. Anxiety eats away at me and I'm scared.

I have good reason to be. I open the door and hear an unfamiliar noise. My senses are confused for a second and I can't place where the sound comes from, but then I realise it's coming from the kitchen so I go straight in there, and on the floor, lying prostrate with virtually no clothes on, catheter bag strewn across the floor, Ellen lies, helpless.

She cries out to me, "I was trying to put my plate in the trash like Greta tells me I have to and I leaned too far forward."

"How long have you been lying here?" I ask, not knowing what to do.

"Since just after you went out. I tried to lift myself up but I couldn't."

I feel utterly sick and I know that I can't lift her myself, so I go back outside to where Greta is still gathering up the scattered credit cards.

"She has fallen. Ellen's on the floor," I cry, panic-struck.

"For fuck's sake."

Her sugar-sweet girliness evaporates in a second and she's like a raging bull, storming past me into the kitchen.

"What the fucking hell are you doing on the floor? You've done it again, haven't you? Whenever I go out you have to ruin it, don't you?"

She walks over to Ellen who cringes as she kicks her.

I'm horrified and sickened to my stomach. "Don't Greta, stop it," I cry.

She ignores me and hisses into the poor woman's face. "Well, *you* did this so you can fucking well stay there until I'm ready to pick you up."

"We can't leave her on the floor," I cry. "Let me help you pick her up."

Ellen looks at us, back and forth, and tries to pull herself up onto her elbow but falls back, helpless. I walk over towards Ellen but Greta stops me in my tracks, her face contorted with hatred.

"Celia, don't!" she says slowly and menacingly. I'm stunned

for she repeats those two words over and over for at least a whole minute. "Celia, *don't*. Celia, *don't*. Celia, *don't*. Celia, *don't*. Celia, *don't*. Celia, *don't*. I said, *don't*!"

I stand there staring at her, my head's spinning in disbelief, and I feel so intimidated and frightened that I don't know what to do. I glance at Ellen who's as terrified as I am. What madness is it that runs through this woman's veins that she can be so full of hate and cruelty towards her mother?

The phone suddenly rips through the stalemate that hangs over us and the surreal scene before me, and it's as if time has stood still. She picks up the phone and hands it to me. "It's for you; it's Des."

I take the phone and instantly he can hear that something's wrong in my voice. I walk out of the room and go into my bedroom and the horror of it all pours out of me.

"Ellen's fallen out of her wheelchair and Greta won't pick her up and won't let me pick her up," I say, my voice trembling with fear, having just witnessed such abuse and pathology that I can no longer kid myself that things are okay with Greta. There is something seriously wrong with her, seriously wrong, and deep within me I know that Greta has just stepped over an invisible line that if I do nothing will act as further *permission* to behave in this way again towards her mother, knowing that I'll just let it happen. I'm trembling.

I feel so agitated sitting on my bed listening to Dessy, who can't grasp the severity of Greta's behaviour, and who is no help as he merely says, "Just go back out there and pick her up."

"She won't let me," I cry, trying to explain, tears pouring down my face.

"Christ, she's sick, she must be. Cely, I'm scared. I want you to get out of there as quickly as possible. Please. Please find somewhere else to live. It's driving me crazy. I can't sleep for fear of what that woman might do. She's not right in the head."

"How can I leave Ellen?" I say, and I can hear the helplessness in Dessy's voice as I tell him I'm afraid to leave her.

I hang up after five minutes and take the phone back out to the kitchen, determined to pick Ellen up even if I have to battle Greta, but as I walk through the doorway Ellen is back in her wheelchair, a shrivelled soul enduring a telling-off from Greta.

I go back into my room, grab my bag and leave the house to go to work, ignoring Greta who calls out sweetly, "Have a nice evening."

I know my silence is passive-aggressive and I reproach myself for not saying more. I tried to help Ellen, I really did, but Greta was so intimidating that I was scared and didn't know what to do, nor did I want to make it worse for Ellen…try as I might, though, I don't know how I could make things any worse.

I feel sick as I walk into the hospital and a colleague smiles a cheery "Hello," expecting one in return. It comes to something when a psychiatric hospital can seem normal compared to the home I've just come from. I don't know how to re-join this normality in the state I'm in and so I hope no one stops me to chat before I reach the bathroom. I'm lucky, and as soon as the door is shut, I fall to pieces and sob with the pain and fear of it all, and vomit up the last all-you-can-eat meal I'll ever share with Greta.

Ten minutes later I stare at my reflection in the mirror and feel a sense of self-loathing that I hadn't done more to try and pick Ellen up from the floor, and the tears fall again.

A small voice inside me says that I need to get to the unit and start my shift but I don't really know how I'm going to manage as I feel splintered into a million smithereens. I splash my face with cold water and kid myself that I look composed.

I share the elevator with a colleague and of course she notices my red, puffy eyes. "Oh, you poor babe," she says. "Are you having problems with your allergies?"

"Yes," I say as I get off at my floor. "I'm allergic to the human race."

The sight of Dwayne and Alex robs me of any restraint I have, and I burst into tears all over again. I'm held by their "sanity hugs" and their counsel, before I can finally get on with the business of taking care of the little ones in my charge. I silence the small voice inside me that I am not honouring the vow I made to myself to keep the core of me safe, and I shake away the realisation that I haven't even *looked* at the doll lying on my bed for ages. My shame is compounded and I feel sick and frightened.

Throughout the shift everyone now knows what Greta did to her mother and their sense of outrage reinforces my belief that Greta is seriously psychologically sick, and all reiterate that I have no choice but to report the abuse to the authorities.

Alex says, "Call the police, right now. That's an offence," but I don't because it's not that simple. I know they're right but I'm scared to death because Greta will know it's me that's reported her and I don't trust what she might do to Ellen, or to me. I have nowhere to go and I'm reluctant to leave because I know that Ellen enjoys having me live with her. I'm also scared that if Greta can behave that way towards her mother in front of me, then what on earth is she capable of when there's no one there to act as a behaviour modifier—not that my presence seems to have modified *anything*. I feel completely cornered; scared to report her and scared not to, and scared to stay but also scared to leave.

As I drive home I have no idea what I'm going to say or do and relief flows through me when I see Greta's car is gone. It's 2330 and she never goes anywhere, so it's significant that she's chosen to be out when I arrive home. I go straight to Ellen's bedroom and poke my head around the door.

"Oh, Ellen, are you all right? I've been so worried."

She smiles at me and I know she's pleased and relieved to see me. "I'm all right," she says.

I decide that I can't pretend anymore, so I say what I think.

"You know, Ellen, what I witnessed today was the most disgusting, abusive thing I've ever seen. It made me sick to my stomach."

"I know," she says, shaking and trying to get her words out to match mine. "She said, 'Have a nice day' and I said, 'I doubt if she will now.'"

"I've had a terrible day," I say, "but not anywhere near as bad as yours. Ellen, this can't carry on, she cannot abuse you in such a way again."

"I know it," she shakes.

"Has this happened before?"

"Yes, she loses her temper. She's always been the same since being a child. I think she takes after her grandmother who was crazy. She had schizophrenia and adored Greta."

My mind does some quick thinking. "Has Greta ever had to see a psychiatrist?"

"Oh, yes," she says, with surprise in her voice that I needed to ask. "She had to be committed to the State Hospital once but it didn't help 'cause as soon as she got out she stopped taking her medication."

I hope she didn't see the fear flash into my face. I knew that my instincts had been right, and I silently cursed myself for not having listened to them. If I had, though, I'd have booked into a hotel when I first met Greta at the airport and I would never have met this beautiful woman.

"Is she taking any medication now?"

"No. She needs to, though. I think she's inherited her grandmother's sickness. She spent a lot of time with her as a child, you know."

"Be that as it may," I say, "it doesn't really matter whether she's suffering from any mental illness, she just cannot be allowed to be abusive to you."

"I know it. I'd be better off in a nursing home."

"You know, millions of people suffer with mental illness and never resort to behaving as abusively as she did today; it's no excuse."

"She seems to hate me and has always been like this. My husband was terrified of her. He used to sleep with a gun under his pillow when she was in the house."

"Good God, has she got a gun in the house now?"

"I don't know. It's probably packed away somewhere."

I feel sick. "Where is she now?"

"I don't know. She went out a few hours ago and didn't say where."

"I expect she didn't want to face me," and as I say it I have a mental discussion with myself. Hopefully she should feel ashamed at her behaviour and that would be why she's made sure that she's out. She certainly should feel ashamed, because there's no hope for her if she couldn't summon up a shred of shame at having been observed being so abusive. It is just as likely, though, that she's stayed out to match my passive-aggressiveness when I didn't speak to her as I left the house earlier, and is letting me know that she's angry with me by not being in.

I'm relieved that she isn't in so that I don't have to say what I'm really thinking and then have to endure her spitefulness. I just don't feel emotionally up to it. It also gives Ellen and me a chance to talk, really talk, for now that I've seen first-hand how her daughter treats her, and have commented and shown my disapproval, we can speak intimately. It's a defining moment, for Ellen doesn't have to pretend anymore and neither do I. From that moment the closeness between us grows to the exclusion of Greta, which serves to change the dynamics in the house and unwittingly places Ellen and myself in a more dangerous position.

I replace Ellen's water and ask her if there's anything she wants before I go to bed. Sleep evades me and I fret over what to do. All my colleagues at work have spelt it out plainly to me: as a professional person it is my duty to report any abuse towards children, the elderly or the infirm, and I could lose my licence if I do not. I am besieged with thoughts that dart into my head like fireflies but do little to light my way. I *know* that I have to report Greta, even more so now because if I don't, my silence serves to reinforce that it's okay for her to behave this way, however, I'm scared. I'm scared for Ellen should something go wrong and nothing or no one comes to her aid, for there's no way that I can carry on living here so she'd be alone, left at the mercy of an even angrier person than before.

I'm also scared to be the one that—should she be taken into a nursing home, which she already said that she'd prefer to being treated like this—initiates that final chapter in her life. Her home is *her* home, and losing one's home to enter institutional living is a monumental step, and I really don't know if she's ready for that. Her level of denial when Greta is merely sullen and neglectful rather than downright abusive, tells me that she's not ready for that final goodbye to her home. I'm scared for myself—scared to say goodbye to this beautiful lady, knowing that having reported Greta will sever all contact with Ellen, and lastly I'm scared for myself as to where I'm going to end up. I feel wretched and so far from home. Could this happen in England? Would our social workers and care staff be so easily dismissed without raising the alarm that something was wrong behind these closed doors? Maybe not to such an alarming extent as it happens in America, but yes, it can and does happen in England. There have been "tragedies" in the past in England where vulnerable children have been identified by the Social Services, yet those children have subsequently been murdered by their carers. (Maria Colwell, aged 7 years, 1973; Victoria Climbie, aged 8 years, 2000; Baby P., Peter Connolly, aged seventeen months, 2007.)

I toss and turn and it's 0300 in the morning when I hear Greta drive up and the intruder bell goes off telling me that she's back inside the house.

I sleep fitfully and when consciousness grabs me back into this hornet's nest, I take out my earplugs and immediately prick my ears to listen for anything.

I don't know what to do, so I run after hugging Ellen. I don't wash but slip into my clothes and go straight out, determined that I will not be around to have to speak to Greta. I know that I have to have it out with her and tell her that what she did was disgusting and cannot be allowed to happen again, but right this moment I don't feel brave enough, so I leave the house and wander around Wal-Mart for hours. I normally love Wal-Mart but today it holds no pleasure. I wander up and down the aisles seeing nothing, and bumping into people whilst mentally rehearsing what I'm going to say to Greta.

The human condition has an amazing ability to defend against all manner of pains and psychological distress. As I walk around Wal-Mart I reframe everything and reach a place where I needn't report Greta, I can stay in the house and be an advocate for my dear sweet Ellen, and lo and behold, not only that but I can help Greta cope with her problems. I decide that when I see Greta I'm going to talk to her from a nurturing stance and try to empathise with her, for there's little doubt that she's very stressed with having to take care of her mother. I vow to ask what I can do to help relieve some of her stress.

Armed with this narration and fierce denial, I go back to the house and immediately I go in to see Ellen. She's lying in her bed, her catheter bag full to bursting and her water bottle empty. I hear Greta coming up the dungeon stairs, so I quickly go to my room, my resolve failing me, and my shame and cowardliness laid bare before me. I throw a towel over "Little Cely" lying on the bed and ignore her presence and the knowledge that I've let myself down, as well as my own integrity. I feel worthless.

Ten minutes pass and I can hear Greta nagging at Ellen to straighten her legs as she transfers her to the wheelchair. Greta barks at her saying there's a sandwich on the table and then not to bother her as it's her day off. When I can be sure that she's gone, I creep back out and find Ellen stuck on the bump in the kitchen doorway, so I push her into position in order that she can eat her sandwich.

"Is this the first thing you've eaten today?" I whisper and she nods.

I can't believe it and I'm more angry than I can say. I know that there's not a shred of shame in Greta, so why did I try and kid myself there is? If she had felt any shame for her behaviour yesterday, she would have tried hard to make it up to Ellen, but instead she leaves her until 1430 the following day before giving her something to eat or drink. I'm sickened and my head is spinning with the anger I feel chasing and snapping at the heels of my denial.

We watch slushy movies all afternoon and I finish knitting the doll for my daughter. Greta stays out of the way and we don't see her all afternoon, which is unusual as she normally comes up and down the stairs to check on what Ellen and I are laughing about or watching on the television. I'm left wondering whether perhaps she does feel some shame for her behaviour after all and can't face me, or whether she's just feeling hostile towards me. Her absence tells me something but I'm not sure what, which is the object of all passive-aggressive behaviour, I guess.

As the afternoon turns into the evening, I wonder what she's going to do about getting Ellen pizza—it's Saturday, and Saturday is always pizza night. The evening wears on and Ellen tells me that she's hungry.

"Do you want me to get you something?" I ask.

"Oh no, Greta has to order the pizza. I don't know what's she's doing down there." She takes her "reacher" and bangs three times on the wooden floor, and I brace myself as I hear Greta stomp up the stairs.

"What?" she demands.

"Aren't you going to order the pizza? It's late and I'm hungry," Ellen shakes, and I'm proud of her for trying to stick up for herself. I continue to stare at the television, cowardliness on my face.

Greta picks up the phone saying, "This is becoming too expensive."

I don't know if her sarcasm is a hint that I should take turns in buying the pizza, but I won't eat any of it, either fresh or old.

She dumps the phone down on the little marble table between us and wheels Ellen around, pushing her into her room, and then closes the door. Something's going on and I strain my ears to hear, but Greta whispers and I can hear only strangled whimpers from Ellen. Five minutes later Greta comes out of Ellen's bedroom and places a cheque on the table and tells me it's for the pizza boy. It's the first thing she's said to me today and the first thing I say to her is "Okay," and I feel ashamed of myself for not sticking up for Ellen or saying something about her behaviour yesterday. The moment seems to have passed and a part of me, the cowardly part, is relieved.

Ellen wheels herself out and I scan her face to see what's there. I see fear. Her face is red.

I kneel at her side and whisper, "What was that all about?"

She whispers back at me, "Greta says that the reason she left me on the floor yesterday is because she's angry with me for choosing my husband over her."

"What?" my voice more a hiss than a whisper. "That's ridiculous, how old is she for Christ's sake? I mean, get over it."

Ellen grimaces, "I *did* choose him over her so maybe she's got a right to be angry."

I can't believe the anger I feel and say as loudly as I can within a whisper, "Look, Ellen, as mothers we all do the best we can and we all make mistakes. We do what we can with what we have at the time and any shortcomings, yes, we feel guilty about, but those flaws in our parenting become our children's personal journey. Greta can't get to the age of thirty-six and still hold you responsible for her life and what happens in it."

I'm so angry that I can feel a pulse beating in my ear. "Even if she had cause to blame you for all kinds of things, nothing, and I mean nothing, gives her or any other human being the right to be as abusive as she was to you yesterday."

Ellen's trembling more than usual and trying hard not to cry. "You're right, I know it." Her voice drops and I lean into her so that I can hear what she's trying to say. "You know, when she had me in the bedroom just now she grabbed my cheeks so hard that I couldn't speak, like this." She attempts to hold her shaking hand out to show a claw-like grasp and now I can see clearly the red marks on her face are where Greta's thumb and four fingers have pinched her face into silence.

"This is terrible," I hiss, "just terrible. I've never known anything like it before. This is abuse, Ellen, no matter what resentment Greta has towards you, this is abuse."

She nods and says, "I know, you're right."

We're silenced by the arrival of the pizza boy and I hand him the cheque and take the two large pizzas (no wonder Greta says it's expensive) and put them on the kitchen table, wanting no part of them or their convenience and lack of healthy nutrition.

I'm sure that Greta knows they've arrived especially as the intruder bell has sounded as I opened the door. In order to head off her criticism that I didn't let her know they were there, I call down the stairs, "Your pizzas are here," and I disappear into my room before she stomps up the stairs.

# 13

I SPEND MOST OF SUNDAY OUT of the house wandering around Wal-Mart aimlessly, and watching a movie that I can't recall as soon as I leave the theatre. I venture back to the house.

Greta's left Ellen in bed all day, and I find her strewn across the bed with all her glory showing, trying to fix a diaper around herself. She's more embarrassed than I am and apologises for her lack of modesty.

"I'm a nurse, Ellen, there's nothing I haven't seen, please don't apologise," I say, my anger flaring at Greta for leaving her mother to try and position the diaper under her, and then attempt to battle with the sticky tapes. It's something that would have taken Greta seconds to do and saved Ellen hours of indignity. I do it for her and she looks up at me and smiles. My heart hurts.

I kneel down and whisper. "What's she been like today?"

"Oh, just the same as usual. You know, I think she's sorry that she left me on the floor."

"Well, I hope so, because she needs to be."

Greta's suddenly in the doorway and there's a flicker of uncertainty in her face, and her voice is light and forced.

"I'll fix the computer now if you like," she says, smiling at me, "so then you can see and hear Dessy."

I'm grateful and say so, but I know that I've just sold my soul to the devil in order to be able to speak to my man, for now I don't feel that I can mention her behaviour towards her mother. I get the sense that she's running, I can't say afraid, because I don't think she is, but she's backtracking, and I like to think that she knows she's gone too far.

I'm wrong.

It's as if nothing has happened and she says, "I'll just go and get my web-cam and install that."

I'm confused because I recall the conversation when she said that it wouldn't work and that I'd have to pay for the damage if I "messed up" the computer through trying to download the web-cam myself. She must have forgotten that she's already told me she can't get it to work. My heart sinks and I feel as if I've just stepped on a roller-coaster ride, one that travels the same journey each time you step on it and induces the same stomach churning anxiety. Why do we have to go through this game again? However, in my naiveté there's still a tiny spark inside me that hopes she's telling the truth, and that the end result will be that I'm able to speak to my man and see him as well ... and that we can all live here happily ever after.

I know how fairy tales are though: tough and raw. She's sugar sweet now that we're talking, and she assumes that leaving her mother on the floor is a thing of the past, a distant memory that when examined later could be called into question as to whether it was a memory at all. I'm being manipulated, I know, and I hate myself for having a price on my head—the promise of being able to speak to and hear my man.

She re-downloads her web-cam, which is old and not mine,

which is new, and I wonder why. She looks so pleased with herself and announces that it's working now. It's late at home in England so I can't speak to my man as he's long gone to bed, but I'm so grateful and a feeling of well-being takes me to a place where my psychologist's hat is hanging on the door of doubt.

The dialogue between us has kick started again without her having been taken to task over her behaviour and with me feeling too afraid and intimidated to call her on it. She has subtly manoeuvred herself into a position where I'm indebted to her; it feels like she's grabbed the baton and is running out front in the race called "control." I feel powerless, manipulated, and stifled. As Greta is now speaking to me and in a good mood, I ask her to come and share a beer with me. I want to talk about ways of trying to reduce her stress, even if I don't have the courage to tell her what I think about her abusive behaviour.

She willingly accepts a beer and I pick up a sense of relief from her that she isn't going to have to defend herself under my gaze and that her cruelty has been swept under the carpet, a hump of hidden trash that we'll all walk around and ignore. I put my therapist's hat on and start to probe.

"It must be very stressful to feel that you're the only carer for your mother," I say. *Especially when you hate her*, I think.

"It wouldn't be so bad if she'd just help herself more," she says. "She's so lazy and won't do her exercises. You know if she doesn't do them she'll lose the strength in her limbs quicker."

I nod, because there's truth in what she's saying.

"I have to force her to do them."

"Doesn't the physiotherapist do them with her?"

She looks at me scornfully. "They're supposed to, but they're useless. I got rid of them, so now *I* have to make her do them. She's supposed to do them twice a day. Still, at least if I make her do them I know they're being done properly."

I wonder when she does these exercises because in the three weeks that I've been here I've not seen her put Ellen through any series of exercises. Perhaps she does them when I'm at work, but I wonder why she would do two sessions within the eight hours I'm out of the house and not spread them out during the day. I guess I'm cynical because I don't believe that she does do them each day, let alone twice a day. I would surely have seen her.

"You know, I could help you with that," I say, calling her bluff. "I don't mind. I mean, if you show me the routine then it's one less thing for you to do, and it should ease your stress a little."

She raises an eyebrow ruefully, as if any help I could offer would be as useless as all the other professionals that come to the house. I carry on, ignoring her scepticism, my beer bolstering my resolve.

"The next time you do the exercise routine I'll watch, okay?"

She goes downstairs and that's the end of that conversation.

I sleep in, hearing no movement in Ellen's bedroom to wake me, or maybe I've slept more soundly having reconciled Greta's abuse into a form that I can cope with. There's no sign of Greta doing any exercises and I get up and make a cup of tea. It's nearly 1100 and I replenish Ellen's water bottle while waiting for the kettle to boil.

Someone hammers on the door. I let her carer in and take my tea into the study to log on. I'm excited because at last I'm going to be able to see and hear my man, and he'll see and hear me.

There he is, his smiling face blowing me kisses. God, how I love him. The sight of him warms me through and through, and I so wish that I could get Ellen's wheelchair into the study so that she could see him, but the room is chock-a-block with different size boxes so there's no way that Ellen could ever be able to get to the computer. It seems gamy that Greta has spent her mother's money on this computer so that she could use it to contact her friends, yet has made it impossible for her to get to it.

Dessy flickers from view again and I don't curse aloud although I want to. What now? We log off and then back on again repeatedly as that seems to bring him back onto the screen, but once he's there, suddenly he's gone again. Greta's downstairs on her computer—the one that works. I know that because she sends me a message whilst I'm trying to stay in contact with Dessy.

The carer leaves and Ellen pushes herself past the study door into the living room. Greta suddenly appears in the study doorway and I don't know how to say "It's not working again" without an edge in my voice, but I try.

"You silly goose," she says. "You only have to ask for help if you need it."

She stands there impatiently while I get out of the chair and she sits there pressing keys, and when she can't produce any sound from Dessy she says, "Well, *I* was able to talk to my friend last night. It must be something Des is doing."

I can't dispute that, as I know that he doesn't really know what he's doing, but then neither do I. Again I feel helpless.

I can see him again and she gets up saying that she doesn't really have time for this right now, maybe later, so I sit back down trying to make the best of it with what we have. Seeing Dessy's face is a gift and if that's all I can have then it's a precious gift, even without the sound.

Greta comes back into the study and thrusts a plate of cold two-day-old pizza in front of me. I'm shocked and dismayed. Of course I refuse it, as I can't eat pizza without suffering with my stomach, but I wouldn't eat it anyway because it's stale and also because I didn't contribute to buy it. I know, though, that by her offering me some, she is offering a hand in—not friendship, never, I know by now that she's not capable of friendship—but a hand in, maybe, collusion. I don't know. She's affronted by my refusal and I try to make it okay.

"Thanks, Greta, I really appreciate it, but I'm not hungry and pizza hurts my tummy." It does no good though, because her face screams at me that she's offended.

I'm aware that the dynamics have changed and I've just experienced that "Gotcha" moment when a psychological game reaches its fruition. Greta is the one who should be experiencing shame, retribution and a determination to do better, but suddenly without warning here I am feeling those things, having just wounded her with my profound ungratefulness.

Dessy and I give up and he types laboriously, "Cely, please get out of there. I've got a bad feeling about all this. It's killing me," and I pray that Greta hasn't accessed the monitoring co-ordinates of the Internet programme that allows her to read others' messages.

I close down the computer and go shopping to find a witch's nose. It's my first Halloween in America in years and I'm determined to get into the spirit of it. I hunt everywhere and can't find one and curse that I didn't bring one from England. It seems strange to me that the one country that celebrates Halloween doesn't have what I want, a nose with warts on it, yet in our country, which doesn't celebrate it to the same extent, you can buy gnarled, warty noses for fifty pence.

I pick up a Kit Kat for Ellen because I know it'll please her, and her eyes sparkle when I give it to her. I'm humbled because it's nothing, yet she's over the moon, and I leave her with it as I go off to work.

Later that night when I get in, Greta's waiting for me in the kitchen and says, "Don't you know how much caffeine there is in chocolate? She doesn't need all that caffeine."

I'm shocked and say nothing as she stomps off down the dungeon stairs. I go straight to Ellen's room.

"Are you all right?" I whisper.

"Yes. Did she say anything to you about the Kit Kat?"

"Yes, she did. What's going on?"

"She was mad because you bought me something."

An awful sinking feeling has dissolved the pit of my churning stomach and my head spins in unison.

"What did she say?"

"She said that you shouldn't be getting me things and that chocolate has too much caffeine in it. She won't let me have any caffeine. She won't let me have any coffee—I love coffee," she says her eyes suddenly dreamy.

"That's mad," I say. "If you can't have chocolate then why does she buy boxes of chocolates and why did she allow you to have the Belgian chocolate shells I brought you from England?"

I know why. She doesn't want anyone giving Ellen anything. She doesn't want her to have anything that will make her happy or her life a little more fun. It's sick and I vow to get Ellen a caffeine-free chocolate bar the next time I'm out.

"Can you pass me some of the chocolate you brought me?" she shakes, pointing to the drawer that houses the half eaten box of Belgian shells that Greta has placed beyond her reach.

I hand them to her and her eyes sparkle again, and as one melts on her tongue I'm thankful for the extra calories and delight it affords her. Her eyes hold something profound in them: joy, fun, gratefulness, girlishness—something. My heart hurts beyond words when I look at this precious lady wasting away in her bed, alone for most of the day and afraid to ask her only *carer* for her basic needs.

I tell her about my day, about Alex and Dwayne, how wonderful they are and how funny they can be at times. She's thirsty for anything outside the house, anything that will let her know that there is still an outside out there. We chuckle and banter about the rights and wrongs of bringing up children, and the motivation that has driven each of us to work in the field of psychiatry. We talk about love, life, heartbreaks, joys, and philosophy—what our small lives could possibly mean in the greater order of things, if anything. She is indelibly imprinted upon my mind and my heart, and to this day I only have to shut my eyes and see her there, with her courage and determination to live yet another day, and with each image my heart breaks anew.

I tuck her in after putting the chocolates back in the drawer, fetch her some fresh water and then go to bed.

I'm awakened by the sound of Greta's irritated voice and I take my earplugs out and strain to hear what's going on. It sounds like she's putting Ellen through her paces, and as I had requested to watch the routine I wonder why she hasn't banged on my door so that I can see the way Greta wants Ellen to do her exercises. This is the first day that I've ever seen her make Ellen do any exercises in the three weeks I've been here. Is this for my benefit, I wonder? Now that I've offered to reduce her workload, suddenly she starts to do it.

With my head in a fog, trying to stay out of slipping into whatever game is set up on this bizarre human chess board, I get up and after going to the bathroom to clean my teeth, I stand in Ellen's doorway. She looks at me beseechingly whilst Greta is wedged into her wheelchair by the side of her bed, barking orders at her.

"I thought you were going to show me the routine so that I can help you?"

"Whatever," she says dismissively, not even bothering to look at me.

I'm horrified when she makes Ellen restart the whole regimen again and speaks abruptly to her, giving her no leeway at all, and demanding more of her than she is capable of. She pins her to the bed by her shoulders, demanding that she move her hips from side to side, and Ellen cries out, "You're hurting me."

I feel sick. I know that I could never put her through such a torturous regimen. What I'm witnessing isn't about encouraging her to use her muscles and strengthen them so that they can sustain her for as long as possible, this is abusive. If Ellen doesn't pull her knee right up to her chin Greta punishes her by making her start all over again. I stand there feeling very sick and not knowing what to say or do. It's a three-handed stand-off, with Greta in complete control. She makes it plain that she doesn't want me there, or my help, yet if I insist on helping she's going to make it so arduous that both Ellen and I will fail. She forces Ellen's shoulders back down again and shouts at her.

"No! That's not right. You *will* do these exercises properly. Now again! One—come on! Two. You're not doing it right. We'll start again. One…"

It goes on forever and Ellen's reprieve is on the tip of my tongue but never makes it past my lips, and I get an awful feeling that Greta is enjoying my reticence, my fear and my subjugation.

Finally I can stand it no longer and walk out of the room. With my departure the torture stops, and she barks at Ellen to get her to sit up so that she can get out of bed. I walk back to the room and, watching Ellen, who is as stiff as a board, I know that I won't feel confident enough to move her, particularly with my "nurse's back." Getting Ellen out of bed is not the help I've offered. I've offered to help watch over her as she goes through her exercise regimen, not get her up.

I say that I'm not comfortable with moving her from bed to chair.

Greta is bitingly sarcastic. "Now, why am I not surprised?"

I can't believe her open hostility and so I pluck up the courage to challenge her.

"What do you mean?"

"Just that."

"What?"

"Just that whenever anyone says they're going to help, they never do."

"I said that I would help with her exercise regimen."

"That's no help to me. I want someone to help so that I can take a day off."

*A day off*, I think. *Off from what? You don't do anything for your mother.*

I don't say what I'm thinking but stand my ground and say, "But the carer comes in the morning so you don't have to get her up for four days of the week."

Her sarcasm is crushing. "Celia, that's new, the carers usually come in the afternoon. We've got a new carer."

She's missed the point. The new carer comes in the morning so despite what has happened in the past, from now on she will not have to get Ellen up herself for four out of seven days. I still stand my ground.

"I said I'll help with her exercise regimen and I will."

"Don't bother," she says rudely.

"It's no bother. What I'll do is this, when I get in from work at eleven thirty I'll go through them then. I always come in and have a chat with Ellen at that time, so she might as well be doing her exercises while we're chatting."

"I said, don't bother. If you can't help me in the way I need help, then just don't bother."

I look at Ellen and smile. "Shall we do that, Ellen, when I get in at night?"

She nods her head and smiles. "That would be good," she says, and Greta storms out of the room.

I take Ellen's hand and say, "I'll turn you into an All-American female wrestler by the time I've finished with you," and she giggles.

That night after work I go into Ellen's room and she's already trying to pull her arms up above her head.

"Good job," I say.

We visit while she points her feet and pulls them up, and I tell her about my family at home and what it feels like to be a grandmother. We laugh until I hear a noise, and although Greta never comes to check on her mother at night, there she is, checking on Ellen and checking on me. I can't believe the level of pathology that drives this woman. She doesn't do any of the exercises on a regular basis yet bemoans her lot and Ellen's motivation, but when help is offered, help that Ellen might enjoy, she has to come and either control it or stamp it out. Her scarcity issues are all consuming. Her life is so barren and devoid of any sustenance, or the ability to take any offered to her, that she can't bear to see anyone else being satisfied in any way. Her presence dampens our nightly banter, our time when we touch base and widen each other's horizons, for although Ellen is virtually bedridden, she widens my horizons by the courage and honesty she shows me.

Greta barks at me. "Has she done them twenty times?"

"Oh, yes," I fib, and Ellen lies perfectly still. She reminds me of the prisoners of war depicted in old movies: fearing discovery of their escape route, everything depends upon looking blank and not reacting. I know that Greta knows I'm lying. I know she knows it by the look on Ellen's face. She's not stupid by any stretch of the imagination, but right this minute she's caught between a rock and a hard place, a place where her oppression is being covertly challenged. She can't question my testimony without engaging in an all-out confrontation, but with the realisation that a lie lingers between Ellen and me, she now knows that our bond is such that I'd lie for her.

There's also something in her face reflecting anger that her cruelty has been discovered, and so she backs off, temporarily powerless, impotent, but fuming. I know that she'll be back and we'll pay for my leniency and Ellen's frailty, not to mention the growing closeness between us. My reason shouts: *This is ridiculous*, but I try to ignore it, and so my sanity slips sideways, resting on a prayer and a lie.

I can barely believe it but Greta comes upstairs again for the next two nights and demands to know whether Ellen has done each exercise twenty times, and as I stand there defending Ellen she becomes more and more accusatory. It seems that the more I protect Ellen, the more persecutory Greta becomes towards us both, and the more dangerous she becomes. She knows that we have bonded, and rather than see it as a means to relieving her of some of her responsibility and stress, she sees it as a betrayal by us both. She is ostracised by her own making.

I'm in denial all week and focus upon finding a witch's costume for the Halloween party at the hospital. Ellen is infected by my excitement and after each shopping trip to find warty noses, long gouging fingernails, vampire blood and spider earrings, she quizzes me, longing to feel a part of life outside her four-wall prison. Her wide eyes and smile give me pleasure.

Each day I attempt to log on to speak to Dessy but the computer is still not right. I can't hear him but I can see him, and he can't see me but he can hear me. So we have a disjointed conversation where everything I say can be heard throughout the house, and he just smiles at me and blows kisses. Occasionally he tries to type something to me but with two fingers and no knowledge of the keyboard it takes forever, and all I can see is the bald patch on his head as he leans forward. It's frustrating and our intimacy is curtailed.

Greta walks past the study door and I call out, "It's still not working."

She renounces all responsibility. "It must be something Des is doing at his end," she shrugs.

I think quickly: "Well, if I can organise for my brother to sit with him would you talk Steve through it, please?"

"Yes, of course. You only have to ask if you want help."

Statements like that drive me crazy and my psychologist's hat tells me that they are part of a *game*. When I ask for help she can cut me down with her caustic tongue, or control me by refusing to help, yet if I don't ask for fear of these things, she can legitimately hold her hands out and reprimand me for not asking.

I thank her profusely and it's the right thing to do, she smiles sweetly and says, "You're welcome."

I feel a glimmer of hope and tell Dessy, who's looking perplexed on the screen wondering what's going on. Then I have a brainwave and say to Greta, "Will you tell Des what's going on?" as I get up from the chair.

She cocks her head to one side and there's that smile again, and I know I've just hit on what she wants—to be included. It costs me nothing to do that, but I'm aware that it's part of the "control" game we're locked into. Now I feel compelled to play my role and again I feel as if I'm selling my soul to the devil merely to get my needs met.

She speaks so sweetly to Des, in the same gentle way she had to me over the Internet. I'm reminded how dangerous the Web can be when judging and meeting people based only on the tone of their voice and what they say. I leave her to it, mindful of the time and my on-going search for a witch's nose.

I rush down to Walgreens but they don't have one. When I go through the check-out I pick up a chocolate bar and read the label but I can't see that it says there's any caffeine in it.

Ellen's eyes are crossed between fear and gratefulness as I hand it to her.

"It's all right, Ellen, it's caffeine-free."

"Oh, thank you," she says, reassured and hungry for the sweet taste in her mouth, without a care about the calories or nutrition.

I get ready for work and Greta's behind me. I can feel her animosity.

"I told you that she's not to have caffeine," her accusation a knife in my back.

"It's all right, I checked. It doesn't have any caffeine in it. She likes it. Greta, it pleases her," I say beseechingly.

Her anger mushrooms. "Look," she snarls, her face twisted with hatred. "I tell you that free gift in the Happy Meal is a collector's item and what do you do, you go and open it making it worthless, then when I tell you she can't have chocolate, what is it you do, you go and buy her more? I don't need you to be buying her chocolate, okay?"

"Greta, the free gifts from McDonald's are ten a penny but I'll gladly go and buy her another one if you want it kept in its wrapper. The chocolate was caffeine-free, I checked. She's hungry."

Her face is still contorted. "Do *not* be buying my mother chocolate, okay?" and she walks off.

This isn't about chocolate, it's about me showing Ellen kindness and her being unable to, so she persecutes both of us for something she won't, and can't, express.

Yet again she gives me plenty to tell Dwayne and Alex, and

they shake their heads recounting their own experiences of the elderly being abused in their own homes by family who can't be bothered to care for them. One nurse tells of the time she worked in a nursing home with those who were lucky to be rescued by the authorities from their families, and we cringe as she describes the state of their bodies. Someone else agrees with her, saying neglect is common here in the US, as families get paid by the government to keep their elderly at home so that they don't swamp the adult services, or cost the government more money by financing nursing home care.

"You know how it is here with children, too," a social worker says. "People who have no career and no real way of earning a living take money from the government to become foster parents, and because there is such a vast need, those people whose motives are mainly financial slip through the net. Some have as many as four or five foster kids in order to bring in an income; they don't care about the kids. It's the same scenario with the elderly or infirm: the government doesn't want to know, just so long as *someone* is caring for them, then it's one less for the over-stretched services to cope with, so they ignore abuse or sub-standard care."

I'm sick at the thought of it. I know England isn't without unscrupulous people whose motives may be less than pure, but the very fact that our carers only get a tiny allowance for their services, assures that very few would do it for the wrong reasons. And the Social Services would never *ever* place four or five foster children in one home. I'm not saying that English foster parents shouldn't be paid much more, but at least it weeds out those who are only in it for the money, a roof over their heads, or their inheritance.

I go home with a heavy heart, and at last Ellen and I can go through the exercise routine without Greta's Nazi-eagle-eye—it seems that Greta has got tired of her surveillance mission. We giggle as she clenches her buttocks twenty times and I say, "God, Ellen, you look like you're having an orgasm."

She stops, unable to exercise and giggle at the same time, and says, "Now, wouldn't *that* be nice," and we giggle some more.

I finally go to bed, warmed at having seen Ellen have some fun, and I read for a while until I hear banging coming from Ellen's room. I jump up quickly, not wanting Greta to come up and inflict a telling off upon her, and I find Ellen hanging over the edge of the bed grappling with her reacher to pick up her medicine tray. One of the compartments has sprung open and there are pills rolling around all over the floor, loads of them.

"Oh, crikey, I hope they're not lost," I say, as I get on my hands and knees to pick them all up from the dusty floor.

There's fear on her face. "Don't call Greta," she says. "She'll get mad."

I hold the pills in my hand beneath her gaze.

"It's okay, they're all there," she says, and starts to try to place them in the container but shakes so hard that she's in danger of knocking the box to the floor again.

"Shall I do it for you?" I ask, and it's as much as *I* can do to jam the lid on for there's so many of them. I can't be sure that they're all there and I scout around to look for stray ones again.

I'm concerned that Greta has left Ellen's weekly pills by her bedside.

"Does Greta give you your pills throughout the day?" I probe.

"No, she puts them out once a week and says that I have to take them myself. It's a bit hard to open the boxes," she says. "That's how I dropped the box. I was trying to open it."

I'm appalled at what she's telling me. As a nurse, the keeping and administration of medication is a serious business and I can't believe that Greta has entrusted her mother, whose thumb and finger co-ordination is impaired, to take her own medication. She can hardly open the boxes, let alone be certain to get each pill to her mouth and wash it down with water, and all this whilst lying flat on her back. I wonder how many times she has dropped the box and how many doses of medicine she hasn't had—medicine she needs—because they've rolled under the bed. More frightening is the notion that more than one compartment could be opened in Ellen's confusion and she would take too many, forgetting what she'd already taken and not knowing what day it was.

As I get back into bed I'm sorely troubled, and again I can't stop the thought that *there's more than one way to kill a cat* from popping into my head.

# *14*

I SPEND SEVERAL MORNINGS OUT of the house looking for a witch's nose and long fingernails, not wanting to interact with Greta any more than I have to. As each day goes by, any effort she's made to be more agreeable after leaving Ellen on the floor dissipates and she reverts back to her sullen, sarcastic self.

It's Wednesday and the trashcan is full to the brim with stinking rubbish, and over the past three weeks I've noticed that she has always put the trash out on Tuesday night. Last night she didn't, and I can hear the trash-man's lorry (I mean, truck) in the neighbourhood. I smell a set-up. She has said on many occasions that there's nowhere in this house that she can't hear her mother, so if I can hear the trash-man's lorry so can she, and I wonder what she'll do. Will she leave it and then be angry that I didn't put the trash out, or blame me for not reminding her? I feel caught in a trap, one that has come out of nowhere and for no other reason than to provide Greta with an opportunity to persecute. My stomach's in shreds as I feel the tentacles of co-dependence trying to ensnare me, so I try to head it off by calling down the dungeon stairs.

"Do you want me to put the trash out?"

She acts dumb. "Oh, is the trash-man coming?"

If I can hear him I know she can, and I resist the urge to call her bluff and say that to her; instead I just say that I can hear him. Being around her is like treading on eggshells, or picking my way through a minefield, terrified that at any moment I may be blown up and annihilated. She stomps up the stairs, her face twisted with sarcasm.

"Do you think that you could *possibly* put the trash out on the last Wednesday of every month so that I don't have to do *everything* around here? That's not too much to ask, is it?"

So despite my trying to head off her game and persecution, it comes my way regardless.

I look at her and say as calmly as I can, "Greta, you only have to ask, that's all, just ask. I'll do whatever I can to help you but you need to tell me what you want me to do."

She huffs unpleasantly and stomps off, back down into the dungeon while I clean up the mess and wheel the green bin to the roadside just in time for the truck to do its work. I stand there fascinated by its no-hands approach to garbage collection while the driver gives me a smile and a wave, which cheers me up a little.

I'm so grateful for work. It sustains me and keeps my sanity anchored to the ground as Greta oscillates between being hostile and then sickly sweet—promising to fix the computer so that I can speak to and see Dessy.

On Thursday at the allotted time I log on and there's my brother waving at me. I feel instantly homesick and tearful, and I can see Dessy dodging in and out of the screen, waving and blowing kisses. I tell them that I'm going to call Greta and that she'll be on the end of the computer in a moment to work things out with Steve.

"I've just seen my brother, Ellen," I say, the excitement squeaking from me as I pass Ellen sitting in her wheelchair in the living room.

"How wonderful," she says smiling.

I holler down the dungeon stairs, "Greta, Steve's on the computer," and she makes us wait five minutes before coming upstairs. I try to ignore it.

I'm dismayed at my emotions at seeing his face; knowing how sensible he is sharply contrasts with the insanity that I've become used to during the past three and a half weeks. I'm aware that there are tears running down my face and while I stand there crying, Greta is talking to Steve, but not about the computer. She's flirting with him and I know he's treading carefully, not wanting to be offensive by telling her to get on with it because his time is precious. When she tells him that I'm crying and insists that he smile and wave at me, he does. His smile is not one of his cosy smiles that would make you feel warm all over; it's more of a grimace, with set eyes that say another story.

Greta fiddles with the mouse and all of a sudden I recognise the click of a photograph being taken. I only know that because my daughter Helen and I played with the web-cam I bought her before I left England, and all my grandchildren pulled faces in front of the camera as their pictures were captured.

"Come on, we've got a homesick person here, smile at her. That's better," Greta says into the microphone, "Go on, show us your toothy pegs, go on."

My tears have stopped, usurped by a feeling of nausea and anxiety. What's going on here? It feels wrong. Steve looks irritated but grins, showing all his teeth and his good looks are erased by a grotesque grimace, which Greta captures on the web-camera.

Steve tries to divert her from her sport and types pertinent questions about settings and such, the like of which is double-dutch to me and Dessy, and we stand by helplessly in awe of their computer prowess. She then tells Steve that she's got to go to the help line, manned by a person who is one of her Internet "friends." We all stand there for thirty minutes listening to her flirting with this man and many others that have joined the chat room, yet not attending at all to the job in hand. I get the feeling that she's enjoying the control and having the pivotal central seat, all of us needing her and being indebted to her. My head is spinning, though, because this feels exactly the same as the past three weeks, and as the man on the help line speaks a technical language I can't comprehend, I get a sinking feeling in my stomach that this is merely a futile exercise. I feel like a mouse that's scrambling after a dangling piece of cheese, that's not meant for my consumption but only my enticement, my desperate dance, entertainment for a cat whose intention has nothing to do with feeding me.

An hour later I have to go to work and ask Greta to say goodbye to Steve and Dessy, who I haven't even said hello to, and I go to work with a heavy heart, feeling as if I've just been had in some way. Yet I reproach myself, as I'm unsure as to whether I feel this way due to my own frustration and homesickness, or whether it's down to a growing sense of paranoia. If she is legitimately trying to make it work then my thoughts are despicable and I reproach myself for them, but deep down the small wise voice within me knows the truth and slices through my brain's need to make sense of the insensible.

It's a long day at work and I'm so grateful for Dwayne and Alex; they are my lifelines and I love them both so much. The shift drags and at last it's fifteen minutes after eleven and I drive home.

The house is in darkness and as I open the front door, there in front of me is a pumpkin, its face carved out and ghostly flickering eyes staring at me from the candle glowing inside the cavity. It's beautiful and I feel a warm glow, wanting so much to experience an American Halloween firsthand. I go into Ellen's room and ask her if she's seen it.

"Why hello, Celeste," she says, obviously pleased to see me. "Greta's been very busy today. She did the pumpkin."

"It's beautiful," I say. "She made a good job of it."

"Also she's been on the computer today while you were at work to try and sort it out."

"That's wonderful," I say, and I ask her if she minds if I log on to see if it works.

The computer is still on, a strange practice, as I always turn mine off after I've finished with it, but the screen saver casts a glow over the cluttered study and draws the eye to the infinity of shooting stars. I shift the mouse and the stars immediately disappear, and I feel instantly sick. There filling the screen is the picture of my brother grimacing, showing "all his toothy pegs" in a pose that's robbed him of his sweetness and handsomeness. I'm not sure what I want to do more, throw up or smash the thing. What kind of human being would put such an awful photograph on the computer as a screen saver knowing that Steve would hate it and that it would cause me pain? Even the first photo she'd taken of Steve where he was smiling would have been painful to me, having him constantly there each time I go anywhere near the computer, but to see him pulling such a grotesque face is unbearable.

I shut the computer down and speak to Ellen, but I don't tell her how I'm feeling. I don't know how to tell her how difficult it is becoming to remain in the same house with her seriously disturbed daughter.

Ellen openly tells me of the abuse she's suffered at the hands of Greta over the years, particularly after her husband died and

Greta arrived with just one suitcase off a Greyhound bus from Mexico, where she'd been living off other relatives. She talks and I listen, and she seems relieved to be able to tell everything to someone who will believe her and who knows firsthand of the extent of Greta's cruelty and pathology. I had feared that she might excuse her daughter's behaviour, for after all they are mother and daughter, and that's a strong bond no matter how pathological it may be. She seems to gain some relief from my understanding.

It's getting late so I drag myself to bed thinking of Steve's distorted face and feeling sick to my stomach that Greta could do such a thing. Her level of pathology is far greater than I had ever dreamed of and not only am I sickened, but I'm scared, too. I know that I'll have to ask her to remove the image tomorrow and I feel anxious. How will I broach the subject? I don't want to offend her yet I can't cope with having such an abusive photograph of someone I love staring out at me all the time.

It's October 31st, Halloween, and I get up and leave the house early, not even able to log on, for I can't bear to shift the mouse and have Steve's distorted face on the screen, reminding me that the dynamics in this house are changing daily and becoming more and more pathological. Something's going to have to give, so being in denial, I do nothing about it and choose instead to go to the hospital to find the recreational therapists so they can apply my witch's makeup and make me really ugly.

I go dressed in black, armed with my broomstick and witch's hat that has long white straggly hair attached to it. I suddenly feel a bit embarrassed as hardly any of the staff have dressed up, but my determination to enjoy Halloween around children snuffs out my anxiety over making a complete fool of myself.

I sit in the classroom and hear gasps as my face takes on a completely different appearance. The recreational therapist sticks her tongue out in concentration and with every sharp intake of breath I stifle a rising wave of panic. She grins, saying, "I think I made you look too ugly," and starts scraping some of the grease off. After daubing and dabbing, and ordering me to shut my eyes lest she blinds me, she stands back to admire her handywork with satisfaction in her stance.

"Good God," her colleagues say, and those who have just entered the room looked really shocked and say, "Who is it?"

I'm suddenly afraid that the wind might blow and I'll stay this way forever more. Other people's reaction to me is enough to make me want to run and hide. I know I can't do that, but I can't deny that I have stage fright.

They lead me to the gym where a Halloween festival has been arranged, and I'm in awe of how the Americans celebrate things in such style. I feel so odd because people I know are shying away from me, looking scared, and showing no signs of recognition. The children look frightened. I want to run and scrub my face and shout out, "It's okay, it's me, Miss Celia," but I can't do that after my colleague has spent so much time and trouble making me up, so I stand behind her like a wallflower.

Gradually as I start to talk to the children and they hear my English accent, recognition dawns on their faces and they smile with wonder.

"It's Miss Celia. It's Miss Celia," they cry, and I begin to feel a bit better.

To my embarrassment there's a competition, and so I have to stand in a line with nine other staff members who are wearing fancy dress costumes, not anything to do with ghosts or ghouls. The children get to vote by the decibels of their cheering and when they get to me the roar is deafening. I resist an urge to cry. It's all too much but behind my greasy mask of lines, wrinkles and warts,

I give myself up to my adopted persona and step forward, shrinking in size, leaning on my broomstick, and cackle, showing two blacked-out teeth. There's pandemonium, the cheers and roaring is colossal and the cheerleader declares me the winner and hands me a steak dinner voucher for two.

I can't believe it. I wanted to partake of their Halloween but instead they've given it to me.

As the children stand up ready to file out of the gym and return to the units, they mob me, saying, "I voted for you, Miss Celia," over and over, and I feel so moved.

There's finally order and the children file out of the gym. I'm left with my exhilaration at having participated, being appreciated, and having fun. And I won something! I never win anything—the last thing I won was a tin of savoury crackers in 1971 in a Christmas raffle.

My exhilaration chases my lack of confidence away and I creep up behind a colleague and tap him on the shoulder. He looks momentarily terrified when he turns around and sees me, and visibly jumps. His fear tickles me but probably humiliates him, for he honestly doesn't know who I am until I speak and my English accent reassures him. He laughs nervously and then says how amazing the makeup is, but more to the point, that once in that role I seem to change shape and become another person.

There's a profound message in there somewhere—something about the reality that we can be anything we choose to be, yet if an identity can be so changed by grease paint and props, plus a wizened stance and a fearful cackle, then who are we? I decide not to ponder too long on the questions my transformation into a witch has posed and go upstairs to the unit, ready to start my shift.

The children are delighted, now that all of them know that it's me. They are keen to let me know that they shouted the loudest for me and that I'm the ugliest witch they've ever seen. I'm so flattered and the incongruency of it all amuses me. A colleague that I don't know very well walks through the door with shock on her face, and says, "Oh, *you're* that ugly witch."

We have a great evening munching Halloween candy while I air my witch's cackle as often as I can. I do it so well that it's disturbing. What's probably more disturbing is that every member of staff stands with their mouths open and says, "God, that's ugly, and you're not wearing a mask either." I can't help but laugh.

As I have my photograph taken, I'm introduced to my colleague's eighteen-month-old daughter who hasn't yet learned to be scared of the ugly, of those who look disfigured or deformed, and as she smiles at me I'm humbled.

During my shift the grease slowly drives me crazy, as the heat from the unit makes the makeup run and I'm desperate to scratch my face. I know that if I succumb to the intense need to claw at my face, my wrinkles and warts will blur into one muddy mess. By 2100 I've had enough and I finally wash it all off, relieved that the old me is still under there. Without the heavy lines of age and maliciousness, my face resumes its sharp angles with high cheekbones and a smile that is complete with all its white teeth. I'm sad that I can't leave the makeup on for the remainder of the evening as I wanted to surprise Ellen, but the itching is just too much.

She's awake when I get in and is enthralled with my tales, her eyes wide as she looks at the photograph. Greta is suddenly behind us in Ellen's doorway.

"Oh, so we didn't get to see your costume," she says sarcastically.

"I'm so sorry, I meant to leave it on all evening but it was just so itchy that I couldn't stand it anymore, but I've got a photograph," I venture.

She glances at it and frowns, saying, "Well, you sure know how to do ugly," and walks away into the living room.

I follow her out and ask her whether any trick-or-treaters had called at the door, as there was a huge bowl of candy on the white marble table.

"Loads," she says.

"Oh, that's good. Did Ellen get to see any of it?" I ask, and she silences me.

"Of course. Duh!"

I use the opportunity to tackle her about the grotesque picture of Steve on the computer and tread as carefully as I can.

"I really appreciate the care you took trying to have my brother's face as a surprise and I hope you don't think I'm being ungrateful, but his face makes me feel homesick, so I'm wondering if you'll wipe it off for me, that's if you don't mind." She bristles. "I realise that it was a kindness but I'm only just coping with being away from home and manage by not thinking about them, but if Steve's face is constantly there, I can't stop myself feeling bad."

She looks really huffy and says, "Well, I thought you'd find it funny. Oh, and by the way, the technical support guy says the problem with the computer is at their end and can't be solved."

Now, I know that I'm not overly computer literate but I know that's rubbish, as she can use the programme downstairs without any problems. It can't be the programme, it has to be the computer and again I feel angry that she didn't just leave the functioning computer in the communal area. I needed only an hour a day, if that, to speak to Dessy.

"Oh," I say, "too bad. Well, as I was saying, it was thoughtful of you to make a screen saver of my brother's face but I'm finding it hard to cope with."

I don't say what I want to say, which would expose every facet of her pathology, so instead I play the game, the one that I've had to learn to play over the past few weeks. She walks off and disappears into the study and fiddles with something for a while and then blanks me as she disappears through the dungeon door.

Everything feels so wrong in this house and I don't know how much longer I can stay here, for as each day goes by and I stay silent, my acceptance is subtle permission for her to continue to be abusive. I get the feeling that she is the replica of Jim Carey in The Mask, saying "Somebody stop me." Ellen can't stop her and I am too scared to, and I don't know what to do, but I do know that my silence infers acceptance. She'll push the boundaries out further and further until someone stops her—that's the nature of such pathology.

I go back into Ellen's room and ask her how her evening went, interested in whether Greta had made the effort and it seems that she had. I'm pleased for Ellen, for her eyes are alight with wonder as she recounts all the neighbourhood children coming past the orange lights adorning the house and knocking on the door. She tells me that Greta had placed her outside on the ramp with a bucket of candy, and as she tells me I can't work out whether Greta was being minimalistic by parking her mother by the front door, with a "that'll do you" attitude, or whether she wanted Ellen to enjoy the experience. Whatever her motives, the end result was that Ellen was enthralled and had more fun than she's had in ages, for which I'm grateful.

I set a package down next to Ellen's bed, Halloween cookies, and she's over the moon.

"Oh my! For me? All for me?"

"Yes, all for you. Can I get you some water or something?"

"Yes, please, then I'll eat two of these cookies and save the rest for tomorrow."

She's like a child at Christmas and she warms my heart.

"Did you see the lights?" Ellen asks.

"No, they were switched off when I got home."

"Go and put them back on and see them," she says, full of wonder.

I don't need telling twice and flip the switch in the bathroom and run outside. It's beautiful, enchanting, and I can see why Ellen is so enthused. I so wish that I could have had the night off so that I could have experienced a neighbourhood Halloween night. I turn them off and go back into her room.

"They are really beautiful," I say. "Greta did a good job."

"Yes, she did," and there's something in her face that I imagine says, *She's my flesh and blood and she's not all bad.* I know about all that. When faced with the deficits in your own children you have to examine what you may have done to contribute to it—it's not an easy evaluation.

"I'm glad she did it for you," I say, and wish Ellen goodnight.

Now that Steve's grotesque grimace isn't barring me from logging on, I go and leave Dessy an email telling him about winning the ugliest witch competition, and promising him that when he gets out here for Christmas I'll take him out for a steak with my winnings.

Ellen's dozing by the time I've finished working on my PhD, so I creep into her room and find the TV remote on her bed to lower the sound so that it doesn't wake her later. It doesn't bother me because I've got my earplugs, and besides, I'm on a high from the kids' reaction to me so I can't sleep. I read instead.

My book is resting on the spare pillow, and as I pick it up I pointedly ignore "Little Cely" lying there, her metaphor neglected, and turn away, reading long into the night.

It's 1330 when I finally wake up and I'm ashamed of myself.

I shuffle to the bathroom and then ask Ellen if she's all right. Her water bottle's on the floor again, lying empty, and I wonder for how long.

"Has Greta been up to see you today?

"No, not yet."

I'm instantly fully awake and angry again. Ellen has no water or food, and the only food that I'm sure she's had since her evening meal, if she was given one, is two Halloween cookies.

"So you haven't eaten anything today yet?"

She nods, smiling at me.

"I ate some of the cookies you brought me."

I pick up her water bottle and fetch her a fresh one, anger coursing through me. Greta doesn't know that I've given Ellen cookies so she has no idea that Ellen has something to eat, yet she's left her without food since dinnertime last night and with only one bottle of water for over fourteen hours. Any generosity I may have felt towards her for making an effort to celebrate Halloween for Ellen is lost, and I'm more angry than I can say. I don't care if she suddenly bounds up the dungeon stairs to strike me down with her sarcasm; I'm going to get this poor woman something to eat. I don't want to go poking about in cupboards so I cut Ellen two large pieces of strudel that's been here on the counter all week but is still within its sell-by date. She's grateful and I'm more irritated by how she's satisfied with so little. How can Greta treat her this way?

Now that Greta hears me walking about she shows herself, and from my bedroom I can hear her barking orders at Ellen to get her into her wheelchair. She then goes out into the kitchen and I follow her.

"The house was decorated beautifully," I say, but she turns on me.

"I didn't ask you to give my mother cake. You've ruined her appetite for lunch now."

I don't believe it. She won't sustain her mother with even a minimal amount of food yet when someone else does, she holds them accountable for her neglect.

"She's starving, Greta. She'll still eat lunch."

I hate the fact that I'm creeping, appeasing, when I should be holding *her* accountable for her blatant neglect and abuse of her mother. She doesn't answer me but huffs, and stomps off down the dungeon stairs.

I go into the lounge where Ellen has placed herself next to the white marble table and is fumbling for the television remote.

"Shall we watch slushy movies?" I ask, and her face lights up. "I'm going to finish sewing up and stuffing the football doll for my daughter today."

"Yes, let's."

And so we do, all day. We watch movie after movie and Greta comes upstairs a couple of times, her face tainted with disapproval but she leaves almost immediately. I sew the doll, peering over my glasses to make it accurate, and I feel like an old granny, which strictly speaking, I am. Ellen's enthralled as the footballer takes shape after I stuff him full of filling, and from being a flattened two-dimensional piece of knitting he suddenly has form and character. She is amazed that he is wearing a pair of shorts and I tell her that his shirt and socks' colours are the Portsmouth football club colours at home in England, the football club that all signed a football in commemoration of Jordan, my grandson who died. Jordan's father, uncles and grandfather all have an affiliation with Portsmouth football club, which has just lately shot up through the leagues of English football—or soccer, to Americans.

We giggle and laugh throughout the day and Greta shows her

face periodically, saying that because I've given Ellen a piece of cake she won't be needing lunch and that she can wait until dinner time before she gets anything else. Ellen isn't too perturbed because I give her a few more cookies and some snacks so that when Greta orders their usual pizza at 2100 at night, her punishment to be denied food is somewhat lost upon us both. I don't know if she detects it or not, but there's the possibility that she has because she's stomping around the house bemoaning the expense of pizza and the waste of buying it if her mother's appetite has been ruined by the cake I gave her at half past one this afternoon.

Ellen and I just glance at each other and I silently "shh" her; she smiles.

Throughout the evening Greta starts to play a deadly game, one that appals me when I think back on it. Ellen and I are having girlie fun and from the expression on Greta's face, she cannot stand it. By now I'm rather past caring—all I care about is Ellen.

The pizza arrives at 2200 and Greta dumps one piece on a paper plate, then plonks it onto Ellen's lap. Greta is up and down the stairs and refills her plate three times. After a while she stomps up the dungeon stairs and walks into the lounge where Ellen and I are tittering at "Queer eye for the straight guy," and she makes an announcement.

"I've just been chatting to Stephen and Helen."

I'm confused. She's never mentioned any friends' names before and I'm suddenly eager to hear more.

"Stephen and Helen who?"

Her demeanour is instantly scathing, "Stephen and Helen, you know, your family. Duh!" (My brother and eldest daughter.)

My head starts to spin but all I say is, "Oh."

It takes every bit of strength I have, which isn't much, to not bite back. I've had enough of her control tactics and try to control the disdain I'm feeling inside. How can she do this when she knows that I can't speak to them? Why would she come upstairs and start bragging that she has the very thing I long for? Ellen looks scared. I instinctively know that placating Greta is as vital as breathing, for any irritation will find its way back to Ellen, and I'm scared and sickened by the realisation that for Ellen's safety I need to keep this woman sweet. I don't think I do a good job though, because somehow something inside me has shifted. I've given up believing that I will hear and see Dessy properly while she's at the helm of this sinking ship, so each time she dangles the carrot of fixing the computer I feel so despondent that I barely react anymore, and that's not what she wants. She wants the same dependence that she's fostered over the past few weeks, and yet as each day goes by, it evaporates.

There's a silent unconscious struggle going on between us, one that has no words but it's there, with her desperate for the urgency in my voice that she's become used to that tells her she has me where she wants me. But I'm burned out. I can't play anymore; I'm just too shot to pieces and too full of hopelessness. All this could have been avoided had she left the working computer in the communal area downstairs; instead it's become a currency, a power, a bargaining tool. Yet as the realisation settles over me that this *is* a psychological game and she has no intention of enabling me to enjoy having contact with my family, I'm steeped in a hopelessness that makes me give up. I can't react anymore even when she continues to attempt to hook me into "playing" by tantalising me with the things she's been saying to my brother and daughter. She walks off, irritated that my reaction to her baiting isn't what she expected. I feel utter despair.

It's late and we're all moved out. The footballer is stuffed and sewn up waiting for his personality to shine through an embroidered expression and a braided hair-do. I wheel Ellen into her room, over the bump in the floor and whip her around in one easy movement rather than leave her to embark upon a lengthy, painstaking three-point turn in such a tiny area.

I lie on my bed with my back to "Little Cely" listening to Greta dumping Ellen into bed. I try to read my book but I feel numb and the words jumble up together.

Half an hour later there's a noise and I whip out my earplugs and listen, alert and scared. I can hear Greta in Ellen's room. Why? She never comes to see to her mother at night. I sit up and there are goose bumps on my arms. I hear Greta hissing while Ellen moans.

I don't know what to do. I'm really scared and I'm also ashamed. How can I get to my age and be this scared? I hear Ellen cry, and I hear a scream that will forever live in my memories; a cry that will surface during every vulnerable moment I ever experience, and one that will rob me of my self respect. I will feel my shame forever, for in this moment I'm too scared to investigate, too scared to leave my room to go out and confront Greta and ask her what's going on, and too scared to go to Ellen's rescue. As I hear Ellen crying, "Stop it, stop it," I hide under my sheet for futile protection, but I'm unable to silence her cries, "Stop it, you've just hit me in the head."

I lie stock-still, straining my ears to hear what's happening, and am relieved when Greta leaves Ellen's room and I see her shadow pass the gap under my door. The television is still blaring so I assume that Ellen's still alive, but even though Greta has left her room I still feel too frightened to leave mine. There are tears pouring down my face, tears of fear, tears of shame, and tears of sadness because I now know that there's no turning back. Greta has placed me in such a position that I have to report her cruelty, and that means leaving this house, and worse, far worse, it means leaving Ellen. It's more than I can bear.

I am torn apart by all the emotions I'm feeling, and I curse the fact that I'm a nurse and have a duty to report the abuse. I could endure Greta's abuse of me if only I could be there to help Ellen, but of course that's an impossible co-dependent situation and one that won't work, a fact that's become increasingly apparent to me over the past ten days. The more I've remained silent and the closer I've become to Ellen, the more abusive Greta has become to both of us, and my silence and inactivity have raised the stakes. There's no choice, Greta has taken the choice away from me by her level of pathology, and I cry into my pillow from fear and shame, but mainly out of grief.

I feel so sick as thoughts cascade into my mind of my not being here to protect Ellen, of Greta having free reign over her, and yet I know that my presence hasn't made or kept her safe anyway. I feel so wretched at the thought of being yet another person who loves and cares for Ellen, chased away by Greta's pathology, leaving the poor woman isolated and defenceless. The images that seep into my mind of her suffering and me not being able to do anything about it turn my stomach, and my weeping turns into silent shoulder-wracking sobs.

I should creep out and see if she's all right, but I can't. I'm in such a state that I know she'll try to rescue *me*, so I stay where I am, hunched up on my bed with my arms around my knees, wiping my dripping nose and tear-stained face on my knees. I feel stripped of everything good about humankind. I can't remember an occasion when I've been so upset and afraid; afraid of what's happening right now and afraid of what I'm going to have to do tomorrow. Out of the corner of my eye I see the doll deliberately turned away from me, facing the wall, cold and neglected. Out of desperation, I reach for her.

I bury my face into her neck and sob harder, remembering my promise to my psychotherapy training supervisor, that I would take care of the core of me, and that the core of me would be personified in the shape and feel of this beautiful doll, "Little Cely." In my shame and fear over the past four weeks, I've come to ignore her and have distanced myself from her by referring to her as "the doll" in order to ignore my emotional safety and my personal integrity. I've done what I needed to do to remain physically alive, but emotionally alive, I'm not sure if I haven't just died.

As I hold her, I know that this is the moment when my personal journey will take a different path. It's painful, very painful, as I hold her in my arms, yet it's strangely liberating too. She flops just like a real baby and she instantly hooks the nurturing side of me and I see her anew. I see *myself* anew. She is a metaphor for the core of myself, a sign to constantly remind me that I have to take care of the core of me, something that I've never been able to do, always having to be the carer, destined to put other people's needs before mine. I feel so utterly scared and bereft that holding her gives me immense comfort and I'm surprised by it. It's a defining and profound moment, one that, when I think back, marks the moment when my personal journey really shifted. It's only since then that I've been able to understand and forgive the awful shame I feel, shame that I couldn't leave my room that night and stand strong in front of Greta for darling, sweet, powerless Ellen.

I hold "Little Cely" for a long time, wondering at the calm that settles over me, and I know what I have to do tomorrow. I'm scared and besieged with grief, but I know now what I have to do in order to do the right thing.

# *15*

I BARELY SLEEP AND AM STARTLED as I hear Greta's low tones in her mother's room. I look at my clock and it's only 0730. Greta never comes up to see to Ellen this early. I listen at the door and pray that she can't see my shadow under the gap. When I'm sure that she's gone downstairs I creep out and go into Ellen's room. I can't believe the sight before my eyes. Her right eye is black and swollen and Greta has tried to put a Band-Aid across it. Instantly I'm outraged but sickened by my shame at not having come to her rescue last night.

"I don't need this abuse," Ellen says. "She needs to take her medicine again."

"This is terrible," I say. "What happened?"

"She got mad and threw the washbowl at me. She says it was an accident."

"That's no accident!" I explode. "For crying out loud."

Greta threw the washbowl at her mother in a temper and Ellen tried to object by crying, "Stop it, you just hit me in the head." How can that be an accident? I'm sickened to my stomach.

My head is spinning, for no amount of fear of being alone in a strange country can enable me to reframe *this* and brush it under a carpet of complacency and self-interest. I know that I have no choice but to report Greta, for she has assaulted Ellen, there's a half-inch laceration on her eyelid. This is an assault, not an accident, and I know that if I continue to be cowardly and say nothing, Greta's pathology is such that left unchallenged, the next abusive incident will be much more severe.

I don't think I've ever felt so much fear. I've got nowhere to go and I know that I can't leave the assault unreported until I find somewhere else to live, yet to report it while I'm still in the house will place me in a very dangerous position. I'm shaking all over.

I go outside and pick up the paper lying on the porch and pilfer the "For Rent" section, carefully putting the paper back together in its yellow plastic bag so that Greta won't notice, then run back into my room. There are a few apartments to rent all needing references, which will take too long. They won't do. I see an ad for "a room to rent, share house privileges and bills with one other."

I call and immediately a woman's voice as bold as brass says "Oh, I just love your accent, and a nurse, how wonderful. I haven't got my car today but if you don't mind picking me up, I can show you the apartment today, if you want."

Driven by desperation, I trust that "what will be, will be." I decide to act this very minute before I chicken out and my subjugation sends a psychological message to Greta that "anything goes" and it's okay to hit your mother and blacken her eye. So even though I'm consumed with fear and am desperate to get out of the house, I race to send an email to my brother to let him know what's happening and ask him to phone Dessy.

I get showered. My hands are trembling as I try to put my contact lenses in, desperate not to come face to face with Greta and be forced to speak to her. I absolutely cannot pretend that everything's all right anymore. I hate myself for being so cowardly and for not confronting her or sticking up for Ellen and myself. I virtually run out of the door and drive away, trembling.

My salvation comes in the shape of a Jamaican black woman brandishing a large handbag, marching up the hill to the Starbucks car park where we'd agreed to meet.

"Yoo-hoo!" she shouts, waving the bag at me. The sight of her defuses some of my tension and I want to giggle.

"Oh, my," she says, panting loudly. "You don't look a bit like a fifty-two year old grandmother, you're beautiful. I bet you get hit on all the time."

Then I do giggle and she gets into my car talking nineteen to the dozen and is unable to fasten her seatbelt. I do it for her and off we go.

She tells me that she's already rented the other room to a pilot. "A nice young man," she gushes. "You'll get on well, I just know it," and I wonder what Dessy will think about that. Still, I'm sure he'd rather I was safe with a sexy young man than at the mercy of a psychopath.

After she shows me around the apartment and then a raggedy old house for rent, I drive along the freeway and venture, "Will you trust me enough to rent a room to me even though you don't know me?"

"Oh, sure," she says, as if it's a foregone conclusion, and I could cry with relief.

We go back to the apartment and sit at the kitchen table; she already has a rental contract in her bag. She's talking fast, and with a slight of hand she crosses out the monthly rental fee and adds $50. "Just initial everywhere where I've initialled," she says, and although I notice that she's just raised the rent on me, I'm so grateful and desperate that I don't mind. Fifty dollars extra is worth it to me to be in a place of safety.

"Now, the pilot's not coming into town for a month so you'll be in the apartment on your own to start with, but that'll be all right, won't it?"

Anything, I think, just anything, as long as I can get out of that house and report Greta to the authorities.

I am so scared, and as I drop her off I wonder how on earth I'm going to do this and stay in one piece. I'm supposed to be working this evening but I'm in such a state that I know I can't work. I go to the hospital and face a supervisor who I've never met before and whose first impression of me is likely to be that I'm a neurotic English woman. I tell her that I've got to go and pack up my things since I daren't leave them alone, for I really don't trust that Greta will not do something to them through spite. I know that I'm not being paranoid for she's so spiteful and has a heck of a lot to lose. She knows that I know what she's doing.

Greta's car's in the drive so I know she's home, as she usually is. The first thing I have to do is to empty out the car boot (Americans call it a trunk), as it's still full of her stuff, stuff that she's bought but doesn't want and has to return to the stores. I'm nervous that if she sees me emptying the car she'll guess what's happening, but I've got no choice so I work quickly.

I'm desperate to cry, for suddenly I fear that something is wrong with the car; I've turned it off but it's still going. Oh, please, not now! Please don't go wrong on me right now.

I'm in such a panic that I bang on the next door neighbour's door and ask him to help me. He reassures me that the noise I hear is the fan, designed to stay on after the car is switched off in order to cool it down. I'm relieved and feel somewhat stupid, but he's very gracious and does his utmost to lessen my humiliation. I want to tell him what's going on but don't. I guess I don't want to voice it because then it'll be real and I'll have to accept it.

I don't have much time so I empty the trunk and stack it all under the carport and out of the line of sight should Greta happen to look out of the window. I'm in luck; she's downstairs chatting to her "friends" on the Internet, oblivious to us upstairs.

I go straight into Ellen's room and I feel so sick, sick with fear, sick with shame, and sick with sadness.

"You know, Ellen, I can't stay here anymore."

"Oh, no, no!"

My heart is breaking.

"What Greta is doing to you is abusive and you know that I'm going to have to report her. I have no choice. My colleagues tell me that it's the law. As a professional, if I know that abuse is going on and I don't report it, then I could lose my licence to practise as a nurse. I could also be prosecuted as if it were me that was doing the abusing."

"I'm so sorry that you've had to see all this," she says, and I'm dismayed and humbled that she's still thinking of me rather than herself at a time like this when she's losing more than all of us. I take her hand and tell her how much I love her. She judders and shakes. "I feel like I know you," she says, with pain in her eyes.

"Me too," I say.

I start to pull away, fear enveloping my sorrow.

"I'm going to start taking some things out to the car," I say. "Please don't tell Greta just yet."

I know I'm begging but she nods and I know that she understands the situation, and I love her even more for it. She's prepared to be silent so that I can get my things out of the house safely, despite the fact that my abandonment will place her in a dangerous, vulnerable position, one where she'll be at the complete mercy of a psychopath. I have no words to describe what I'm feeling. There's bile in my throat as I throw my clothes into my suitcases and take pile upon pile of books out to the car.

I've wedged the front door open so that Greta won't be able to detect how often the door is being opened. I know she'll come upstairs to investigate if the bell keeps going off every time I go in and out of the house with armfuls of my things.

I know that I can't hold off telling her any longer, and after I've done as much as I can, I sit in my chair and turn the television on, hoping she'll get Ellen up so that we can visit and watch slushy movies for one last evening. She hasn't made any attempt to get her mother out of bed all day. The first time I see her I find the strength from somewhere to say, "I need to talk to you."

She says, "Fine," and goes into Ellen's room and almost immediately comes back out.

It's now. I have to say it now.

"I can't stay here anymore."

She just says, "Right, that's fine."

"The reason is that I cannot stand by and watch you be so abusive towards your mother. You can't expect me to sit by and watch it."

"That's fine," she says abruptly, and walks off towards Ellen's room again and moments later walks through the living room and rounds on me. "You said that you would pay for the network machine and you haven't paid for it. You might want to think about that."

I'm so astounded that she has nothing to say about her abuse towards her mother or my departure, which I know will hit them hard financially, that I shamefully resort to sarcasm.

"Oh, believe me, there's plenty that I'll be wanting to think about."

She disappears through the dungeon door and I creep into Ellen's room and ask if I can use the phone.

"I've told her," I say.

"I know. She just came in to say that you're going and that she wasn't sorry."

*I bet she isn't,* I think. *She knows that I know too much about her, and the abuse towards her mother and her plans to transfer all of Ellen's money and assets into her name...quite aside from her pathology of wanting to isolate Ellen and make her "pay" for the "demeanours" she holds against her. She wants anyone who could cast doubt on her motives to be removed from the picture.*

I wonder at her stupidity in revealing all her plans to me—a total stranger—during those first few days. She must have been very arrogant or very comfortable in her self-imposed martyrdom. Fear of being exposed must surely have been a factor in her withdrawal from me during the past three weeks.

I take the phone from Ellen and squeeze her hand.

"Try not to worry too much," I say, knowing that my words mean nothing. They are hollow and empty, designed to make *me* feel better.

I phone Alex and ask him if he'll come and help me move out of the house in the morning, mainly for some moral support. He says that he'll be glad to.

"Will 0700 be okay?" I nearly choke and ask if he can make it a bit later. He says that he'll see me at 1000.

I hand the phone back to Ellen and say how wonderful it would be if she could get out of bed (it's now 1700 in the afternoon) so that we could spend our last evening together, but of course Greta won't consider getting her up.

I try desperately to control my mounting anxiety, so I park myself in front of the television in the lounge and start watching nameless, faceless movies, alone, except for the little woollen stuffed footballer on my knee.

Greta arrives in the doorway and stands with her hands on her hips, saying, "Just when are you thinking of moving out?"

I try to keep my voice even and present myself as being calm. My stomach's in shreds.

"Tomorrow morning," I say assertively.

"Fine," is all she says, and walks back into the kitchen, taking two pieces of cold pizza into Ellen's bedroom, before disappearing downstairs into the dungeon again.

I force myself to start embroidering the footballer's face and he's a perfect distraction. Every half an hour I take the doll in to Ellen to show her how he's suddenly coming to life with his own little character, so that we can spend our last evening together, despite Greta's refusal to get her up.

Greta comes upstairs time and time again, which is so unlike her, and walks past me with her nose in the air. She goes straight to Ellen's room and shuts the door. There's nothing I can do, so finding some courage from somewhere, I hold my head up, determined not to let her see that she intimidates me. I braid the doll's hair and pretend to be interested in the movie that's flickering across the screen. She comes back out and doesn't speak directly to me but says loudly, with sarcasm dripping from her, "Oh, she thinks she knows about a lot of things, but she doesn't know anything. She says she cares about you, but even after I've told her that we've got a drawer full of McDonald's collector's items, she takes the doll out of the wrapper, making it worthless."

I'm stunned by her thinking. How bizarre it that? I ignore her as best I can but it's difficult as I'm scared silly now that her hostility is blatantly laid out in front of me. I'm not sure what she's going to do. Her pathology is an unknown quantity—she must surely be panicking knowing that she's revealed her plans for her mother's estate, and the chips are down. Her anxiety is revealed as she comes up and down the stairs over and over. She can't leave Ellen alone, and for the first time since I walked through the door four weeks ago, she's checking on her as she should. It's a tragedy that her motivation for such attention is not borne out of caring. She's running scared, and seeing her in such a state helps me to hang on to what little strength I have left.

I carry on braiding the doll's hair and work systematically, determined that I'll have it finished before I go to bed so that Ellen can see it.

She's in awe, and he really is a fine little man, a black football player with cornrow braids from forehead to nape, very fashionable right now. Nothing I watch on television registers and my pseudo cheerfulness is a sham, designed to bluff. Greta is up and down the whole evening, yet I refuse to show the fear I'm feeling.

I'm so desperate for my man and long for him to be here to make this all better, but I know that I have to do this on my own. I'll be away from a phone and unable to contact him for some time. I know it's going to feel like the same "blackout" that astronauts experience every time they hurtle back to earth. This is something I'm going to *have to* do on my own. I want to cry but I can't afford the luxury, so I force myself to appear light-hearted.

I go in and out of Ellen's room to show her the doll's progress and Greta catches me in there on one of her checks.

"My mother needs to sleep now," she snaps, with something akin to panic in her voice, but it's difficult to discern through the open hatred emanating from her.

"We're almost done," I say cheerfully, believing that I should be nominated for the next Oscar. "She wants to see the doll in its finished state."

"She's seen enough," and I know that's the end of our disjointed evening together, and to reinforce the fact she shuts Ellen's door, a thing she never does.

I stay up a while longer to finish the doll's last braid, and with a jaded sense of achievement I put the finished doll in my room and turn off the television and lights. I head for Ellen's room and open its door.

"Goodnight, babe," I say, my heart hurting beyond words.

"Goodnight, Celeste," she says with sorrow etched on her face.

"I've finished the little footballer."

"Really? Can I see him?"

I fetch him and creep into Ellen's room. She's enthralled. He really is beautiful and such a transformation from the flat, odd, un-stuffed shape he started out as.

I go back to my room having shut Ellen's door as quietly as I can and get into bed. I don't know why I think that sleep will de-scend upon me—I'm a fool. Sleep is evading this house, with each of us separated by dry walls, but united by anxiety and insomnia. As I toss and turn, I hear Greta come upstairs once more to check on Ellen, and her movement outside my room fills me with trepida-tion. I sit up, vowing to tiptoe across the room and lock the door as soon as she's gone. She isn't in Ellen's room for more than a minute when I see her shadow pass my room and she's gone.

Intuition speaks to me. I leave the light off and creep silently to my desk, picking up a pen and a piece of paper before open-ing my door with the stealth of a cat burglar. It's dark in the hall and I strain my ears to listen for movement from the dungeon or on the stairs. There's none, so I gingerly turn Ellen's door handle and creep inside, bobbing down beside her.

"Is there any one you would like me to call?" I ask, whispering in her ear, knowing that Greta is immediately below us. "Is there anyone that you think will be able to help you?"

She nods her head and points to a writing tablet on her table.

"These people," she whispers, and I have to lean forward to

hear what she's saying. "They have my best interest at heart."

"Do you want me to call them?"

"Yes, definitely. I can't take this abuse, I'd be better off in a nursing home than suffer this every day."

I put my finger to my lips, terrified that Greta will hear and come rushing upstairs to investigate.

She points out the number of her friend, her financial advisor, her sister-in-law and her niece. I jot them down as quickly as I can, cursing the fact that I'm dyslexic and am prone to writing the wrong numbers down. I try to check the numbers but I swear that I can hear movement downstairs, and fearing that Greta will appear at the doorway at any moment, placing Ellen and myself in a very vulnerable position, I squeeze her hand and close her door behind me before creeping back into my room.

I lock my door and put the valuable piece of paper in my bag. I get into bed and hold "Little Cely," whispering affirmations that I will take care of me and do what's right for Ellen no matter how scared I am or how much it hurts. I gain comfort from her in my hour of need.

I try to lie down and succumb to sleep, but it evades me for most of the night. I hear Greta come up to check on Ellen twice more during the night. It all feels utterly ironic that only now, when she's fearful, does she do what she's supposed to do, actions that would have allowed me to stay here. It all seems such a waste of a situation that could have been beneficial to us all.

I can see that the dungeon lights are still on as they reflect into the yard beneath my window, so I know she can't sleep either. We are like isolated beacons, all giving off signals, all needing help, but all waiting in vain. I'm so frightened that for the first time I sleep without my earplugs in; I need to be able to hear—to be alert.

I drift off and before I can register any time passing, it's morning, very early in the morning, and I can hear Greta in Ellen's room. Now, this is unheard of. For the past four weeks Greta has left Ellen until the afternoon before she replenishes her water bottle or gives her anything to eat, yet today she's seeing to her at the crack of dawn. I don't want to go out there yet as it's too early; Alex isn't coming until 1000 and I need him for moral support, so I lie on my bed and watch the minute hand move indiscernibly before me for an hour.

Now, I have to get going; I can't put it off any longer. I shuffle my way to the kitchen and put the kettle on. As I go back to my room, I see Greta wedged into Ellen's wheelchair right by the side of her bed. I say, "Good morning," but Greta ignores me whilst Ellen is her sweet self.

Greta sits in the wheelchair refusing to leave, obviously desperate to prevent Ellen and me having any contact. I'm so glad that I had the presence of mind to creep back into Ellen's room last night to get her phone numbers. I feel as if maybe I *do* have a guardian angel with me. I had no idea what made me think of creeping back out to see Ellen last night, for I didn't expect Greta to "stand guard" so diligently this morning. She seems determined that she will witness *everything* that's said between Ellen and me, and I imagine that somewhere behind her hostility she's feeling mortally afraid.

I shower and fetch my second suitcase from the study and begin packing all the last minute bits and pieces in it. Well, I don't *pack* as such; I just throw everything into the suitcase, urgency chasing away the need to be orderly. There seems so much to have to move. I've only been here four weeks. Where has it all come from?

It's only nine thirty and Alex isn't coming until ten, so I strip the sheets from my bed and take them downstairs into the laundry, but

I can't wash them as Greta's left mouldy clothes rotting in the washing machine, so I leave them in the wash basket.

I say goodbye to the poor caged dog as I walk back up the stairs and grab a broom and a damp dishcloth in the kitchen. Greta sees it and tells me to leave the cleaning, but my self-respect won't allow me to do that, nor can I have her saying that I left my room in a mess. I finally stand up for myself.

"It's my mess, Greta, so I'll clean my room."

She says nothing but is fuming.

I wipe *all* the surfaces, some that obviously haven't been cleaned for years and then sweep the wooden floor, depositing the clods of dust in the trashcan. I notice that she's parcelled my tea bags up in a Zip-lock bag and so I say, "Thanks for parcelling up my tea bags," trying desperately to remain civil and respectful.

She's still wedged into the wheelchair and ignores me.

I ask her what to clean the bathroom with and she bites my head off.

"I said, just leave it."

"Greta, I'm not leaving it, I have my self-respect. I will not leave a mess or not clean up after myself."

This is just terrible. She's openly hostile and poor Ellen is cowering in her bed. I can feel myself starting to cry.

"It's in the same place the last time you asked," she sneers, but I know that I've never asked before. I'm ashamed to say that cleaning is not something I do until I notice it needs doing. I recognise the same defeating circle that ensnares Ellen every day, damned if you do and damned if you don't.

The chips are well and truly thrown down on the table and there's nowhere else for me to go other than to stand up for myself, even though my insides are screwed up with dreadful fear and anxiety.

"Greta, if you won't help me by telling me where things are, then I'll just have to use whatever I can."

She's the spider I've been dreaming about and I'm struggling to free myself, knowing that my dear sweet friend is ensnared and bound by her daughter's poison. I'm crying really hard. I suddenly feel very grown up, set adrift in this "earth re-entry blackout," where there's no Dessy, yet with fear and grief driving me, I hear my mother's voice in my head: "Do the right thing."

I open the linen closet door and grab a face cloth. If she won't tell me where she keeps the stack of dishcloths, this'll have to do, and as she taunts me from her mother's wheelchair, I hunt under the kitchen sink for something to clean the bathroom with. There's nothing, so I pour washing up liquid onto the washcloth and go to the bathroom and start scrubbing, bubbles blossoming all around the taps.

"Celia, get the fuck out of my house," Greta shouts at me.

I'm crying so badly that I've nothing to lose, and all my shame for having been silenced by my fear and dependency bubbles to the surface; I don't care anymore. Despite my fear of her pathology I *will* stand up for myself and I *will* leave my room and bathroom clean.

The timing's all wrong. I was praying that Alex would be here in case this happened and she would unleash the vileness inside her that she's barely able to keep in check at the best of times, but I guess hatred knows no time, and it arrives unannounced. I should have accepted his offer to be here at 0700.

Despite feeling as if I'm falling to pieces, as the past four weeks' oppression, fear and shame overwhelm me, I stand without inhibition and I stick up for myself and for dear, beautiful Ellen.

"This is not your house, it's your mother's," I say, without any concern for myself.

"Get the fuck out of my house."

I'm desperately trying to wash away the bubbles that refuse to pop and slither down the drain.

"Celia, get in here!" I go into the bedroom and the sight screws my very soul, for I know that whilst I've been sluicing bubbles off the taps, Greta has wielded her whispered potent hatred over her mother.

Ellen looks utterly terrified.

Greta says triumphantly, "She's got something to tell you. Go on, tell her," she barks at Ellen.

Ellen is trembling, her eyes beseeching me.

"Celia, leave the cleaning, you can go now."

For someone who usually has a lot to say, I am speechless with misery and compassion. I totally ignore Greta, who is still wedged into the wheelchair.

"It's okay, babe," I say to Ellen, with all the love I can find, which isn't hard because the sight of her takes me to a place where I've never experienced such compassion or respect. "I've nearly finished."

I see the red marks on her face, evidence that Greta has silenced her whilst hissing into her face telling her what to say.

I turn to Greta, fully aware that it's not 1000 yet and I'm desperate for Alex to arrive for moral support, so I say, "I'm not finished packing yet."

"Well, hurry up and get the fuck out of my house."

I stop in the doorway in command of strength I didn't know I had. I look at her wedged into her mother's wheelchair, the first time in a month that she's been with her in the morning and spent more than a few minutes with her. Her mother, so gentle and sweet, having given to her all her life, receives her daughter's attention only when she fears being exposed or having her "meal ticket" wrenched away from her. Greta has a lot to lose, and in a bizarre moment that is reminiscent of a poorly acted silent movie, we stare at each other, and I feel a fleeting glance of compassion as strength momentarily rests upon me.

"It's not that I think you're a bad person," I say. Her face twists with an incredulous frown that surpasses any of her "Duh" expressions. "I can see that you're out of your depth here and you're not coping."

"Celia, I'm sick of it. Just sick of it."

"I know. Well then, do something about it."

She looks at me as if I'm completely stupid and I hurry on while I have some strength and her attention.

"You told me that it's your greatest wish to go out to work; well, do that."

Her face is twisted with contempt.

I look at Ellen whose eyes are hopeful.

"Ellen, there are other things that you can do. Get someone in to take care of you."

Greta all but explodes with scorn.

"Don't you think we've thought of that? It costs twelve hundred dollars a week."

I'm determined not to get embroiled in the arguments she has poised on her lips, ready for anyone who dares to challenge her parasitic existence, as she sucks and drains the life and finance out of her mother.

I do my best to blank her and talk to Ellen, whose face reflects such silent gratefulness.

"Ellen, there *are* many things that you can do. I've seen it in the papers. There are people who will come and live in. You have to give them their room and board, but they'd be with you all the time to make sure that you're all right."

I then look at Greta who is so angry that she can barely contain herself. I carry on, bolstered by Ellen's anticipation and the sight of Greta being cornered.

"You'd have to vet them of course, but there are many people who'd help in return for room and board. Then that means you," I look pointedly at Greta, "can go out and get the job you keep saying you're desperate to get."

I then get overly brave, or if I'm truthful, sarcastic, and say, "Then you can put five hundred dollars into your mother's estate each month so that you don't live here free of charge."

She looks like she's about to explode and I know I've hit a raw nerve.

"You think I live here for free?"

"Well, you do," I say, with complete candour.

Ellen's face is full of hope. "It sounds like a good idea," she stutters.

Greta snuffs her out. "We'll talk about it later," she says, dismissing me. I go back to sluicing the bubbles around the bathroom sink and within seconds Greta calls me back into Ellen's room.

"Go on, tell her," she demands.

"Celia, you can leave now," Ellen says with tears in her eyes, and her cheeks are even redder where Greta has obviously grabbed her face again.

I grab her pad with the phone numbers written on it and write my work phone number.

"Ellen, if you want to talk, doesn't matter what time it is, call me on this number."

I look at Greta and I'm disgusted and realise I lied, she *is* a bad person, bad through and through. I'm consumed by grief, revulsion, anger and relief, yet I stand tall with a height that doesn't reflect my internal processes.

"I shall be coming around here once a week to bring Ellen lunch," and Ellen smiles and nods, while I hold my gaze beneath Greta's scathing disdain. "What day would suit you best?" I ask Greta.

"I don't care," she says, so I tell her I'll phone with a day and time.

# *16*

———

Alex is still not here and I wish with all my heart that I'd accepted his offer of getting here earlier. All my stuff is still in my room, but I can't stay in the house so I start lugging all my bags and boxes out onto the front porch. I pick up "Little Cely" and stroke her face, whispering, "You'll be all right, I promise," and gently wrap her in a sheet and place her inside a Wal-Mart bag, then in a laundry basket for protection, and take her out first. I'm panting and wheezing, my asthma constricting my airway, as I go back and forth taking my stuff outside the house, and all the time Greta's still wedged in her mother's wheelchair, watching. As I go back into my room for the last time, I hear Alex blowing his horn outside and I've never been more relieved to see anyone.

I give Greta the key and ignore her look of disgust as I lean over and place a kiss on Ellen's forehead and tell her I love her. As I stand in the doorway I say, "You know, Greta, your mother's a very special lady. You should treat her better."

"Whatever!"

I'm bolstered by knowing that Alex is outside.

"Have you any idea just how abusive you are?"

"Whatever! Just get the fuck out of my house."

Ellen looks terrified and has tears in her eyes as I walk out of the house.

Alex is driving his elderly friend's Mercedes and has already started loading my things into the car. I scan my things to note where "Little Cely" is. I'm vaguely aware that the metaphoric core of me is locked in the trunk of a Mercedes wrapped in a sheet, stuffed into a blue Wal-Mart plastic bag, jammed next to a pile of psychology books about attachment theory. There's no time for me to be sentimental or to ponder the irony and metaphors about being abandoned in a handbag or in a trunk.

Alex puts his big arms around me and gives me a "sanity hug" and I love him dearly. I know that Greta is looking out from behind the blinds to see who is invading her world, and I'm sure she must be panicking like crazy—it's not just the three of us now, locked together in co-dependence. The cavalry is here.

Alex leads me over to the Mercedes and introduces me to Ben, who is such a gentleman, despite having been dragged out of bed in the morning to come and rescue an English woman. He has trouble breathing and has portable oxygen tubes up his nose, yet his manners are impeccable as he introduces himself, and adds, "You have a wonderful accent."

The contrast of the relationship between Alex and Ben to Greta and Ellen's relationship is profound and hearing them banter, with Alex's constant watchful care of him, emphasises the abusive manner Greta has shown her mother and which I have become accustomed to. I realise that I've become numb to it and have let so much more slide past me than I would have had I not become *tolerant* of the abuse around me. I now know firsthand how the tolerance of "enablers" maintains a drug addict's and/or alcoholic's dependence, and I'm aware that I have been an enabler in this household because I turned a blind-eye.

"There's good news and there's bad news," Alex says.

"What?" Fear slivers down my back as Greta watches out of the window.

"The good news is that I've called the abuse in to the hotline, but the bad news is that they said it's a matter for the police, so they're on their way."

"Oh, my God!" That's absolutely the last thing I wanted. I dreaded an all-out confrontation, or to be anywhere near the house if the police were to be involved. I'm cowardly, I know, but I'm also scared. I believe Greta is capable of *anything*, and although I keep saying it, it's true, she really does have a lot to lose, and she has a gun in the house.

Alex can see the panic in my face. "It'll be all right," he says.

I don't know what to do. I want to just drive away, but I can't do that now as Alex says the police will want me to give a statement. I feel in an utter state of panic. This isn't going how I planned it, yet I realise it's "the right thing," and doing the right thing isn't always easy or comfortable.

Alex sustains me with his constant quips, and he tells me to get inside the Mercedes as they have the benefit of air conditioning— it's hot even though it's November. Despite Ben having trouble breathing, his own quips roll off the edge of Alex's as they attempt to calm me down. I feel safe with them both, they are my knights in shining armour and they contain the frightened child inside of me that knows Greta will be fuming and wondering why we're still sitting outside the house. I'm suddenly anxious about the neighbour and what he will think when the police arrive, so I get out of the car, and note Ellen's curtain move as Greta watches while I go to the neighbour's house.

He takes a while to come to the door but is instantly concerned by the distress on my face. I tell him what's been going on and that the police are on the way because Greta has assaulted Ellen.

He shakes his head, and says, "Oh, no. No! Not against that sweet lady. You never know what goes on behind closed doors, do you?" He seems a really sweet guy. "I'm worried about my daughter going in there to sit with Ellen now."

"Oh, I don't think she's in any danger from Greta, and Ellen loves her company so. She looks forward to her coming to visit."

I'm ashamed of thinking that if his daughter continues to visit, there will be another person watching out for Ellen. I know that's not right; we shouldn't have to rely on a sixteen-year-old child to be society's eyes. He's anxious and so am I.

We wait and I know that Greta must be freaking out from behind the curtains and poor Ellen will be beside herself with terror. My heart hurts but I'm powerless to do anything other than face it all head on. "Do the right thing" blares in my head, and it hurts. I'm trembling, but I have to do it.

I love Alex, standing there talking to the police on his cell phone, strong and right. I don't know if I'll ever be able to express my gratitude to him for being there for me when I've only been working with him for three weeks.

He tells me that the police have been held up and may be hours, so I suggest to him that they come and interview me at work in the afternoon. He conveys the message but the duty police officer says that won't be possible as a different shift will be working and they "can't leave loose ends for the next shift," so they need to interview me now or disregard our call. I can't believe what they've just said! "Disregard our call because of paper work?" Where's the right thing in that? The neighbour is standing there with us and all the time I know that Greta is watching and raging. There's nothing I can do other than to give the police my new address and ask them to interview me there.

I'm actually grateful; anything to get me away from Greta and her wrath. I beg the neighbour to keep a watchful eye open for Ellen and tell him where he can contact me at work, should he need to. He goes back into the house, his shoulders slumped, and it's true, you never know what goes on right under your nose.

Thankfully we drive off and I pray that Greta hasn't heard me give my new address to the police from the open window. Then I tell myself not to be so silly, as she knows where I work if she should want to confront me. My head is spinning so badly that I'm not aware of my bearings and I take the wrong turn. In my mirror I can see Ben gesticulating, but I assume that he's waving his support for me so I wave back.

I stop at a junction, lost, and suddenly desperate to cry. Alex gets out of his car and says, "Ben says it's that way," and he points down the road.

I look in that direction but shake my head. "No, it's this way," I say pointing in the opposite direction, up the hill.

We drive up the road in convoy around neighbourhoods that I didn't even know were there until I realise that I'm hopelessly lost, and after Alex gets caught at a red light I pull into a gas station to wait for him. I watch him drive past me, wait for a few minutes for him to turn around but he doesn't come back, and I realise that I haven't told him the exact address. I've told him which neighbourhood the apartment is in, but not the actual address. I'm never usually this dippy and it's a measure of the stress I'm under. After waiting a futile ten minutes I know that we've lost each other, because if he'd noticed I pulled into the gas station, he'd have come back. He obviously hasn't seen me and could be anywhere by now. I curse that I didn't give him my new address.

I do the only thing I can think of and that is to go to the new house, as I need to be there to meet the police. I try not to think of "Little Cely" being so far away but console myself that she's safe with Alex and Ben, and having a ride in a Mercedes!

When I finally find the apartment I wonder whatever made me take the wrong turn, as it was so simple and I usually have a really good sense of direction. I can only assume that I'm in such a state of fear and stress that all reason and spatial awareness have fled me, along with my possessions and metaphoric self in the back of Ben's Mercedes.

I pull up onto the drive and look around. There are virtually no cars parked outside the houses and I feel alone. I tell myself to grow up and be a big girl—it's going to be all right.

I don't know what to do because I don't have a phone and I need to call Alex to let him know the address. I see a man outside his house and I run over to him. Heaven only knows what he must think of me, with a weird accent, panting to get my breath and fear alive on my face.

"Have you got a phone I could use? My friend is helping me move in and somehow I've lost him and he doesn't know my address."

He looks at me as if I'm from another planet, but is very gracious and pulls out the cell phone from his shirt pocket. "What's the number?" he drawls.

I know that my face is vacant. I have no idea. The number is in my handbag, which is in my car two hundred yards away.

"I don't know, hang on a min," I pant, and I run back to my car to retrieve Alex's phone number from my handbag. The man's grinning by the time I return, and I can't be sure whether it's because of my accent and my dippy behaviour, which would betray female kind everywhere, or because my boobs are bouncing all over the place as I run towards him. Who cares? I know I'm past it.

He dials the number because I have no idea how to use his phone and I leave the address on Alex's voice mail. I back away as gracefully and as thankfully as I possibly can, which is hard, particularly as the police screech around the corner with their sirens blaring, and pull up outside my new home.

"It's okay," I say over my shoulder as I run over to the officer who is getting out of his car, and I pray that he's not about to draw his gun.

"I've had a report that there's an old lady being hurt at this address," he says.

"Come in, come in, I'm so pleased to see you. She's not here."

He looks confused, but no more so than the neighbour who leans against his car watching with a bemused expression, wondering what the neighbour-hood's coming to.

I open the door and invite the officer into the living room and he sits at the table while I explain what's happened. His mother would be so proud of him, as he is one of the most respectful young men I've ever met. After asking numerous questions and taking notes, he stands up and says, "I'm going to go straight back to the office to speak to my supervisor, and Ma'am, I can assure you that we'll have Ellen out of there before you get to work this afternoon."

I want to cry. There's something final about the end of an era. My own era with Ellen and Greta was short and painful, but the thought of the end of Ellen's era of living in her own home is painful, yet she can't stay there at the mercy of such a woman. I feel mortified and helpless, yet thankful that the powers that be are now going to take over and put Ellen's best interests first, even if the consequences are painful.

The officer leaves and I prop the front door open with an old rusted metal chair and begin to transport my possessions from the car into the house, wondering where Alex has gone. As time goes on I figure that he must have taken poor, sweet Ben home, and with him my "metaphoric self" in a Wal-Mart plastic carrier bag. It's an image I can't afford to dwell on for I'm still shaking and terrified.

I know psychopaths, they are my business, and I know what they are capable of, especially those who have a lot to lose. Now that the pretence has gone, I know that Greta will bitterly regret having told me that she is systematically transferring all her mother's assets into her name, or that I have witnessed such abuse that would curdle any decent American's stomach. The knowledge fills me with fear and I don't feel as if I'm functioning properly. I look around me and realise that this is the first time I've ever been totally alone in my life. I'm ashamed of my fear though, because I know that Ellen will be more afraid, and *has* more reason to be afraid. I'm out of the house, she isn't, and until the police and ambulance arrive, she will have to endure Greta's anger and fear of being exposed. I'm more scared than I can begin to describe and I long for Dessy, and something deep within me is glad that the core of me is locked in the trunk of a Mercedes somewhere else. It feels safer than I feel this minute.

I put all my things in my room, which isn't much, as half of it's with Alex, so I decide that a trip to Wal-Mart to buy some sheets and pillows is what I need to do. It's good therapy, Wal-Mart shopping, so I set off. As I drive close to Ellen's neighbourhood I hear sirens and my stomach does a somersault as I picture Ellen being rescued from that place and Greta being taken into custody for her cruelty. I imagine Ellen nestling into a warm bed with nursing aids helping her to eat a proper meal, and pumping up her pillows so that she can sleep properly and be comforted in body and spirit. I also see Greta locked into a cell, probably bigger than the tiny room she allocated to Ellen, and being fed the same stale sandwich or cube of stale cake and water she forced upon Ellen day in and day out.

I'm so sick in my stomach but my mother is with me in spirit, I know I've done the right thing—Ellen will be safe and that's all that matters to me. I miss her already, but I can't even begin to visit those feelings for they're just too painful, and I tell myself that I'll go and see her when she's settled in the nursing home and it'll be all right. The words of Desiderata are in my head: "Whether it's apparent to you or not, the universe is unfolding as it should," and the thought comforts me.

I concentrate on buying sheets and pillows, and get to work a few minutes early. I go to the nursing office to apologise for calling in last night; last night seems so long ago. I know that the supervisor can see I'm in a state, although *I* thought that I was doing okay having tried to orientate myself in Wal-Mart. I'm desperate to cry but chase the need away. There are thirty children upstairs who need me to be strong. I need to be strong for me too, but at this time I'm not sure just how much strength I have left. Although I'm out of the house, the situation is still potentially dangerous. My Ellen has been taken from her house, Greta has been exposed and she has no hiding place. She has everything to lose, and I don't know what she'll do. She doesn't think like normal people, losing everything could send her over the edge, and I'm scared that she'll be waiting outside for me when I finish my shift. I mean, if the police actually let her go, she'll have nothing to stay at home for, as Ellen will be cared for in a nursing home.

Alex and Dwayne nurture me all evening, and when the kids go to bed and Alex is due to leave, he takes me downstairs to transfer all my stuff from Ben's car into mine. We go into the parking lot, scanning around, but can't see anything untoward so he helps me with my bags.

"I'll take that one," I say, trying not to sound too urgent as I pull the Wal-Mart bag out of my washing basket. I lay the bag with "Little Cely" in it on my back seat, and I refrain from whispering, "It'll be okay, not much longer," although I think it. It's oddly comforting to perceive the core of myself, which is so frightened at the moment, as something external to myself. It allows me to access the part of me that can be strong and also nurturing, and it prevents me from succumbing to the fear. I make a mental note to later examine the therapeutic process I'm going through when I feel safer, for it feels profound.

There's so much to do during the shift that I'm very late finishing work and everyone's gone home. My hair stands on end, because I know that there will be no one in the parking lot, and if Greta's going to wait for me, now would be a good time. The only man on duty is a guy I don't know, but I feel compelled to ask him if he'd walk me to my car. He's the perfect gentleman and I feel safe in his presence.

Dessy had called me during the evening and warned me to drive round the block several times if I feel that I'm being followed. I pull out of the parking lot and scan around to see if there are any lights that suddenly come on, or any car behind me that seems to be going as slowly as I am. There's nothing, and with nausea in my throat, I drive to my new home. I try desperately not to allow my fear to take me to a place where paranoia enflames my panic and grief, yet it's hard and I don't know how to stop it coursing through me.

I pull up outside my new home and more uneasiness spreads through me—there's a car in the driveway and there shouldn't be.

It's not Greta's, but whose is it?

The Jamaican landlady had said that the pilot wouldn't be coming into town for another four weeks, so perhaps it's her car.

Perhaps she and her boyfriend have had a row, a fight. If she's not expecting me to move in until tomorrow, maybe she's spending a last night in her leased home.

As I walk in, my senses are alert and fearful. Greta's momentarily forgotten as snores shake the house. They don't sound like a woman's snores, not unless she has severe sinus trouble. I'm scared, but I have nowhere else to go and I figure that whoever it is in the next room to me has to be less pathological than Greta, so I force myself to get a grip. I leave everything in my car apart from the plastic carrier bag, and as the house rocks rhythmically with guttural snorts, I retrieve "Little Cely" from her bag and sheet and hold her in my arms.

Thinking of my psychotherapy training supervisor, I do a quick spot of "re-parenting" and whisper "I swear I will never let this happen again. I will take care of you in the future, I promise." For the first time since I found her waiting for me in her box a month ago, I own what she represents, and own my responsibility for myself, my safety and my place in this world. I spread out one of my white towels and lay her gently on top of one of the beaten scrappy, second hand, trashy chests of drawers, and the fear I've felt is momentarily usurped by the love I feel for this inanimate object that represents so much.

I turn the door handle very quietly and make my way to the fridge to get a beer—God knows I need one—and there before me is a half-eaten chicken, and I'm confused. Call me prejudiced or stereotyping, but I just can't see my female landlady, or a preppy pilot, tearing their way through a chicken, with no plate, no vegetables or gravy, just a fingered grab at the breast and thigh. Something is not right, but I'm so tired and so distraught that I really don't care. I get my beer and lock myself in my room as the house rocks to the sound of snoring.

I jam my earplugs into my ears and don't wake until 1300 the next day. I poke my head out of my door and listen. The safety chain is hanging limply down, telling me that whoever was here has gone. I shower and as I potter about the house, I can't believe the sense of relief that's beginning to settle upon me, knowing that I don't have to brace myself to ward off Greta's passive-aggressiveness or irrational hostility. It's only then that I realise just how much stress I've been under. There's still some anxiety nibbling inside me though, as I wonder what happened to Ellen yesterday, and of course, whether Greta is in or out of police custody. I may be out of the house but this isn't over yet. I open the front door and the sun is shining. There are no cars parked on the street and I feel safer than I've felt during the past four weeks.

Everyone at work asks, "What happened to that awful woman? Is her mother safe?" I can't answer those questions, so I try over and over to reach the duty police officer, and I don't know if it's because of my English accent or because they're busy, but I just can't seem to get any information. I'm transferred from one department to another and I still don't get any answers. My colleagues tell me to go to the City Police Department downtown and get a copy of the police report. I find out where it is and am determined to get up early and go down there tomorrow. I have to know where Ellen is and that she's all right.

We spend the evening giggling about the phantom snoring and Alex cracks me up by saying, "We've only got eight weird people in this state and you seem to have met all of them in only four weeks."

I leave work with Dwayne and he escorts me to my car. There's no one around, and his parting shot to me is to put my earplugs in to muffle the snoring.

As I pull up onto the drive the car is there again, and this time

I'm more anxious, as my landlady knew that I would definitely be moving in by Tuesday, so why would she be there tonight? I open the front door gingerly and the house is rocking to the same guttural snoring. It has to be a man, it can't be her, surely, but who is it?

There's a pot of miniature roses on the kitchen table and I read the card. It says "To my new roommate—Mark." I don't know what the pilot's name is so I assume it's him. I write on the card and say, "Wasn't expecting you for a month, but hi. I work three to eleven—call me tomorrow to say hello on..."

I get up early and drive downtown, finding the Police Department easily. I take a number and feel as if I'm in a deli waiting for a slice of cheese. The precinct is full of people with complaints, some arrogant and others subservient. I'm subservient; police with guns scare me. I'm used to the village Bobby armed only with his helmet and truncheon riding his push bike around town.

Finally it's my turn and I explain that I want a copy of the police report on an assault upon an infirm lady that I filed two days ago. They can't find it. I complete the details again—is it my accent? Is it their incompetence? I stay calm, thinking only of finding out where Ellen is.

After waiting thirty minutes the young woman returns to the window and gives me a copy of the police report.

I start to read it as I leave the building and cross the road to where my car is parked. I can't believe it—my head starts spinning and I feel sick.

*Subject One, not related to Subject Two and Subject Three advised that while renting a room at the residence thinks that Subject Two was abusing Subject Three, her mother. Subject One advised that Subject Three has unexplained bruising on her body. Subject One advised that she heard Subject Three one night tell Subject Two that she had hit her in the head. Subject Two, daughter of Subject Three, advised that Subject One moved into the residence to help take care of Subject Three and never provided any assistance. Subject Two advised that Subject One became mad at her and decided to move out after staying there for approximately one month. Subject Two advised that Subject Three has a bath aid that comes three times a week as well as a nurse once a month and nobody has accused her of abuse before. Subject Three advised that she has not been abused. She advised that she has Multiple Sclerosis and falls often when trying to walk. Subject Three advised that Subject Two hit her in the head by mistake when cleaning her. No further action at this time.*

I'm sick to my stomach. It's all lies. I still have the email from Greta saying that my role in their house was to provide financial aid and to be a different face as company for Ellen. I was never there to "help take care of Ellen," and Greta will never know just how much assistance I gave the poor woman because I did so when she wasn't there. Any assistance I gave Ellen in front of Greta she always criticised and said that Ellen was to do everything for herself. I wasn't to help her. I had not moved out because I had "got mad" with Greta—it's unbelievable. Ellen doesn't "fall often when trying to walk," she *can't* walk, and the only time I've ever seen her try to walk was while holding onto her frame with her physiotherapist standing immediately behind her with her wheelchair so that she *couldn't* fall. The reason poor Ellen has so many bruises on her body is because Greta insists that she does things that are beyond her capability and she falls out of her wheelchair. How is it possible that while giving someone a bed-bath you can lacerate and blacken an eye "by mistake"?

So while I was consoling myself with retail therapy at Wal-Mart and being lulled into a false sense of security hearing an ambulance siren that I assumed was rescuing Ellen, the police were being hoodwinked by Greta's inevitable use of her sugar-sweet victim voice and Ellen's terror-driven denial.

So Ellen is still at home under the control of Greta, and everything Alex and I did counted for nothing. I feel utterly sick. Poor Ellen must be terrified and resigned that help will never come.

I'm more sick and worried than I can begin to say, for now there'll be no stopping Greta, and Ellen will be completely at her mercy. No wonder Greta hasn't been sitting in the parking lot waiting for me; she's been at home guarding her territory, her inheritance, probably scared to put a foot wrong, knowing that her actions are in the balance. Should she attempt to be a dutiful daughter perhaps the accusations levelled at her could be deemed as "retaliations" by me, as she's inferred in the police report, but should she slip up, the allegations will be confirmed. She's too clever for that, and has far too much to lose, in fact she has everything to lose, but the one thing she would lose that would make not one iota of difference to her is her mother.

I'm so sick, too sick to eat or sleep, wondering what is going on in that house, and not knowing what else I can do to help Ellen, as the police and the Department of Human Services have conveniently swept it all under the carpet.

## 17

THE EVENING SHIFT IS TENSE with the outrage we all feel at the way Ellen has been left in that same abusive situation and everyone offers a course of action to take next. I should write to the police and explain that I know their hands are tied if Ellen won't, or can't, stand up for herself to confirm the abuse, but to alert them to what is really going on. I should call the abuse hotline again and insist that they do something. I should speak to the financial advisor and tell him what Greta's intentions are. I should call all her family and friends. Dwayne scares me by raising a wise eyebrow and saying in his own shrewd manner, "You know, Celia, the world is full of sick people. You got yourself out of there safely. You don't know what that sick woman is capable of. Maybe you should just move on with your life and let it be."

"What about Ellen? I can't sleep at night thinking about her being stuck alone in that house with that awful woman."

He nods his head, knowingly. "You did what you could. You did much more than most people would do."

"It's not enough. There has to be something else I can do," I say, with my heart as heavy as it could possibly be.

A child tugs on his leg and as he walks out of the nurses' station, he taps his head and says, "You be careful, girl."

I call the abuse hotline again and am frustrated beyond belief with their attitude. "Well, it sounds like it's a matter for the police," they say. I tell them that the police aren't able to take it any further at this time. "Well, is she in full control of all her faculties?" Mainly, I tell them, provided she's getting the right medications, and who knows if she is, half of them end up on the floor or else she takes double amounts after becoming muddled. "We can't do anything until she's deemed incompetent." I tell them about the neglect, the bruises and the assault, but rather than be concerned, the woman on the end of the line becomes defensive. "Our carers are highly trained to look out for non-accidental injuries and would report anything suspicious." Is she calling me a liar?

I tell her that it's highly unlikely that any carer would report anything because as soon as they get too close to Ellen, Greta gets rid of them, finding some insignificant or non-existent deficit in their care. That's the way abusers work—they alienate and isolate their victims, then discredit anyone with any savvy who may suspect something's not right in order to sow the seeds of doubt on their testimony. The hotline tells me that all the time Ellen is considered in possession of all her faculties, and won't make a complaint against Greta, they can't do anything. They hang up on me as I'm telling them that Ellen is intimidated by her daughter and is scared of what she would do to her if she should tell.

Well, that was a fat lot of good.

I call Ellen's sister-in-law, Carla, and I'm full of trepidation, wondering what her reaction to me will be. She is sweet and wonderful and is so glad that I called. She tells me that she's been worried sick about Ellen for ages and tells me things about Greta that scare me even more. She sounds relieved to be able to offload her pent-up fears and outrage at the injustices she's witnessed over the years. This sweet, caring woman is the same one that Greta had called a "prize bitch," who was as bad as her brother, Ellen's husband. She confirms what Ellen told me, that her brother was so intimidated by Greta that if she ever stayed in the house, he would sleep with a loaded gun under his pillow. She tells me that she witnessed Greta pushing Ellen over whilst in a temper, but owns up to being too scared to report her to the authorities due to what Greta might do to Ellen or her brother in retaliation.

"I don't want to scare you, Celia, but do you have someone that can walk you to your car each night, because there's nothing I wouldn't put past her?"

She succeeds in scaring me, not that I wasn't scared already. She tells me things that Greta had conveniently failed to tell me, like having been married; a major omission. Apparently she *met* an Arabian man on the Internet and she brought him over to the States, changed her religion to Muslim and married him. So that's why she was able to put the headscarf on so proficiently when we were in the Salvation Army shop weeks ago. I recall that she signs her signature in Arabic, and Carla tells me that she went through a phase of wearing the same clothes that Arabian women wear. It's all starting to fall into place.

"The thing is, though, that she had no money and all of a sudden four thousand dollars went missing from my brother's account."

"My God," I say, shocked, but not really surprised. "Surely that was a matter for the police?"

"We couldn't prove that the money she withdrew, bit by bit, hadn't been spent on Ellen and my brother, so she got away with it."

"She's slippery and treacherous," I say, thinking that there seems to be no end to the woman's lack of morality.

She tells me how Ellen was reluctant to tell Greta that her husband had died for fear that she would return to live with her mother. She knew that once he was gone, Greta would come back immediately and expect Ellen to support her.

"She's never had a proper job, you know," she tells me, and I think about how she constantly says she's desperate to get a job. The reality is that she doesn't want one, and with such poor interpersonal skills she wouldn't be able to keep any job. Carla tells me about how she had arrived from Mexico with one suitcase once she heard that her stepfather had died, and yet by the time she was about to go to England to marry her fiancé, she had crate loads of things to ship. "All bought with my brother's inheritance," she says. "And he loved Ellen so much that he left her all that money to take care of her, not to support her daughter, who's perfectly capable of supporting herself, but refuses to."

"I know that she was hospitalised in the State Hospital once, but do you know if she's ever been in trouble with the police?" I ask.

"Not that I know of," she says, thinking hard on the end of the line. "There was one occasion when she had to go to court because she pressed charges against a young girl who had slapped her after Greta called her 'trailer trash.'"

"You're kidding! That's great coming from her," I say uncharitably. "So she's abusive towards someone else and they end up being taken to court by her. She plays a dangerous game. Has no one ever gone to the authorities about everything she's done?"

"No, she always manages to get away with it. She's so intimidating that, I'm ashamed to say, I've always felt scared to do anything. I know this may sound awful, but I think she's trying to kill Ellen. She's a burden to her and she wants my brother's money before it's all used up in caring for Ellen."

She voices what I've felt all along, and I tell her about Greta starving Ellen, leaving her lying down in the bed to eat, the windows open and the fan going full pelt when it was freezing outside.

"Has she still got the catheter in?" she asks.

"Yes."

"I thought so. It was supposed to come out so that she didn't get a urinary tract infection, but Greta argued like a thing possessed to have it kept in."

"But a urinary tract infection in her malnourished run-down state could easily kill her," I say.

"Exactly."

I feel compassion for this sweet lady and I tell her that I know exactly what she means.

We talk at length on several occasions, and she knows I'm genuine and I know that she is too, yet knowing that, we still feel stumped and don't know what to do. She gives me the phone number of Ellen's financial advisor and also her dear friend Jill, but it's a few days before I pluck up enough courage to phone both of them.

In the meantime while all this is going on, I'm coping with wondering who Mark is and what he's like. Alex, in his indomitable style, rescues me from the horror of Ellen's helplessness by focusing on the snoring and the ripping of chicken limbs.

"Maybe some pilots don't have good table manners," he laughs.

Another colleague says that I should "have it out" with my new landlady as things don't seem quite right. I'm getting used to things being not quite right in America.

All of a sudden I receive a phone call; it's from my landlady and she's talking fast, guilty-fast, saying she's sitting with my new roommate. She puts him on the phone (she's obviously in our apartment).

"Hi," he says.

I feel caught off guard and burble. "I wasn't expecting you for a few weeks, but now's fine."

"I'm not who you think I am," he says, and my heart sinks—what now?

"I hope you liked the roses," he says. "I didn't know how to say 'hello' so I thought I would buy some flowers. I hope they didn't give you the wrong idea. They're meant as a 'hello,' that's all."

I'm relieved that he's said that, and I reassure him that I didn't see their presence in any other way.

My landlady comes back on the phone and continues to talk fast.

"Mark's a really cool guy, a real family man. He loves his wife. You'll really like him," and then she hangs up.

She's put someone else in the apartment other than the person I agreed to live with. I could have sworn she said that the pilot had already paid his monthly rental fee. We talk about it around the nurses' table and they're right, my landlady's behaviour *is* outrageous, but compared with the injustices going on in Ellen's home, it's nothing.

I talk to Mark, my new roommate, during the week on the telephone, and knowing that we are going to come face to face on Saturday, I ask him if he'll stay up late on Friday evening so that we can say "hello" face to face, while I still have my clothes on. I don't relish the thought of meeting him in the morning in my nightie, with my hair flying all over the place. I mean, a girl has her principles! He says "Yes, of course," but he chickens out by the time I get home and leaves me a note saying that he's tired and we'll meet tomorrow, on Saturday, after he finishes work.

It's a strange experience, having been so wired up for the past four weeks, to now wake up on a Saturday and be carefree with nothing to do other than to wait for the arrival of my new room-mate. It occurs to me how the act of living our lives changes what we see as being okay and acceptable. If someone had said that I would be sharing an apartment with a complete stranger, a male at that, I would never have believed them, nor would I have done it. Yet life and circumstances placed me in the position where it was acceptable, and it turned out to be an experience that I wouldn't have missed for the world. It's something I love about the adventure of life, like Forrest Gump's box of chocolates, "You never know what you're gonna get." Yet it's more than that, more than making a random selection from a box of chocolates, it's about making decisions based on the place or situations you find yourself in—choices that lead you to experience a life that may never have been yours had you stayed at home watching television or cat-napping on the sofa.

Mark is utterly respectful and adores his wife, and we engage in a dance of who loves their spouse the most, which subtly defines the limits of our new roommate relationship. He's only working in the city because he couldn't find a job in his home town, and tries to go back each weekend, although he can't always make it due to struggling to earn enough money. He misses his family and I understand where he's coming from. I'm grateful to him and he brings something good into my life. Having Mark around gives me a feeling of safety at a time when I'm truly fearful, for although I'm out of Ellen's house and Greta's claws, I know it's not over. We sit up on the weekends that he doesn't go home, discussing the rights and wrongs of Social Security and the Department of Human Services. I learn from him and he learns from me, and we're ships in the night that mean something fleeting to each other, timely placed air-sea rescue boats in a tide of betrayal and persecution.

The one thing we inevitably come back to is Ellen, and Greta's treatment of her. Mark wants to go to their house and raise Cain. He says that he'll come with me to visit her each week in order to keep my promise of lunch, but after we discuss it for hours, we realise that Greta's pathology is so profound that there's no way I can visit Ellen on a weekly basis. Greta wants me out of her life not only because of the threat I pose to her, but also to be rid of anyone who could bring joy to Ellen's life. In the cold hard light of day I know that I can't go round to her house as I'm too scared that she'll "stitch me up." It would be so easy for her to slip something into my bag and then say I'd stolen it, or feed her something noxious after I'd gone and say that I was trying to poison her. It's tragic but true. Greta's pathology is so great that I can't ignore the possibility, and I'd be stupid to place myself in that position. Yet as I realise it, sadness settles over me, because Greta's got what she wanted yet again by intimidating everyone who comes in contact with her mother. She isolates Ellen and maintains the pathological dynamics that ensure her financial security and a rent-free roof over her head. It is equally as sick that she soaks up a limitless supply of strokes by bewailing her lot on the Internet to the poor gullible idiots like me, who will hear only her sugary voice and the apparent self-sacrifice she claims to make.

• • •

As the days go by I work hard, supported by Dwayne and Alex, and being around children whose lives have been so awful, and I feel more focused and grounded. With my anger and helplessness as raw as ever, I pluck up the courage to call Ellen's friend, Jill.

I start by apologising for the imposition of calling unannounced and immediately she puts me at ease, saying that she's glad to talk to someone about what's going on in *that* house, and that she's had firsthand experience of Greta's abuse towards her mother.

"It's been going on for years," she confides. "She doesn't care one little bit for Ellen—never has. I think she hates her, and d'you know what, I think she's trying to kill her."

We discuss that Carla and I feel the same, and there's a strange comfort in our collective perspective. She is obviously pleased to have the opportunity to vent her outrage at Greta's treatment of her friend.

"You know I've got Multiple Sclerosis myself," she says, and I admire her spirit, that despite her own ailments, her friend's problems are foremost in her mind. "Well, when they moved house, yet again..."

"Yet again," I interrupt.

"Yes, Greta has never been satisfied with any of Ellen's homes and she has always insisted that they move to somewhere that suits Greta. Well, when they moved into the house they're in now, Greta brought Ellen to my house overnight, or so I thought. She left her with me for four days. I can barely look after myself let alone someone else who can do as little as Ellen can."

I don't know what to say.

"I was round there the other night for dinner. Not that I eat the food Greta makes because I don't trust that she hasn't put anything in it, but Ellen was in a terrible state. She didn't know what day it was, or the year, or who was president, and that's not like her. So even though Greta objected, I insisted that we take her to the Emergency Room, and good thing I did because it turns out that she'd been overdosing on her medications."

I know I gasp. I had a feeling that something like that was happening—another way of "killing the cat."

"Of course Greta said that it was an accident and that her mother was a law unto herself and had forgotten that she'd already taken the medications, and had taken them by mistake. They kept her in for observation, and after the drugs were out of her system, she was as alert as you or I. While she was there the doctor insisted that her catheter be removed, as it has been inside her for more than six months and he said she'd get a urinary tract infection. But you know what, Greta got hold of a catheter and put it in Ellen herself when they got home. She said that she wasn't having her pee everywhere. It's terrible. I swear she's trying to kill her."

I listen to her, and although she sounds old and repeats herself—probably out of relief to be able to express her fears to someone who will listen—she is of "sound mind" and not as Greta has described her. It dawns on me that to cover her tracks, Greta has attempted to divide and rule, for by stating that Jill is crazy, any testimony she may offer describing the abuse in that house will invite ridicule.

Everything she says heightens my anxieties and sense of helplessness, and I really don't know what to do. I'm scared for Ellen, and for me, yet despite feeling fear and mind-numbing anxiety, I feel a sense of relief that someone impartial has witnessed the same abusive behaviours I have. I've never doubted that Greta's behaviour towards her mother was abusive, but it's reassuring to hear other people equate the same behaviour as being totally unacceptable, and I have an insight as to how Carla felt when I voiced my fears. I ask Jill if she minds from time to time if I call her to see how Ellen is, and she very sweetly says that she doesn't mind at all.

Although nothing's changed I feel slightly better. Now to speak to Chester, the financial advisor, and I feel even more nervous about speaking to him, and chicken out several times within the next hour. I try to figure out why, and when I strip it all away I think it's because Greta told me that afternoon, after I'd only been there a few days and she'd hidden me in the dungeon while Chester was there, that he thought she was "doing a good job." Did he really think that, or was it what she wanted to believe, bolstered by Ellen's Pollyanna optimism?

I finally pluck up the courage to call him and his secretary says that he's out of town until Monday; a part of me feels relieved.

I sit at the nurses' table with my thoughts, the unit silent as the children are down in the cafeteria. The phone rings and it's Ellen. My heart leaps and I'm over the moon to hear her voice, but my jubilation is quickly snuffed out.

She says, "Celeste, don't be calling my friends."

I do a mental appraisal that tells me Jill has just called her to say that I'm as concerned as she is, and my stomach jolts as I'm sure that Greta would have been listening to their conversation from the phone extension in the dungeon. Her voice is shaky and clipped and I'm so shocked that all I say is "okay" before she rings off. My hands are trembling and I feel sick and stunned. That wasn't my dear Ellen; she wouldn't speak that way, not to me, or anyone.

The image of Greta pinching her cheeks until Ellen was either silenced or said what she was dictated to say flashes into my head. I can't stop the image of Ellen being completely overpowered during my last morning in her house when I was cleaning up the bathroom, knowing that Greta was sitting in her wheel-chair and had silently intimidated her into saying what Greta demanded she say. I don't believe that such a sweet woman would say, "Don't be calling my friends," especially after begging me to call people to alert them of her plight.

The line goes dead and she is gone before I can say anything other than "Are you all right?" which falls upon the silence of the dead line.

I'm alone in the nurses' station; my thoughts are my only companion whilst the children are all downstairs eating dinner, a world away from a square of stale cake and cold water. The phone rings a minute later and it's Ellen again.

She sounds different. "How did you get my friend's number?" I can hear Greta hissing in the background and my fears are confirmed; it's the same as the day I left. Ellen in bed, an invalid, a helpless puppet answering to the demands of a cornered, fearful woman who holds the reigns of Ellen's life or death in her hands.

"Babe, you gave me the number, you remember?" I say, anxiety eating at me, as I know that Greta will punish her mother for having given me any numbers that might bring about her freedom. But what am I to say? If I lie, Greta will know it, she's far from stupid. I try to change the subject.

"How are you? I miss you terribly."

"I miss you, too," she says before the phone suddenly goes dead. I want to howl with grief and fear, but at that moment the elevator opens and out pour eighteen cussing children, hell-bent on getting my attention.

Later, when they are in bed, Dwayne and Alex hear my story and shake their heads, not in disbelief for they say that it's all too common, but with the tragedy of it all and a sense of helplessness that matches my own. Yet all the time they try to reassure me and throw a lifeline to rescue me from drowning in a sea of despair. I'm suffocating in self-recrimination, for I have yet to "do the right thing." I've made a noise, drawn attention to Ellen's plight but nothing has been done, averted by Greta's cleverness and manipulation, and poor Ellen's terror and isolation.

There are too many demands on social funds, too many officials who want or need to "pass the buck," or not enough places in nursing homes, not enough advocates for the infirm, the sick and the dying. I'm sickened. How can this happen in the most powerful country in the world?

I spend the rest of the shift feeling wretched. I feel like I'm making noises to the authorities that are bouncing off sheer, imposing cliffs, the echoes of which are deafening me and making my head hurt, but are making absolutely no other difference at all.

The director of nursing comes onto the unit and diverts my attention away from my sense of helplessness by holding an impromptu meeting about how to change the ethos on the children's unit. He wants us to teach the children how to gain positive attention rather than the negative attention they've been used to all their lives. "I mean," he says, "which child in a class gets the most attention, the naughty one or the good one? The naughty one, of course. What incentive do our kids have to be good, or to learn a new way of behaving?"

Everyone makes suggestions, and each of them is foiled by other staff members who mutter, "We've tried that in the past." When he leaves the unit some of the staff berate him, saying that all these kids need is a "good whooping." My heart hurts that they can talk that way, and I wonder if one of Ellen's old boyfriends or her crazy grandmother had given Greta continuous "good whoopings" that made her the way she is today. Kids need structure, very firm boundaries, but lots of love and security.

I leave work, distracted but still heavy hearted. As I slip into my room, I pick up "Little Cely" and hold her to me, stroking her hair. I'm overwhelmed by the sense of love that comes over me and I think of Dr. Claude Steiner's short story called "The Warm Fuzzy Tale." It's dated now, but its message is just as profound as when he wrote it in the 1970s. It's about needing and seeking strokes and, depending upon the scarcity of them in a family, a child would behave positively or negatively in order to be noticed.

I think back to when my children were little—they would *eat out of my hand* in order to get a cuddle or a treat. Steiner called positive strokes warm fuzzies and negative strokes cold pricklies, and the whole premise of his tale was that any stroke was better than being ignored. Children who believe that they can't receive warm fuzzies from their parents will act out in order to get the attention they need. I see it all the time at work. The little ones in our care don't believe that they can get any warm fuzzies, so they act out.

I force Greta and the development of her pathology out of my mind, and feeling the tingle of creativity course through me, I put "Little Cely" down and turn on my computer. I begin to write a children's story entitled "What's inside your fuzzy bag?" It pours out of me and for the first time in weeks I feel animated. It's morning before I finish it, and I go to bed for a few hours before I have to be at work at 1500.

I bump into the director of nursing as I walk through the hospital door and tell him that I've written a story to try to help the little ones learn that there's a better way to get the attention they deserve. He raises an eyebrow and says, "That's great. Let me have a copy."

That evening after the children have showered, we sit them down and I tell them that I'm going to read to them, and at the end I'm going to ask them four questions, so they better pay attention. They sit up, their backs straight as I begin.

• • •

*Long, long ago in the land of sunshine, there lived a wise old doctor called Steiner who sat in his round house in the middle of the woods where people lined up to listen to his wisdom, and the creatures of the forest knew his name.*

*"There are but two truths," he said, his eyes twinkling. "Just two."*

*"Why so few?" a small child asked.*

*Dr. Steiner laughed and said, "That's what keeps life so simple."*

*"What are they?" asked the child's parents.*

*A hush spread through the circular room as the crowd waited to hear the great man speak.*

*Savoring the moment, he scanned the sea of faces before him, while kindness rested upon them.*

*"The first truth is," he went on, "that from the moment of birth until the moment of death, every human being, everywhere, seeks Strokes. They have to have them for they are as vital as air, water and food."*

*The crowd looked confused.*

*"And what's the second truth?" a little boy asked.*

*Dr. Steiner fell silent for a moment before speaking.*

*"Ah, the second truth is the wisest of all wisdoms and shows us the way; how to be happy and healthy throughout life."*

*"What is it?"*

*"The second truth is that any stroke is better than no stroke."*

*"The man's an old fool," cursed a man who had been dragged to the round house in the woods by his family. "I don't believe in all this sloppy stuff. What's he talking about?"*

*Dr. Steiner heard him, but he smiled gently and began to tell his story.*

*"Far, far away in the land that bobbed in and out of view, depending upon the sea mist, lived a race of human beings that were blessed with a precious gift. Each child was born with a brightly colored, fuzzy bag that was full to the brim with warm fuzzies.*

*"Old fool," the doctor heard the man say. "What's a warm fuzzy?"*

*"A warm fuzzy is something given to you by someone else that, once received, makes you feel warm all over; it makes you feel val-*

ued and special, as special as each of you are."

The man fell silent, to the relief of his wife and children.

Dr. Steiner leaned forward, his eyes glowing, and he wagged his finger, shaking his head.

"The warm fuzzies weren't meant to be kept for themselves. Oh, no. They were to be given to other people. And as everyone had a fuzzy bag full to the brim with warm fuzzies, there was lots and lots of sharing, and people felt happy and valued, so they had a massive party, one that went on for a lifetime."

Dr. Steiner's face suddenly became solemn.

"But not everyone gave out warm fuzzies though, for some believed that if they gave them away freely, then they'd have none for themselves, and their fuzzy bags would be empty, a feeling that would be intolerable. But they were so wrong," he said. "A fuzzy bag never runs out. It's like a magic porridge pot, always full, no matter how many times you dip into it."

The man in the back of the circular room shifted uncomfortably.

"Those people who were scared of giving them away, for fear of running out of warm fuzzies for themselves, were frightened at the thought of being fuzzy-less and alone. Although they were at the great party of life, they began to notice that, because they weren't able to give warm fuzzies away freely, they were being ignored and left alone. They weren't having as much fun as everyone else. So they devised a way of being able to give so that they would be accepted by the other party revelers but wouldn't have to give away their warm fuzzies.

"They hid their fuzzy bags and sat up through the long, dark night and sewed another bag, one that looked like a fuzzy bag, yet was full of cold pricklies. With that bag in their hands, they were able to give to the people who gave to them at the party, which made them feel a bit better. But as they pulled out jagged cold pricklies and gave them *away freely, little by little a shivery feeling spread through the great party. Children who had expected only warm fuzzies now had doubt on their faces and a tinge of fear, wondering whether they were going to receive a wonderful warm fuzzy, or whether a cold pricklie would pounce upon them and shrivel their sense of worth."*

*The children and their parents sat at Dr. Steiner's feet in awe, their mouths open, and even the man at the back of the round house was silent.*

*Dr. Steiner coughed, and something between sadness and joy settled on his face, as he looked at the adults before him.*

*"You know, warm fuzzies and cold pricklies have another name. They are called 'strokes,' and there are two kinds of strokes: positive ones and negative ones, warm fuzzies and cold pricklies. Every human being from the moment of birth to the moment of death seeks strokes; that's the first truth. Yet the second truth is the one that will determine our growth as human beings, for if the only strokes we have to offer are negative ones, cold pricklies, then they are the only ones available to our children. Remember the second truth, 'Any stroke is better than no stroke.' Our children will learn how to obtain those cold pricklies, as they need strokes to survive as human beings. If you are unable to give warm fuzzies, you force a child to seek the only alternative, cold pricklies, in order to feel validated and alive."*

*An old woman in the middle of the room shouted out, "But how do you know the difference between a positive and negative stroke?"*

*Dr. Steiner didn't get a chance to answer, for the children called out, "I know, I know. I know what cold pricklies are."*

*The smile on his face reflected a further truth: children need no words to know what's in the heart of those before them.*

*They jumped up and called out one by one.*

*"A cold pricklie is when you're shouted at, and told to 'shut up,' or called 'boy' instead of your own name."*

"*Another cold pricklie is when you're ignored or nagged, or disbelieved.*"

"*My worst cold pricklie is when I'm promised something but, because my mom and dad are in a mood, they won't let me have it and don't keep their promises,*" cried another child.

"*I hate it when I'm told to 'go away' for I feel like I don't matter.*"

"*My worst cold pricklie is being shamed in front of my friends and made to feel stupid.*"

"*Sometimes I feel like I can't win, so why even bother to try,*" another child said sadly.

*Silence hung in the air in that round room full of people in the woods, as the children sat back down again, and the man at the back was the quietest.*

"*The easy way to know the difference between positive strokes and negative strokes is that positive ones make you feel good and negative ones make you feel bad. There are a million and one positive strokes that you can give, like 'Good job,' or 'Well done,' or 'I'm so proud of you.' And you don't even have to say anything to give out positive strokes; you can smile, pat someone on the back or give them a safe hug. The only way to help children grow healthily and to feel valued,*" Dr. Steiner said, without any reprimand in his voice, "*is to give warm fuzzies. For even those children who have never known the warm, fuzzy feeling of being valued will respond, in the end, to being given warm fuzzies. They will give up their search for cold pricklies once they're shown another way.*"

*The man at the back of the room found his voice again, and he asked a question that hung on the lips of other parents.*

"*Yes, but giving children these …things, whatever you call them…*"

"*Warm fuzzies,*" Dr. Steiner prompted.

"*Warm fuzzies,*" the man said, as if the gentleness of their name *was repugnant to him. "But if we give these …things… to our children when they're acting up, it'll only reward them for their bad behavior. Give them a whooping, that's what I say. It never did me any harm."*

*Sadness spread over Dr. Steiner's face and he said, "Tell me, sir, look into your own fuzzy bag and see what's there. Does yours hold warm fuzzies or cold pricklies?"*

*The man went very red as he looked inside his fuzzy bag, his heart, and found hundreds of cold pricklies all fighting to get out, to spread a shiver to whomever they landed upon.*

*"You see, "said the doctor, "receiving cold pricklies as a child, or even as an adult, does do harm. It means they are unable to give out anything except cold pricklies in the future."*

*"Then where is the hope?" the man's wife asked, with anxiety etched on her face.*

*"Ah, there's always hope," Dr. Steiner said kindly. "Even if the bag you hold at the moment is full of cold pricklies, you can throw all your cold pricklies away and only accept warm fuzzies. Before long your fuzzy bag will be full of warm fuzzies to share and give away."*

*Another man shouted out, "But if our children are out of control, then how will these warm fuzzies gain control and keep them safe?"*

*A murmur of ascent rippled through the room.*

*"Yes, our children will walk all over us if we keep giving them warm fuzzies."*

*Dr. Steiner waited until the crowd became quiet, and then he said, "There is not one human being alive that doesn't need boundaries, or who doesn't have to follow rules, we all do, but that's got nothing to do with the giving of warm fuzzies or cold pricklies. It's what we give within those boundaries that either helps us grow or not."*

*"What shall we do?" a young mother asked. "My bag is full of*

*cold pricklies and I don't know how to give warm fuzzies. How can I change?"*

*Dr. Steiner smiled at her honesty and reached into his pale green, fuzzy bag and threw a smiling, sugar-pink warm fuzzy at her, which settled around her shoulders, melting her anxiety.*

*"You are very honest, my dear, and brave. All change is difficult and gradual, so why not practice giving just five warm fuzzies per day until it feels more comfortable. Then gradually increase the number you give until giving them becomes as natural as breathing."*

*"But what happens if the cold pricklies pop out when I'm not looking?"*

*"They almost certainly will to start with, after all they've been spreading shivers for years. But now that you know all about warm fuzzies, each time a cold pricklie escapes, you'll see it and the harm it does, and so you'll be on guard. Gradually they'll wither and die. Trust me, it's true."*

*The children began to fidget, as all children do, and Dr. Steiner stood up.*

*"Just remember the two truths and you'll all be okay. 'From the moment of birth until the moment of death, every human being seeks strokes' and 'Any stroke is better than no stroke.' And if you remember these truths, life and loving will be easy. I'm tired now, my friends, I need to sleep."*

*The crowd showered him with warm fuzzies and gratitude, then filed out of the round house in the woods, leaving to go forth and spread his simple words of wisdom, while the old doctor nestled into his bed surrounded by the creatures of the forest."*

• • •

I look around at the children and say, "Okay, remember that I said I'd ask you some questions after the story. Are you ready?"

I ask them what colour their fuzzy bag is (their heart) and what it's made out of, and I explain that it can be anything because it's unique to them. Then I ask them what their worst cold pricklie was, and to end on a positive note, I ask them what their best warm fuzzy was. Their answers are so sweet and poignant that I want to cry.

The next day a dear little boy has made a long paper sword and queues up for dinner as a staff yells at him to be quiet. He has no idea how profound he is when he says, "Miss Celia, I've made a sword to chop down all the cold pricklies around here, because there's lots of cold pricklies here." I feel totally humbled.

The story gives Alex, Dwayne and myself a way of avoiding confrontations, which the children are used to getting into, and I even get them to go on a stamping rampage to get rid of all the cold pricklies that might be lurking about.

The story and the change in the children's behaviours offer me a diversion from the ever present anxiety I feel for Ellen. I wistfully wish I could share it with her as I know she'd love it. I'm plagued by nightmares about Ellen and Greta and, now that I've started writing again, I keep a journal and document everything that's happened since I arrived in America two months ago. It seems to help me a little. I also write two more short stories for the children: "The play-mad imps," and "My horse is my behaviour," and when the children love them, it lightens my heart if only for a moment.

I'm also distracted from my ruminations by what's going on at the apartment, which becomes weirder every day. One evening my landlady calls me at work. "I'm worried about you," she says.

"Oh? Why?"

"Well, Mark said something that's made it clear he sees you as becoming more than a friend and I just wonder whether you'd feel more comfortable staying at the house rather than the apartment."

She's talking about the ramshackle house she owns, which she said a couple of weeks ago was totally unsuitable for me.

I think quickly; what's going on here? I know with absolute certainty that Mark is devoted to his wife as I am to Dessy, and there's no way in heaven that he would have designs on me. Then I have a sudden flash of insight; the pilot has come into town and she's freaking out, having already taken his month's rent and spent it, along with mine and Mark's, three rents for just two rooms. She wants to scare me into leaving so that she's let off the hook and the pilot gets the room he's already paid for. This time I'm glad I know the psychology I know, and I play her at her own game.

"Oh, no, I'm really comfortable at the apartment and Mark's being a perfect gentleman. I don't see any problem at the moment, but thanks for being concerned." I know I'm manipulating her.

I hear her backtracking, "Oh, okay. I was just worried about you, that's all," and then she hangs up.

It's the end of my shift and as I drive home I decide that open communication is the only way to go, so when I get in I knock on Mark's door, even though it's late, and tell him what the landlady has said.

He's outraged, instantly awake, and not wanting to offend me by saying that he wouldn't fancy me if I was the last woman on earth, he does a diplomatic job of reassuring me. Bless him. He tells me that he is sick to the back teeth of her and that every night there are messages taped to his bedroom door demanding work to be done at the old house.

"I did her a couple of favours and ever since she thinks she owns me. She's out to make trouble," and he susses out exactly what I'd figured out too, that she needs one of us to move into the old house in order to keep the pilot happy, and not have to find his month's rent to return to him, not to mention the consequences of breach of contract.

He can't sleep now and gets up. He drinks a glass of milk and he draws my attention to something that I haven't noticed before: everything in the house has a tiny price tag on it. How weird. I don't get it for a moment as my Englishness blinds me.

"She's obviously either bought all this rubbish from garage sales or is going to sell it at one."

"Well, I'll be jiggered," I say, suddenly realising that he's right and I hadn't noticed. We don't have garage sales at home—the vast majority of English people don't have a garage. Everything does have a tiny tag on it and I feel as if I'm living on a stage set, and Mark and I are participants in a reality show.

Mark and I discuss how every day our landlady lets herself into the apartment and moves things around or tapes urgent "do it now" notes to Mark's door. Bolstered by each other's belligerence we decide to confront her, and he calls asking her to come round. In the meantime he makes me dinner, saying that he loves to cook.

She arrives with a friend, a shady character whose eyes scan everywhere, and Mark fires questions at her while I tell her that it feels as if there are three of us sharing the apartment; our privacy is being invaded. She whines, saying that all her personal things are in the house and she needs to get to them at times. It all feels very strange and she's incredibly defensive. She changes the subject as she leaves, telling Mark that he must fix the pilot's door, as it has no lock on it and he's concerned about the safety of his stuff.

"He's very comfortable at the old house," she says as she leaves, as if she needs to justify her backtracking, with a silent *It doesn't matter that neither of you would move out, he's okay where he is— thank the Lord.* None of it needs saying and Mike and I look at each other after she's gone and shake our heads. What *is* she like?

After a few days I pluck up the courage to call Chester, the financial advisor. He answers immediately and my stomach knots. I explain who I am and he knows nothing about me.

"Greta made me hide downstairs while you were at the house during your last meeting."

"You're kidding."

"She told me how pleased you were that she had tried to save money by buying canned goods with blue stickers on them."

"I remember," he says.

I tell him how concerned I am and that Greta told me she was "systematically transferring all her mother's assets into her own name," and he wasn't at all shocked.

"You know, I was just about to hand the case over to my senior because I can't cope with Greta's abusive nature towards her mother. Sometimes it's been so awful that I've had to leave early because I couldn't stand it."

His verification is distressing and reassuring at the same time—yet another independent person validating what I witnessed, and what is really going on in that house.

"I can't tell you any of the things I've seen or that have upset me due to confidentiality..."

"I quite understand," I say, understanding perfectly.

"But I've been concerned for months and months and it's played on my mind, so much so that I really was about to hand the case over."

His honesty is wonderful. He sounds young, and I make assumptions that he is far from experienced in dealing with such a person as Greta.

"Please don't give up," I beg. "This is how cases such as this slip through the net. I don't know what to do, but I can't just walk away and do nothing. Believe me, I want to. I want to run far away and not have to deal with it, but that's not the right thing to do, and we have to do the right thing by Ellen. She can't do it for herself and is stuck in that house on her own with an angry, vindictive psychopathic daughter. I know it feels wretched but we can't just walk away to reduce our own discomfort."

I'm preaching, but I'm desperate for someone to do something, for there seems to be nothing I can do other than report Greta to the police and to the Department of Human Services.

Chester says that he needs to speak to his supervisor, as it's "such a difficult case."

"She didn't tell me you were there," he says, "or that you'd paid her five hundred dollars. That's technically an offence against the IRS."

"I bought a car off her too, an old banger, for two thousand dollars as well."

"You did? She never told me."

I think, as he's being incredulous. "Oh, heck. I made the cheques out in Greta's name."

"But it's Ellen's car."

"I didn't know that when I first arrived. That means that I've paid the wrong person for a car that doesn't belong to her. Isn't that against the law?"

"Hmm," he mutters.

We seem to be at a stalemate, because I don't want Greta to know that I've been speaking to Ellen's financial adviser, or Carla for that matter, yet should Chester act upon my information it will tell Greta exactly where the information has come from. That will place Ellen and myself in an equally vulnerable position. He's at a loss at what to do and so am I. I tell him that I'll send him a copy of the police report as he's another witness, other than Carla and Jill, who has seen Greta being abusive to her mother. All this time, as ripples of injustice and helplessness flow through me, I pray that Ellen will survive this. I miss her so much.

# 18

ALEX COMES TO WORK LOOKING EXHAUSTED, and Dwayne and I are worried. He insists that he's fine but we can see that he's not.

"I'm okay. I just didn't get much sleep last night. Ben's been real sick lately, so I've been sitting up with him 'cause I can't bear to think of him coughing or needing something when I'm asleep." He reminds me that Ben tends to sleep while he's at work and is then awake during the night.

"Alex, be careful babe," I say, feeling concerned for his health. "You need some sleep."

"Oh, I'll be all right. I got a couple of hours. He needs me, he's really sick."

I marvel at the sight of this young man who has put his life and career on hold to care for this man who is his friend—not his family, but his friend. I stand on tiptoes to hug him and pat his back, moved by the stark contrast between him and his care for someone to whom he has no familial obligation, from whom most people in the same situation would have just walked away, and Greta's complete lack of care towards her mother. While he's weighed down with weariness and an impending sense of loss as Ben deteriorates daily, he continues to care for the children, bringing them pizza and soda, and has us in stitches with his unique quick wit. He leaves work thirty minutes before Dwayne and I do, and during that time we share our worries about him, wondering how he's really feeling behind his generosity and humour. He leaves us reeling with laughter, yet is weighed down with anxiety, for he's starting to look very haggard and low when he thinks no one is watching him.

Day after day he soldiers on because it's the right thing to do, and I'm in awe of him. I'm humbled and yet angry at the same time, as my sense of helplessness being unable to help Ellen increases, and the disgust I feel towards Greta is magnified by the love shown by Alex towards his elderly, frail friend.

I stay in regular contact with Carla and she tells me that Ellen says she's all right. When she prompts her to find out how Greta is being towards her, Ellen says, "Well, you know she's sick. She doesn't mean anything by it." Carla tries to encourage her to talk about "what happened to the lodger that Greta invited into the house after answering that ad," but all she says is, "Well, you know, it didn't work out. She left." Carla's hands are tied. If she reveals that she knows what really happened, Greta, who would likely be listening on the other line, would bully her mother for having revealed so much to me and for having given me the phone numbers of people who could *interfere*. Carla is well aware of the depths of Greta's spitefulness, and it leaves her feeling as helpless as I feel. She asks me to contact other members of Ellen's family, but try as I might I can never get through.

I speak to Chester again and he urges me to speak to Ellen's sister—immediate family who would have some say in her care—but they must be continually on the Internet, as I still can't get through. I feel more and more helpless.

Alex sits in the classroom with children all around him and his shoulders are slumped. I wave to him through the window as I come into work and I can see that it's an effort for him to smile back. When the children have their bathroom break I grab him and search his eyes.

"What's wrong?" I ask.

"Ben's in hospital. It's not good. His daughters flew in today. They're with him now. We don't know if he'll last the night."

"Oh, babe," I say, feeling so inadequate and not knowing how to help my dear friend, who seems so dejected and lost.

He's indomitable and forces a smile upon his face.

"He's peaceful though, and has been able to say everything he wanted to say to his daughters. They're fine people, you know."

"They're very lucky to know that you've taken such care of their dad. You're a wonderful man, Alex."

He looks awkward and doesn't want to hear me praising his devotion, so he shakes his head.

"I just did what anyone would do."

"No, you didn't. You did a very wonderful thing. You've made a scary, frightening and potentially lonely time in Ben's life better. You've given him a wonderful, priceless gift. You've nurtured him and chased away any fears he may have had about becoming old and sick alone, or worse, dying alone."

I'm thinking of my mother as I speak to him. It was her greatest fear, dying alone, with no one to hold her hand and to tell her "it's okay, don't be afraid." I try not to sharpen the memory of her death, yet it's there in the fore of my mind, as it is constantly. She was lucky, for when death came to her, she had enough time for all her children to be at her bedside, and although it was terrible for us to watch her struggle and drown in her own secretions for sixty hours, her fear of dying alone never materialised, and for that I'm eternally grateful.

I'm overwhelmed with love and concern for my friend. He's just as low the following day and says that Ben has been "made comfortable" but the doctors aren't sure how long he'll last. It could be hours or weeks, or he could get better. Alex looks annihilated, exhausted, yet still his only concern is for others.

"I've been at the hospital all day," he says, "and his daughters are with him, so he's happy." He tries to smile. "They really are wonderful people," he says again.

The next day as I clock in, Alex is already sitting in the classroom with the children, keeping order yet nurturing them, and I watch him for a moment, searching for signs of how he's feeling today.

Dwayne walks by me and says, "How is he?" I shake my head. I don't know, and yet something about his pose tells me that I do.

As the children tumble out of the dayroom and race down the hall, he walks heavily behind them and I tug on his arm.

"Are you okay?"

"Ben died last night."

Even then as my face contorts with sorrow for the man I barely knew, but who was a knight in shining armour who had rescued me with Alex from Greta's abuse, Alex is thinking of others rather than his own pain. He forces his face to smile. "He was happy, he had his daughters with him and he couldn't have asked for more. He was very peaceful. It's as he would have wanted it."

I hug him and he accepts it, and I'm grateful, for at this moment when memories of my own mother's death are triggered, and the contrast in care for the vulnerable and infirm never more apparent, I need the hug as much as I think he does.

The children break into our moment and he shrugs.

"Gotta go," he says, and he lines the children up ready to take them to the gym, their heads bobbing in a jagged line of impatience and frustrated energy, and I'm left standing, humbled by his ability to give to others when his own soul is in pain.

I'm left with my thoughts, which are fostered by the growing silence on the unit, as the elevator sinks towards the ground floor and the echoes of the children fade. I can't help it; I wonder how it will be when Ellen dies—almost certainly alone—either from malnutrition or choking on a piece of stale food whilst eating lying down. Will it be from catching cold through either not wearing enough or not having enough blankets, or not being able to pull them over her when the window's left open with the fan going full pelt? Will it be from being unable to fight a urinary tract infection, or a fall after trying to meet expectations beyond her capabilities? As I muse over these heart-wrenching demises, I know in my heart that she will meet her maker alone, without the love and care that Ben's been given by Alex and his daughters, care that everyone deserves. I feel sick and anxious.

I stay in regular contact with Jill and she tells me that she can see no change in Greta's behaviour or Ellen's state of neglect. I pray that Greta is sufficiently spooked by Alex reporting her to the police that she'll stop her bullying.

I continually try to contact Ellen's sister and niece, but their phone lines are still constantly engaged, and I'm ashamed of myself as part of me is relieved that they don't answer. I'm scared that Greta, in her pursuit to absolve herself, will have worked hard to discredit me so that Ellen's family will be unlikely to believe what I've seen, or anyone else who dares to challenge Greta. I'm sickened by the strength of Greta's determination to protect her own interests, and I'm also sickened by my own fear. I know that as human beings we'll do what we need to do in order to survive, so with fear bombarding me like an angry hailstorm, I'll shiver with inertia and retreat while Greta performs an Oscar winning performance of Pollyanna. I feel that we're all stuck, for if Ellen turns round and says to the police and the Department of Human Services that she's okay and nothing's wrong, what can anyone do? What can *I* do?

Greta's behaviour reminds me of the classic grooming procedure of paedophiles, who discredit and alienate their victims so that no one will believe them. So sick, yet impenetrable. I feel a scream deep inside me that longs to be let loose but is smothered for fear that once voiced it will never stop.

I call Alex often during the weekend, concern overriding my fear of being intrusive, my intention being to give him a "sanity phone call," and I act like an overbearing mother hen asking him if he's slept or eaten. He says yes to both and I feel that he's being buoyant in front of Ben's daughters, who are staying for a few days to sort out their father's affairs before having to return to their commitments interstate.

He arrives for work looking shell-shocked. "I didn't do it for any reward," he says, shaking his head in disbelief.

"What?" I ask, holding on to his arm, feeling the need to put some boundaries around this precious man who is as lost as he is dumbfounded.

"I only wanted to be there for him; he was my friend."

"What?"

"He's left me his home, his truck and his Mercedes."

He looks wretched and I understand. This is a man who would do anything for anyone and would abhor payment of any kind, yet in this moment he has been given a wonderful gift that he fully deserves.

"He told his daughters that he wanted me to have it so that I could put myself through college after putting my life on hold to care for him, and they agreed."

"It's nothing more than you deserve," I say, but he's not listening. He just looks wretched, and again I'm reminded of the awful contrast between Ben's passing and the way it'll be when Ellen dies.

He takes a few days off and I call him to see if he's all right. He tells me that he has some tough decisions to make as to whether to stay in town and finish his education here or return home and go to school there. He sounds lost and probably needs more time off to grieve, yet duty calls him back to work before he's ready. The children need him and so do Dwayne and I, not only for his quiet strength with the children but also for his spirit.

Dwayne and I share moments of silent concern, looks that flash between us, which let each of us know that the other is keeping an eye on our friend.

• • •

It's nearly Christmas and I've never been away from home at Christmas time before and I feel bereft, even though I know that Dessy will be flying in soon. Not even that cheers me up, and I bewail my lot at work saying that I don't feel in the slightest bit Christmassy. I try to explain what Christmas means to me and how different it is in England, being our one major celebration as opposed to America's "Holiday Season" spanning from Halloween to New Year. Americans seem tired and exhausted when Christmas eventually arrives and the event does not seem to be the same in America as it is in England. I feel far from home, very homesick, and I long to feel the winter chill and make a Christmas cake and mince pies.

Alex demands that I visit him the next day and he'll take me to a place that is purely "Christmas" in the hopes that it'll ignite the spirit in me. There he is again, immersed in grief yet thinking of others. He takes me to a store that feels like a Christmas theme park. He ignores me as I protest and buys me two glass Christmas tree ornaments of angels, priceless treasures to me, and then we eat turkey and dressing, laughing at the differences in our cultures. What's *dressing*? "Dressing" to us Brits means putting clothes on.

Alex tries to stay buoyant, still caring for everyone else, and yet I know that he's hurting, finding himself at a crossroad in his life where he has to make decisions that will shape the way his future goes. Wherever he decides to go to college, I know that he'll be the most wonderful counsellor, as he has a gift, the gift of knowing, and the gift of being able to offer a rescuing hand to those buried in their past.

A week later he sits on the edge of the nurses' table after the children have gone to bed and it's finally quiet.

"I've made my decision," he says. "I'm going home and will be selling up," and then he offers me first refusal to buy Ben's and his home. I'm lost between two places; one that is full of sorrow to see my friend leave and another that is steeped in gratitude and a sense of disbelief. For the first time since I arrived in America thirteen years ago, I could have my own home and I need never have to worry about where to stay, or inadvertently find myself in a dangerous situation, ever again.

Alex leaves work to organise his affairs and his absence leaves an empty hole on the unit. Dwayne and I miss him terribly and the children show their sense of loss by acting out.

The days race by and Dessy finally arrives and I'm scared. It's been three months since I've seen him and I don't know if anything has been changed by our separation; it's an unknown quantity for me and I don't know the answer. But within hours I know that nothing's changed and the magic between us is as acute as ever.

We creep into the apartment trying not to wake Mark, and yet I'm sure he must be awake. I know I would be if he was bringing his wife into the house. We giggle as we try to be quiet and whisper at each other in bed, unable to say *hello* properly as the walls are like paper, so we share a drink and stare at each other, amazed at the bond between us.

It's 0500 in the morning and Dessy needs to visit the bathroom. I hiss at him to be quiet so as not to wake Mark. He creeps out and after a few minutes I can hear him struggling with the bathroom door. Oh dear, I forgot to tell him about the wonky lock. I know that he's locked himself in the bathroom and can't get out.

I creep out and try to whisper through the door, as Mark's door is inches away and I don't want to wake him, but to no avail. Mark appears in his doorway dressed in his "Sponge Bob" sleep trousers.

"Here, let me help," he says, and I go back to bed, giggling at the absurdity of it all and listening to him barking orders through the door at Dessy, who knows that he's going to have to meet my roommate dressed only in Mickey Mouse briefs.

I'm so proud of Dessy and his interpersonal skills, and giggle as I hear him shake Mark's hand and say, "Hello, it's great to meet you. I had hoped to meet you with my clothes on," and I know that Mark instantly likes him, as they both laugh at the ridiculousness of their first encounter.

The next day I take Dessy down to meet Alex and we all go to lunch. Two hours later I leave in tears as Alex agrees to allow me to pay for the home in four instalments, saying that he's not desperate for the money. He has given me more than he knows and I don't know how to thank him, other than to tell everyone who reads this book just what a wonderful, caring, generous, trusting human being he is.

• • •

Over the next few days Dessy, Mark and I thrash out how we're going to deliver Ellen's Christmas present, the Belgian chocolates from England that she loves, so that Greta won't stop her from having them. Mark is as bold as brass and keen for a confrontation, and as they plan what to do I hope that the sight of two men will force Greta to back down and treat Ellen better, if only for show. I'm so stupid though, and I underestimate her determination to sever the ties between Ellen and me.

What cancer of the soul makes one human being, devoid of love in her life, rob her mother of any friendship and kindness in order to make her pay for the wrongs she perceives have been done to her?

Mark and Dessy choose the following day to deliver the package, and during the evening they bang on Greta's front door. As they recount the tale my heart is in my mouth, because I know that Ellen will have been afraid. Greta refused to answer the door and Mark, not being one to be thwarted, went around to the back of the house and hammered on the dungeon door while Dessy knocked on the front door. Mark told me that he could see her downstairs and when neither of them would stop knocking, she finally went upstairs to open the door.

I feel proud of Des as he recounts saying, "I'm Celia's husband and I've come to see Ellen and to give her a Christmas present."

Greta responded by saying, "You can't see her as she's had a bad turn this weekend."

Undeterred Des says "So I can come back tomorrow then," and chooses not to leave the present, as he wants to see that Ellen is all right.

He tells me all this during a beer at a neighbourhood bar where he's been entertaining the locals with his English accent. I feel vaguely irritated that Ellen still doesn't have her present, and Dessy tries to minimise my concerns by saying that he'll take it round tomorrow. I try to tell him that it wouldn't be a good idea and I don't think he quite realises the depth of pathology he's up against.

I drive home and Des's kindness takes my breath away as I open the front door and find the apartment glittering with English decorations, beautiful garlands hanging from the ceiling.

"I wanted to make you feel at home," he says, and I love him more than I can say. It is truly thoughtful and I want to cry, but daren't or I'll be overwhelmed by homesickness for my family at Christmas time, and that would hurt my man, who has made so much effort to please me. I sit and savour the red and green chains criss-crossing over the ceiling as they glint in the Christmas tree lights while Dessy goes to bed, the worse for wear having sat in the pub for two hours waiting for me to finish work. Mark wanders out in his Sponge Bob sleep trousers.

He tells me that Greta was desperate for them to leave and was determined that neither of them would enter the house. He feels that she was like a child having been caught doing something wrong, and he reassures me that he'll go with Dessy again tomorrow after work rather than let him go on his own. I feel anxious as the element of surprise has now gone and there's no telling what she'll do to protect her patch, or to prevent her cruelty being discovered. She knows that Dessy was listening on the phone the day she forced her mother to lay on the floor as a punishment for falling out of her wheelchair, so she must know that Dessy knows what's going on. It's no surprise to me that she was desperate for them to leave and wouldn't let them in the house to see Ellen. I'm very concerned by what she means by "a bad turn over the weekend" and I can only imagine, but would rather not.

I have the following day off work, and we wait for Mark to get home but he doesn't arrive, so we decide to drop the present off at the neighbour's house. It's on the way to the restaurant where I plan to take Dessy out for a steak with my winnings for being the ugliest witch at Halloween. I pull up outside the neighbour's house, but despite his car being parked on the drive, they're not in. I feel sick with fear as I see Greta's silhouette in the window, and I wonder if she's been there all day waiting to send us away with a flea in our ears. As I creep back to the car, I'm more perturbed than ever about Ellen and whether she's had to suffer because Dessy and Mark went around to the house, daring to bang on the door to deliver her a Christmas present.

We go out for our steak but I don't really enjoy it, as I feel agitated and worried out of my mind.

It's Christmas Eve, so I give Jill a call and tell her that Greta wouldn't let Dessy see Ellen. She's up in arms again about Greta's treatment of her friend and tells me that she told Ellen's doctor that Greta has reinserted the catheter and mistreats her. She gives me his name. Jill says that she's going to pick Ellen up on Christmas night and take her for a ride so that she can see the lights, because Greta can't be bothered to take her anywhere. I tell her about the present and she says in a deep southern drawl, "Now, I have to tell you this, okay?"

"Yes, go on," I say, with my stomach churning because something in her voice tells me that this is going to hurt and sit in my head all day to nibble its way into any Christmas cheer I hope to muster.

"I spoke to Ellen last night. She called me after your husband visited and she told me that she'd have to return any gift from you, and that she didn't want anything to do with you because Greta says that you've 'got problems.'"

"You're kidding?"

"No, that's what she said, okay? I needed to tell you that, okay?"

I want to cry. I don't believe that Ellen would readily believe such a thing—we love each other—and for her to say it tells me that she has been browbeaten at best and at worst is terrified to anger Greta. A sickness sours my stomach and I resist the urge to validate my sanity by brandishing my credentials to Jill, but pray that she can hear in my voice how sane and concerned I am for our mutual friend.

"Okay?" she says again as if it's a punctuation mark, or a breathing space to think what to say next. "I just needed to tell you, okay?"

I think quickly, working out the connotations of what she's just said. If I persist in trying to deliver her Christmas present, I am going to place Ellen in a more volatile situation. Greta is obviously feeling encroached upon and she will vent her anger upon Ellen, and that's the very last thing I want to happen. Greta would take delight in sending the gift back, which would feel awful but I'm big enough to be able to stand that. However, it would be nothing compared to how Ellen would feel. There's no choice as far as I can tell—we can't deliver the gift, but I hope that merely knowing that we tried will be gift enough for Ellen.

Jill agrees with me, saying that she thinks Greta will make Ellen's life hell, and we *visit* for a few minutes saying how sick it is for someone who *should* be loving to be so hateful, especially at a time of giving.

"Would you like the gift?" I ask. "It'll only go to waste."

"What is it?"

I feel girlie again. "Oh, it's wonderful. It's come all the way from

England, exquisite Belgian chocolates in the shape of shells—gorgeous. You could have them if you'd like them, or maybe if you're going to see Ellen tomorrow night you could both share them like two schoolgirls at a pyjama party."

"Why not?" she says, and I'm glad. I don't need any thanks for the gift, I just want Ellen to benefit from it, and if she thinks it's from Jill, that's just fine.

"Are you in right now?" I ask, thinking quickly about getting to work on time.

"I'm not trying to put you off," she says, "but I've got to get my hair done today, and tomorrow I'm spending Christmas Day with my son, but Friday morning will be all right." She gives me lengthy directions to get to her house and tells me to call her first, but when we arrive we can just open the carport door and walk in. She's given me a gift that she's unaware of; by trusting me enough to just walk into her home, she's validated me. I feel weepy.

We go shopping. It's a last-minute craziness—the roads and shops are stacked—and I feel bereft being away from my children and grandchildren, yet shamed for appearing ungrateful in front of Dessy who's making such an effort. I *am* grateful, very, but this is the first time I've been away from home at Christmas and I vow never to do it again. It feels surreal, but I try to make the best of it. I can't help thinking about Ellen, despite it being so painful. I had wanted to make her a Father Christmas stocking, just as my mother used to, with a rosy, shiny apple all the way from Greenland wedged in the toe, a pink sugar mouse, chocolate coins, an orange, multi-coloured bath salts, knitted woolly socks, trinkets of all shapes and sizes that bulged mysteriously through the sock, and wedged in the top of the stocking, reigning over everything beneath him, a home-made soft toy. Greta's robbed me of the pleasure of giving and robbed dear, sweet Ellen of the pleasure of receiving and having childlike fun on Christmas morning.

The wonder of it is timeless, and as Dessy and I battle with the crowds standing in line I recall the last soft toy my mother made for my stocking, Tommy Golly. I smile to myself and blink back the tears. She'd sat up long into Christmas Eve night with my elder sister helping her, trying to finish the soft toy in time for him to sit at the top of my Christmas stocking. In my sister's haste and inexperience she'd sewn his arms on upside down. Tommy looked spread-eagled with his arms outstretched to the heavens instead of at his sides, and I loved him with a passion for what he was and what he represented—two women who cared about my Christmas morning.

There will be no one caring about Ellen's Christmas morning, and I try hard not to think of her being left in the bed for hours and hours with no fun to brighten her day. Knowing Ellen as I do, she'll be grateful for small mercies and if questioned will say, "Oh, we had a good time," but compared to what? I know that Greta will do the minimum and will spend most of her day down in the dungeon, either asleep, or more likely visiting with her Internet *friends*, leaving her mother alone.

I shake the thoughts away as best I can, which isn't very well, and I throw myself into finding a gift to take to Jill on Boxing Day, the day after Christmas. We English have a three-day Christmas: Christmas Eve, Christmas Day and Boxing Day, and I smile as I think of my efforts at trying to explain the origins of Boxing Day to my American colleagues. It is the day when historically all the men and women "in service" to the wealthy would go from big house to big house to have a tip placed in their boxes. Boxing Day is my favourite day of Christmas, as the stress has dissolved, presents are played with and stomachs are full of turkey and Christmas pudding—it's a day for adults, a day to relax and enjoy family and friends.

Finding Jill a present for Boxing Day seems therapeutic and we find a beautiful throw, one that will keep her knees warm throughout the cold winter. It is in American "Christmas colours," something that we don't have in England. Christmas is Christmas without assigned colours, and I can't help but think that "Christmas colours" refers to interior design and has nothing to do with a stable and humble birth, where the only colours were of musty darkness and the light of a shining star.

I'm so homesick that I succumb to an act of extravagance and buy a five-foot singing and dancing Santa and Dessy walks off shaking his head, laughing at me. I can't help it, he'll cheer me up, and he sings the song that is a special bond between my granddaughters and me. I have to have him, and poor Dessy has to sit in the back of the car, usurped by Santa sitting in the front seat. Other drivers hoot at us and I wave, feeling a sad giggle spread over my face and ignore Dessy's complaints that he's squashed and that he has never before taken second place to a bearded gentleman dressed all in red.

It's almost time to go to work and I leave Dessy on his own on Christmas Eve; my heart is heavy. The phone rings and it's my beautiful granddaughter telling me that she's just put the mince pies out for Father Christmas and a carrot and sprout for Rudolf.

"I want to come to your house like we always do," she cries, and I feel my heavy heart break.

I drive to work and enter the unit where chaos reigns. Half the children have gone home and those that are waiting act out, sick with fear that their parents won't come; such is their level of mistrust in their caregivers. My heart aches for them. We have a hard evening trying to be nurturing and hold it together to provide

boundaries for the children who've lost theirs. It's hard though, as my strength has left on the last greyhound bus and I feel stranded with my own misery.

My salvation comes in the form of five small children who have been left at the hospital and who are not going to hang up a stocking over a fireplace or at the end of their beds, and for whom Father Christmas isn't going to come. Their abandonment bites deeply into the core of me as I look at their sweet lost faces, and although they aren't my beloved family, they are tonight.

We're summoned to the gym and I pull the children away from their movie, but for once they don't groan and we all line up ready to go downstairs, and I'm as excited as they are. I have no idea what to expect. Carol singing in England is a sedate affair as I remember, having been in the Brownies and Girl Guides, and I can't believe what awaits us in the gym. I suddenly feel ashamed of my homesickness.

There are oodles of people milling around in the gym, people I've never seen before, and after each unit joins us, one of our staff stands in front of us and says, "At this time I know that all of you will be thinking of your families. Christmas is a time for valuing our families and I want you all to think of us staff as your families until we've helped you work out your problems and you can return to your own, or find a new caring family."

I've got tears in my eyes and I know that this moment is going to make my own "home alone Christmas" special.

"I wanted to share with you my own family, so they've come along to entertain you and to let you know that family matters, and that you're family to us right now."

I scan the crowd before me and there are infants right through to a dotty old granny who can barely stand, and I marvel at their generosity. My feelings are compounded when I hear my

American colleagues say how wonderfully generous they are, considering how important Christmas Eve is in America. I ask, eager to know different customs, and I'm told that Christmas Eve is a day for a huge family get-together, as big as Christmas Day is in England. I feel humbled by this woman and her family's kindness, and I know their Christmas spirit will be with me forever. I have an image of a nine-year-old black girl dressed in a Santa suit dancing all on her own in a huge gym just to entertain us. It is a precious vision that I'll never forget; sometimes gifts don't come wrapped in gaudy Christmas paper.

I wish above all else that I could share this with Ellen; she'd be enthralled and would be sustained by their goodness, but it's impossible. I try to chase away the images of her being alone in bed on such a wonderful evening. I need to hide those images, as I know they'll suffocate what little energy and resolve I have and which I need to nurture these beautiful children on a night that heralds the love of a mother towards her child. Although I'm not in any mood to be faced with the lessons of life, I can't help but see the stark contrast before me: the unconditional love of a united family generously putting others before their own needs compared to abandoned, lost children whose families are too busy satisfying their own needs to make Christmas special for their own children.

# 19

WE GO BACK UPSTAIRS AND RESUME watching the movie and I dig into my bag for the treats I've brought the children. The bag of candy is easy to share, but I've underestimated the number of oranges I need. Christmas is quintessentially a large orange to me and just the smell can take me back to being just five years old at my first school Christmas party, where a rotund parent volunteered to dress up as Father Christmas and gave me a jewel in the form of a large orange. I sobbed as my mother cut it open for me to eat; she broke it. I didn't want to eat it; I wanted to look at it, because I'd never seen one before and Santa had given it to me.

I don't know what to do. I have four oranges and there are five children. Perhaps I should peel them and share the segments, but to do that would take away the magic of a whole, perfectly round orange. I go to the eldest child and ask what I should do. She tells me that she really doesn't mind not having one, as the others are just "little kids." I'm moved by her ability to do the right thing despite her age and the trauma she's endured, and the comparisons of those who don't do the right thing are never far from my mind. Particularly so when a child is brought to the unit sobbing, having been admitted at bed time on Christmas Eve because she'd had a temper tantrum. She's six years old and I think of my granddaughter's annual rituals on Christmas Eve. That's what this child should be doing, not being dumped in a facility because she had a paddy, a tantrum.

What is wrong with this nation, the most powerful in the world, that when their children act up, as most children do at times, parents don't deal with it as they should, but hand the child to outside agencies for them to fix their child? We don't have such places in England and my colleague stare at me in disbelief when I tell them. They say, "Well, what do you do with your kids who act out then?" We parent them, put boundaries around them, teach them right from wrong and how to get their needs met in a positive way. I don't believe we English have it totally right, of course not, because there are scarce resources in England for children with genuine problems, but we don't add to their problems by institutionalising them, or condone the lack of parental responsibility by making it acceptable for parents to take their children to facilities for "someone else to *fix*."

I shake my head in disbelief as I watch the little girl sob for her mother, so I distract her by reading one of my silly little stories, this one about a huge Christmas tree, and she smiles. I share out candy and ignore a heartless worker who tells me I'm doing wrong as candy is bad for kids. He says I'm spoiling them. "I never had anything at Christmas and it didn't do me any harm," he mutters passively-aggressively, proving himself wrong.

The evening passes quickly and I tuck all six children into in bed, something I don't usually do, but tonight is different, special. The little girl slips her candy under her pillow, a stash that by its presence validates Christmas for her. Eating it would make it just another day when someone had given her a treat. I understand totally, remembering my orange. I feel compassion and anger at the same time. This precious child is just six years old, lying in a strange bed, surrounded by strangers. Where is her mother on this night of perfect motherhood? Doesn't she feel the hole in her arms left by her child's absence? Why is she not here to do the right thing?

I spend the remainder of the shift trying to understand some of the hidden side of American culture: the underbelly of a nation where the unspeakable exists and thrives. My colleague tells me about his life in a Chicago ghetto and he looks at me as if I've just stepped off another planet when I ask him what Father Christmas used to bring him as a child. His face is full of scorn as he says, "Santa doesn't come to the ghetto."

I look at him in amazement and try to explain how different it is in England. Every family celebrates Christmas unless it's against their religion. If a parent wilfully did not make an effort for their children, such behaviour would be seen as neglect and could be reported to the social services. He looks at me in amazement and shrugs, again saying, "It didn't do me any harm." But I think about the way he shouts, and his reluctance to give the children any treats, or even encouragement, and I see that although he survived his tough beginnings, he's devoid of play, of being able to have fun or nurture anyone else.

I think about the psychological experiments on infant monkeys carried out by Harlow and Suomi in 1970. They sought to explore how important the role of attachment is between infants and parents upon the developing infant. Although the baby monkeys were fed via a cold "wire" mother through a teat, they continually clung to another wire mother, covered in soft foam and cosy towelling material, to gain comfort and security. Harlow and Suomi's research explained the effects of maternal deprivation—when parents don't interact in return to the infant's attempts to interact with them. They observed that when the monkeys were fully grown and had their own infants, they were unable to parent their own babies. Their research can draw a parallel between the current trend of "babies having babies," teenagers who have not attached properly to their parents because *their* parents weren't attached to their own and have never learned parenting skills. With each generation, in pockets of society, babies suffer the same fate as Harlow's and Suomi's monkeys, growing into adulthood physically yet deficient in emotional intelligence, or the ability to attach to their babies and form mutually satisfying relationships with others. And so it goes on. This is what's lurking beneath the underbelly of this powerful, great nation, and I see it happening in England, too.

• • •

Dessy's snoring when I get in, slumped in the chair and I gently sidle next to him. He stirs, and I tell him about the beautiful extended family that gave of their time to make the children's Christmas as special as it could be.

We try to replicate our English Christmas traditions but we both know that it's not going to work, so we do something different and resign ourselves to the difference. For the first year ever we don't have a Christmas stocking and choose instead to have a sack, and at my insistence, every single thing inside the sack is to be wrapped. I curse my tenacity, for Dessy's had all evening to wrap the titbits he's bought for me, but I have to hide in the bedroom at this late hour to wrap all the things I've bought him. I long for my eldest daughter who wraps with such finesse but shake away her image, as it's too painful to think of her.

Resignation settles over me and I'm aware that Dessy is "as happy as Larry" having me all to himself. Every Christmas I'm busy with my family to provide them with the Christmas my mother made for us despite being dirt-poor, paying for it with pennies throughout the year. Every Christmas is a tribute to my mother. During Christmas Day when I speak to my children they tell me that Christmas is nothing without me. I'm moved. Yet the praise belongs to my mother for her sacrifices and insistence on doing the right thing for us as children, despite the awful hardship we all endured and the stress it caused her.

Dessy and I have a good day although deep down my heart hurts with longing. We laugh at the trinkets we've bought each other. He put Bird's Instant Custard in my sack knowing that I adore custard and America doesn't sell it (it's hot yellow pudding). I put an oil funnel and Peppermint Patties in his. I stifle the feeling that I'm merely going through the motions, but I can't stifle wondering what Ellen's doing and whether she received any gifts other than the second hand trinket Greta bought for pennies at the Salvation Army store during my first week here.

We visit friends armed with English "crackers" and some that Dessy has made for their children. I smile as I tell Dessy how puzzled my colleagues are when I try to explain English Christmas traditions, which are so utterly different from America's multicultural society. (When I first arrived in America in 1990 I was fascinated that American Christmas traditions were unique to each family's origins and ancestors—one of the cultural difference I embraced.) Every Christmas in England each household does much the same thing; their table is set with crackers—long cardboard tubes covered in paper with a strip of gunpowder running through the length of them, which goes "bang" when two people pull them apart by tugging on the ends. Inside the cracker is a toy, a motto and a paper hat, and Christmas isn't Christmas without wearing your paper hat like a crown until it rips or drops off.

Nor is Christmas complete without half the nation listening to the Queen's speech or sleeping in front of it. Amusing!

My friend's children pull apart the shop-bought crackers from England easily but when they're given those made by Dessy, the strong wrapping paper is resistant to tearing and they pull and pull, leaning back at forty-five degree angles, but they're so well made that they just don't pull apart. We laugh and wonder at the fun children get from simple home-made gifts compared to expensive shop-bought ones, before returning home to check on the dinner.

We go through the motions and set the table, but before we sit down to eat our feast, we do a mercy dash to a colleague who's working a sixteen-hour shift at the hospital so that others can have the day off, and who has no Christmas dinner. It's his first taste of English cooking and his eyes are wide as I point out our traditions on his plate. There is turkey, sausage meat, stuffing, pigs in blankets (real sausages wrapped in real bacon), roast potatoes, roast parsnips, carrots, Brussels sprouts, peas, bread sauce, cranberry sauce and gravy. No green bean casserole, macaroni cheese, candied yams or mash potato in sight. We have a rich steamed Christmas pudding with brandy butter for dessert and gently set it alight by putting a flame to a spoonful of brandy poured over the top of the pudding. Its blue flames flicker in the dusk, and the rest of the day is steeped in wine, love and homesickness.

My granddaughters leave their table to sing to me across the Atlantic and it's so funny, yet sad, that I laugh as tears run down my cheeks. I can't see them as I don't have Internet but hearing them is precious. Hearing them sing reminds me of last year when we were making mince pies in the kitchen and were singing "Walking in a winter wonderland," without knowing any of the words until the last line. They sing the same into the phone, "do-de-do-dedoing" the verse and whistling the refrain until they get to the only line they know; again, a precious gift that cannot be wrapped in seasonal paper.

I call Alex late on Christmas night and he's alone. I'm shocked, but he blows it off and says that he'll be back in a few days.

We awake the next day, Boxing Day, and I'm anxious but am unable to place why. I phone Jill and I instantly know why; she's cold and evasive.

I say, "Is it still okay for today?" and she sounds clipped, saying, "I think I'll pass on that."

I say, "Okay, take care," but I feel devastated. I know what's happened. She's spent the day with her son and told him all about what's going on with Ellen and Greta, and he's told her to stay out of it. For all she knows, perhaps Greta's right and I do "have problems," after all she wouldn't want to have such a person just walk into her home.

I understand but it's so utterly sad. Her son did what any loving son would do—protected his mother from the unknown; my family would have said the same.

It's hard to express what's going through my mind. I'm sick through and through, and I feel totally helpless, knowing that Greta has worked hard to divide us all even further, which is the perpetrator's mission. I want to cry, but I'm aware that for Dessy this is his holiday and he's gone to such an effort to make things nice for me, so I bottle it all up instead.

I know that I've come to a crossroads, a place where the day of reckoning resides. I don't know how I can do any more, and it's at this point that I try to switch off, but it's hard as I'm not very good at kidding myself.

I've learned much. Perhaps it was a stupid thing to do to put a flyer into strangers' mailboxes to advertise for lodgings, but I did so in good faith, believing the American people to be as straight as those I've met so far. The flyer said "Let's share in each other's cultures," a sentiment I still believe in today, a sentiment that Ellen and I enjoyed. I couldn't know that our growing closeness would enflame Greta's pathology so that both Ellen and I were left in uncompromising, dangerous positions.

I know that this is the end, the end of this chapter in my life, a moment when I accept one of my failings, that I can't fix everything, and that having done the right thing doesn't mean that I can move mountains. The thought does nothing to make me feel any better, yet we humans have the ability to repress or project. Freud was right in so many aspects of his work; when psychological stress threatens our stability we subconsciously find a way to live with it, and this is what I'm trying to do on Boxing Day. Dessy assumes that Boxing Day was so named due to the amount of sport shown after Christmas. Although this isn't so, I feel as if I've been in a boxing ring and had the sensibility knocked out of me. I know I'm re-framing, repressing and projecting but there's nothing else I can do. I can't go hammering on Ellen's door or Greta will have me arrested, and with Ellen denying any abuse, where do I stand?

As defeat threatens to take me down I hear my mother's voice: "Do the right thing," so despite feeling despair I force myself to find another way. I'll write a letter to everyone I can, so although I can't do anything to stop Ellen's misery or demise, I can draw attention to her plight and that of thousands upon thousands of others like her, left by the state and their families to endure at worst, abuse, and at the very least, neglect. I can write letters to the police disputing their "no further action at this time" report yet understanding that their hands are tied. I can write an official letter to Chester, the financial advisor, to let him and his company know what's going on. I can also write a letter to Ellen's doctor expressing my fears that it is Greta's intention to allow her mother to die so that she will be rid of her and inherit her mother's estate. I can also inform the police that should Ellen suddenly die, they should not take it at face value but to order an autopsy.

I can write this book to highlight my love for dear Ellen, to let her know that I did what I could but that it wasn't enough, and I'll have to live with that. By the time it's published she'll be dead, killed not by Multiple Sclerosis but by slow, torturing neglect. A legacy to a mother who did her best with what she had at the time, from a daughter whose heart was so shrivelled with bitterness and blame that her mother's death was the only acceptable payment she could entertain. She will reap her mother's inheritance, left to her by her stepfather whom she despised, and who felt so afraid of her that he slept with a loaded gun under his pillow, an inheritance that would make him turn in his grave. It was intended to be an inheritance for Ellen, to pay for a carer to ensure her comfort as she had ensured his. Greta will inherit "blood money."

My heart feels broken as I think such thoughts, but I keep them to myself as I go to work on Boxing Day—just another ordinary day to Americans, but not to me.

• • •

It's been a terrible year, full of anxiety and uncertainty, yet one that has given me many priceless gifts, and as New Year's Eve approaches we wonder how to see the next year in. I know that I want to spend it with Alex, and Des invites him to come to dinner and sample his famous roast potatoes.

I'm so fortunate to be given the night off and begin to help Dessy set the table when the phone rings.

"Change in plans," Alex says breathlessly. "I've got tickets to go to a flash New Year's Eve party downtown and I want you two to come. Get dressed."

An hour later he's at our door with his friend, Brenda, waving from his car. He steps in and begins to dance with the singing, dancing Santa and my spirits begin to soar for the first time in months.

"Come and see 'Little Cely,'" I say, excitedly, wanting to share something so precious with him.

"Oh, my God!" he gasps in shock as I put her in his arms and take a photo. There's something very comforting about seeing my metaphoric self being held by someone as caring as Alex and the sight suits him. I know that one day he'll make a truly wonderful father.

We meet Brenda and by the end of the evening it feels as if we've known each other forever, and we sing and laugh all the way home. Dessy says it's been the best New Year's Eve he's ever had.

The first day of the new year is our last together as Dessy flies home tomorrow. We spend much of the day holding each other and I cry like a baby. He truly is my dearest friend, my soul mate, and our separation has reunited the passion that's always been there behind our exhaustion and work commitments. I know that I'm going to miss him far more than when we said goodbye three months ago.

It's painful to take him to the airport and I cry all day until I have to go to work. I hold myself together until I exit the hospital and then start all over again.

Mark comes back after Christmas and I'm pleased to see him; it's lonely without Dessy. Each time we meet in the kitchen we mull over the latest antics of our wayward landlady but then things take an unexpected turn; we learn that she doesn't have permission to sublet to Mark or me. I'm reminded of Alex's quip, "What bad luck, we've only got eight weird people in this state and you seem to have met all of them." I'm on tenterhooks, as the real landlord wants repossession of his apartment as soon as possible, so we are going to be homeless. Mark decides to go back to his family and work nearer home and I'm pleased for them all.

Alex is in the process of sorting out his move interstate so we keep missing each other and I begin to panic, wondering whether I really am going to be able to buy his humble little home from him. And as my homelessness looms nearer, my anxieties grow by the minute. I've missed him so much since he left work, and even though we've become ships in the night, I've valued his friendship and support during the three months since Alex and Ben rescued me from Greta's clutches. We say goodbye when he leaves town and I feel very sad.

The house-buying legalities are finally sorted out and I feel immense relief, and vow to myself and Alex that I will honour the four post-dated cheques I've given him. His trust in me is a precious gift, almost as precious as the humble home and place of safety I now have. I honour Ben in my prayers for the gift he gave Alex and for fate having brought us all together at precisely the right time. I try to ignore the fear I feel when I realise that this is the first time in my life that I've ever lived alone and focus instead on the fact that for the next few months I'm going to work my socks off and live on pork bones, liver and porridge so that I can pay my debt to Alex. I *will not* fail.

It's pouring with rain the day I move everything from the apartment into my new home and I feel a bit lost. I know I'm not truly alone for "Little Cely" is there to remind me of my pledge to myself and my supervisor that I *will* take care of me. I prop her on a pillow as I have no furniture. My bed cannot be delivered for days and so I go on a futon-hunting mission.

It's freezing and getting dark as I pull into the same car park where Greta bought the pine corner seat all those weeks ago, and dear Keith was browbeaten by her ungratefulness. I start to walk towards the store and turn around when I hear someone shouting at me. Instantly fear prickles down my back as a hooded youth marches straight towards me, and I know that I'm about to be mugged.

My head's spinning as he cuts immediately in front of me, still shouting, but without touching me, and behind me is a policeman with his hand already on his gun. We look at each other and then at the young man, and after a confusing pause where we look at the youth, we both laugh at the same time; he was oblivious to either of us as he was singing along to aggressive rap music blaring through his headphones.

"I thought I was going to have to go to work then," the policeman quips, and I tell him how thankful I am that he's there.

We grin as we keep bumping into each other in the store and I'm reminded that, although I've sampled some of America's pathology, I have met some wonderful Americans and wouldn't have missed the experience for the world. My thoughts are reinforced after I buy a futon but have no way to get it home, and Keith's not around. I try to explain that I have no bed to sleep on if I can't take it home now, and the man next to me in line says that if I trust him he'll drop it off on his way home after going to a family dinner for a few hours. Of course I trust him, and I'm reminded that my bad experience with Greta has not robbed me of the gift of trust, and I'm glad.

Later that evening he arrives outside my house and we struggle inside with the large heavy box. I try to pay him but he refuses, such is his kindness, but I stuff some notes into his young son's hand and tell him to buy some candy and something nice for

Mummy and Daddy. The child grins at me and his dad shrugs as I thank him over and over.

Hours later my hands are raw from trying to put the futon together, and I sit on it, proud but exhausted. My possessions are in an untidy heap on the floor waiting to be put away, and under the pile I see an unopened Christmas present. I know what it is; it's the velour wrap in "Christmas colours" that I bought for Jill but couldn't give her. I keep it for myself, not as a gift but as a reminder of the lessons I've learned; that invaluable gifts cannot be wrapped, and also as a reminder to stay focused upon loving and giving despite rejection or persecution. I fall asleep exhausted and rather shell-shocked.

The next day it storms so I stay in all day until hunger forces me out into the driving rain, but it's so bad that I get lost. I almost enter the highway going the wrong way and I'm crying by the time I get home, my appetite gone. I feel very alone and decide that the only thing to do is to sleep.

It's late and there's someone banging on my door. My stomach lurches.

"Who is it?" I ask nervously.

"It's me, Brenda."

I open the door and the sight of her is like seeing an angel. She's breathless. "I'm *so* sorry that I wasn't here to help you move in. I had to visit my parents and take care of them, and then I had to take care of my nephew. I usually only get one weekend a month free. I'm *so* sorry. Are you all right?"

I've only ever met this lady once, on New Year's Eve, and she's greeting me as if I'm family. She makes me feel very special and nurtured, and chases away the isolation that was threatening to drown me.

"What can I do to help you, just name it," she says genuinely.

"There's nothing, really."

"There must be something?"

I think. "Well, I'm flying home next Saturday for a week, would you be able to take me to the airport?"

"Of course, I'd be glad to, and I'll come and pick you up, too."

I'm so grateful and we visit for a while before she leaves, and suddenly everything doesn't seem so bleak anymore.

She's true to her word and takes me to the airport and we giggle over the officials peering into the singing, dancing Santa's box, as he's too big to go through their x-ray machine. They all rush over to investigate; perhaps they think it's a terrorist's bomb, so Brenda and I walk away quickly before they tell us that he can't be shipped. He really *is* just a bearded old man that dances just like everyone's granddad. He's not a bomb, but I'm glad of their pedantry for as we ascend the escalator my fear of flying begins to mount.

Brenda stays until it's time for me to go through the gate and pats me on the back reassuringly as the Valium starts to kick in. When will I get over this? They say that it's the safest form of travel.

• • •

As I sit on the plane flying back to America after spending a week with Dessy and my children, I muse over the difference just four months can make. The last time I flew this way I was going into the unknown, meeting a person that I'd only seen once on the Internet.

This time Dessy and I had followed our ritual of eating McDonald's at Gatwick Airport while waiting for the flight, but I only ate one sausage McMuffin and he wasn't consumed by doing his paperwork. This time we seemed able to say goodbye properly, but there was a "see you soon" attached to it. I even managed to sit quietly in the departure lounge and control my panic, finding my seat on the plane without knocking into people or running my hand up my neighbour's thigh while finding my seat belt.

I smile. This feels very different to four months ago, even though my fear of flying is still there and I yank my belt as tight as I can, with the same thought in my head as last time: that if the plane goes down they'll find me stuck in my seat. This time, however, I know what I'm going to: my new home, my new friend, Brenda, and my job with all the same children waiting for me to get back armed with English chocolate. Despite my niggling fear constantly present as the plane drops and judders, I smile at the thought of the children and Dwayne all missing me, and although it's been wonderful to see my children and grandchildren, I've missed the eighteen feisty, lost souls on the unit, and my steadfast partner, Dwayne.

I mull over the differences in my body and psyche. I feel less exhausted than I was four months ago, having stepped off the "hamster treadmill" that consisted of driving for hours, attending appointment after appointment in body only, and scribbling court report after court report, with my case load ever increasing. My life now consists of living within a ten-mile radius of my workplace so I don't waste my time driving. When I get home each evening, I've finished for the day and the work isn't backing up waiting for me to do the next day; someone else has taken over. Most of all I have the precious gift of being instrumental in the lives of the numerous children that pass through my care. Yes, this feels very different to the life I was living four months ago and I feel satisfied with myself for having had the courage to change the way my life was heading, and not just sticking with it because it was familiar and there was a pension at the end of it.

My hands still leave nail marks in the arm rests as the plane buffets around while my thoughts take me to a place where I'm faced with the reality that four months ago I'm ashamed to say I only prayed in aeroplanes. I've done much praying in the past four months, a little for myself and my own safety, but much for Ellen and all the poor helpless, vulnerable people in similar situations. Along with the metaphoric core of myself, my doll, and my increasing dialogue with my concept of God, I have embarked upon a spiritual journey of self-discovery, learning firsthand of the starkness of good and evil; each residing so close to each other in every human being.

I am reminded of the words of wisdom a friend uttered after my mother died. He believed that in death, humans return to their perfect form, unsullied by human pathology derived from our inadequate childhoods or defective genes. I believe that all true wisdom is ultimately beyond human comprehension, being limited by our humanness and the limitations of our human brains, but his words make the most sense to me. As a psychologist and psychotherapist, I am well aware of the nature versus nurture debate and the role genetics and socialisation have in the formation of pathology. I also know of Freud's concept of the Id, the part of ourselves that seeks immediate gratification to the detriment of anyone else or even ourselves. Watching Greta abuse Ellen has been like facing the raw, driving greed of the Id, spiteful and self-serving, determined to gratify itself to the detriment of anyone else. As I think of Ellen's plight I'm still sick to my stomach and the fear is never far from my consciousness. It visits me as terrifying nightmares night after night; this I'll have to live with. But the kindness, strength, generosity and faith I've witnessed in the American people throughout this past four months help to balance my perception of the human condition.

I'm reminded how vital religion and spirituality are to curtail the Id's determination to consume, satiate the senses and promote the self. Only with the pursuit of spirituality will human kind be able to control the capacity for evil that resides in each of us through the mere act of being born human.

I rest my head back and force my own Id back into submission, willing goodness to take its place. It would be too easy to succumb to feelings of hatred towards Greta for the spiteful things she does, not only to Ellen but also to me and anyone that threatens to get too close. I refuse to raise my blood pressure when I think of her holding on to the cheques for the car for months only to cash them in when they could bounce and cost me a small fortune in penalties. And heaven forbid she could then have me arrested for non-payment of the car. Paying Alex left me so short of money that when Greta cashed all four cheques together, I had nothing—no money for petrol or food. But a precious elderly lady at work loaned me two hundred dollars to help me out until payday. While I recognise Greta's shrivelled spirit, I also see goodness all around me and I refuse to let enmity impact upon my life or sense of serenity. I have a choice, as all humans do; I can choose to react, retaliate and sink to a place where the Id is set free to wreak havoc upon the self and destroy others, or I can rise above it and "turn the other cheek," and keep the core of myself safe.

Whilst I struggle with the ongoing grief at having been forced to abandon Ellen, I know that my life is a journey, one where I learn and try to do the right thing. I know I'm not perfect, not at all, but I have integrity. I was terrified but I tried to help. I was unable to make a difference, being thwarted at every turn, but I tried, yet even as I think these things they do little to ease the pain of grief and longing for my friend, Ellen.

I know I've done my best though, and the way in which I can

best come to terms with having been forced to abandon Ellen·is to tell everyone. I will let the world know of these silent, stifled victims, whose last moments in life are touched by retribution and greed. The care they receive during their final days fails to reflect the struggle or sacrifice they've made to bring up their children with the skills they had at the time, but instead reflects the vengeful, base nature of the human being without spirituality, without goodness or love.

I no longer pray only in aeroplanes, for having been touched by something evil, I seek goodness and peace to counterbalance the darkness. Deep within me I hear my mother's voice telling me to do the right thing, my supervisor's voice saying I did all I could, and an even deeper, profound voice that tells me I must be an advocate for all those who are abused and suffer in silence.

I continue to pray as the plane's engines change key and sing in a tone that would herald an impending disaster to the phobic ear, but my prayers this time aren't only bargaining prayers to ensure a safe landing for me, and three hundred other passengers. They are full of thanks. My prayers, even as my nails leave their frenetic indentations on the armrest, are of gratitude for having had the opportunity to meet Ellen, Alex, Ben and Brenda, and for the ongoing support from Dwayne and my precious friend, Vicki. My hurt is as raw as ever and I daren't even speculate as to what Ellen may be doing right this minute, or if she's even alive, as the plane roars its angry touchdown. I know that the hurt will be with me forever. I may be able to stifle it in my waking moments but it'll visit me in my dreams for the rest of my life, dreams that are filled with fear, for her image, frail and awkward in her bed, is always with me, and I know that I have to live with the horror of it all forever more. The clever planning and discrediting that Greta has cultivated may succeed in killing off her mother undetected or unchallenged, but she takes a deadly chance on the possibility of a Day of Judgement existing. It doesn't trouble her as she's a non-believer, but merely not believing in something doesn't mean to say that such a thing doesn't exist.

As the roar of the aeroplane slamming on its brakes filters into my thoughts I'm suddenly desperate to see "Little Cely," left alone on the sofa in my new home.

It's over, I'm back and as the engines slow and we taxi to the terminal, my thoughts are full of thanks, not only for my safe journey but for the strength to do what's right, and for the gift of meeting such wonderful people in my life. I know that I'll probably never see Ellen alive again, and pray that there is such a thing as heaven, for if there is she'll be there with her sweetness and dry wit, for her loyalty and determination to weather her pain, and for her insistence on trying to be a good mother, despite everything. I shall know her spirit. My prayers have a different feel to them, and I allow calm to rest over me while the other passengers scramble for their bags in order to be first in line, and they become irritated when the doors remain closed and they have nowhere to go.

I slow my breathing and look out the window at the lights. Again I think about the differences between this and my last trip. How as I waited for the cabin door to open I was terrified of meeting Greta or facing what would be waiting for me as I tried to assimilate myself into their household. Although I feel sad, as I did four months ago at having to say goodbye to Dessy and my children, there's a peace about me this time. I know that Brenda is going to be there at the gate waiting with an unconditional smile and hug for me. I've only known her for six weeks and "visited" on only three occasions, yet I know deep within me that she is a precious human being, as precious as Alex, Dwayne and dear Ellen, and knowing she's there helps me contain my homesickness.

I don't hurry, what's the point? I'm virtually the last person off the plane. I have none of the anxieties I had four months ago as I walk towards the arrivals area, although the ghost of Greta lingers as I look up the ramp searching for Brenda among the bobbing heads beyond the barrier. I see her immediately, as I had Greta, although Greta's stance had been one of "this must be you, hurry up," whereas Brenda's is one of excitement and welcome.

Despite being exhausted and homesick for Dessy and my family, I smile for there she is, this beautiful person who I would never have met if not for Alex and Ben, and being in the right place at the right time, as fate dictates. She's waiting for me with a smile on her face and two large "welcome home" balloons floating above her.

I laugh, my exhaustion forgotten, and I give her a hug. She's so far removed from Greta, whose body had instantly frozen with human contact when I'd greeted her, and we hug and laugh at the balloons bouncing around, a tangible, colourful welcome.

"Well, I had to do something to make you feel at home. Did you have a good trip?" she asks. "Are you okay?"

"It was bumpy but okay."

"So you coped okay with it?"

"I had lots to think about," I say, feeling as though I've travelled more than the four thousand miles from England to America in my mind.

"Do you want to stop for a drink of some sort? Here, let me carry your bags, you must be exhausted."

It's all a far cry from when Greta picked me up, her curt "Good flight?" and the discomfort I felt as she marched off ahead of me to the baggage claim ordering me where to go. There's no awkwardness between Brenda and me, and we chat and giggle while waiting for my bags. There's no impatience in Brenda, nor foot tapping or eyes rolling heavenwards while we wait as there had been with

Greta. Neither does Brenda storm off ahead leaving me to struggle with my heavy case, battling my asthma, but instead she tells me to stand at the curb and she'll fetch the car. I know that my gratitude is accepted by Brenda and not scathingly rejected. As she drives I say the same as I had said to Greta. "It's so beautiful," as we pass the landmarks that all hold sweet memories for me, but I say it not out of desperation to dispel the awkwardness and anxiety that hung in the air in Greta's car. I say it because it *is* beautiful; it takes my breath away and it feels like coming home.

"Yes, it *really* is. Welcome home," Brenda says, with sincerity etched on her face.

"Thank you so much."

We pull into my new home, and I'm overwhelmed by it all; the stark comparisons between goodness and evil. This has been one of the most traumatic periods of my life, yet despite that, I have been given the precious gift of friendship and of generosity and trust by Ben and Alex who have enabled me to buy a home, one without fear, where I can be peaceful and safe.

I open the door and warmth brushes my face as I fumble for the light. There she is resting on the couch, "Little Cely," the metaphoric core of me snuggled up in a fleecy blanket. We laugh as I pick her up and Brenda quips about being left "home alone," but tells me not to worry. "She's not dead, she just needs some tender loving care," and I smile to myself after she leaves and ponder on the depth of what she's just said.

Four months ago I left England with my psychotherapy supervisor's words ringing in my ears: "You take care of everyone else yet have trouble taking care of you. Who is going to take care of you?"

It was a tough question, one that I wanted to sweep under the carpet with a nonchalant "Me, of course. I'm okay. Don't worry about me. I've got this far in life, I'll be fine," but I said nothing as she was too perceptive to be swept aside with shallow words. Yet there was some truth in my unspoken answer "Me! I'll take care of me." My psychotherapy training has shown me that even though a person may have suffered inadequate or abusive parenting and they cannot rely upon someone else to take care of them, there is always the one person who's constantly with them—themselves.

I don't know what made me buy my doll or to use her as a "therapeutic tool." I hadn't intended to when I bought her, it just happened. The impact upon me has been profound and I know that in the future I will use the concept in my therapeutic work with others. I have seen teenage girls so despairing that they start to cut themselves and yet are instantly soothed when the doll is placed in their arms. It seems magical but there are scientific reasons for the changes in behaviour and emotions.

In the pursuit of controlling the Id, each of us has assimilated masses of psychological non-verbal *messages* from our parents or caregivers and those *messages* may be positive, *affirmations*, which subconsciously encourage us to be the best we can be, or else they may be negative. The austere non-verbal negative *messages* from our caregivers step in like irritating computer pop-ups to crush us whenever we try to nurture ourselves. Nurturing ourselves isn't the same as giving free-reign to the destructive forces of the Id, it's about nurturing the very core of ourselves and replacing affirmations, or instilling those that perhaps were never part of our development. Holding a doll and attributing her to your core self overrides the austere parental voices inside and allows the nurturing part of your personality to give you permission to be spontaneous and creative, to laugh and love, to play and have fun, facets of the self that may have been stifled during the act of socialisation. It has the same feel to it as Philip Pullman's creative trilogy, *Northern lights*, *The subtle knife* and *The amber spyglass*, where children's souls are externally manifested as animals attached spiritually and emotionally to them to nurture and enjoy; the personification of intuition.

I *know* that "Little Cely" is an inanimate object, one that has been lovingly created through hours of work, but it's what she represents that is so important. As I sit on the sofa holding her, thinking about the past four months and the trauma of it all, I become aware that there's silent reassurance emanating from me and I feel strong. It dawns on me that in order to love other people you have to love yourself, a statement I heard often enough as a child but which I thought it sounded selfish or meant *being* selfish. As I've learned, I realise that it has nothing to do with being selfish, it's about recognising your own self-worth and your right to be here, a part of this universe. If that feels difficult to accept, using symbolism, by the act of separating "your core self" and perceiving it as an external object, will enable you to love yourself safely until you are ready to assimilate those affirmations into your own psyche. It's utterly powerful.

I recall the repugnance in Greta's face when she first saw my doll, and as I muse and ponder, I allow the first shadow of jetlag to creep over me. I think about Greta's core self, how totally buried it is, so that she's unable to love or have fun. As I have my psychologist's hat on at this moment, my hostility towards her abusive behaviour is overshadowed and I'm saddened, thinking what my reaction would be towards her if she were to sit next to me with her metaphoric self in *her* arms. I know that I would be filled with love and compassion for this person who is so hurt and damaged that any love or passion to celebrate life has been squashed out of her, for whatever reason.

I sit for some time, the aeroplane still humming in my ears, along with my grandchildren's cries of goodbye and Dessy's sadness, and I look at "Little Cely" in my arms; she is truly beautiful.

I think of Brenda's words "She's not dead, she just needs some tender loving care," and as I hold her with my heart full, I recognise a truth: By learning to take care of the core of yourself, you will be whole and emotionally healthy. It is only then that you will be able to love and care for others, and be able to *do the right thing*.

# Epilogue

This book began as a journal, started a couple of days after my escape from Ellen's and Greta's house. I was having terrible nightmares about Ellen and whether she was all right, and writing down my thoughts seemed to help keep the nightmares at bay. However, I still had to wake up and be there for the children in my care, each one a wounded soul. As each chapter evolved, I questioned everything I'd done and said, left undone and unsaid, and I recognised just how life-changing that month in Ellen's home had been for me and my personal development. I acknowledged my strengths and weaknesses with raw clarity, and much of that was very painful. I questioned everything. Had I done the right thing, even though it took me so long to pluck up the courage to report Greta's abuse? Had I made Ellen's suffering worse by reporting it? Had I made Greta more dangerous by exposing her? Could I have done more to help Greta—or Ellen? It made me question doing the right thing and what "the right thing" might be with all its "shades of grey."

I spent much of the time terrified, which may surprise the reader. How can someone with that amount of academic and clinical knowledge be afraid and become embroiled in such a pathological situation? The answer, I guess, is that I'm human, with human frailties beliefs and fears. I was driven by wanting to help

Ellen *and* Greta, a facet of my personality which I'm still working on: the need to please and make things right for everyone else. Those readers who find my indecision and sense of fear incongruent may wish to know that no matter how educated or celebrated a person becomes, they are still on their own personal journey, battling the remnants of their own unique childhoods, good and bad, and their genes.

It was easy to be driven to help Ellen because she was so frail, sweet and funny, with such an indomitable spirit, but I was *always* mindful of trying to help Greta because I could see that she was struggling to actually *live*. My academic knowledge has served me well when trying to put aside my negative feelings towards her and the way she treated Ellen, for I have asked myself, "How did Greta become that way?" The academic world recognises the nature versus nurture argument, whether who we are is dependent upon our genes or our upbringing, and most agree it's a bit of both. Greta had family members with severe mental illness, but I don't believe that in itself could account for her behaviour.

With childhood being the cornerstone of everyone's emerging personality, I had to temper my feelings towards her and try to understand what had gone wrong for her. I felt compelled—driven—to reach out to teenagers with feelings similar to Greta's, lost, angry, bitter, full of hate and self-loathing—to help them not become a person who could abuse the very person who gave them life.

During the last eight years, while this manuscript lay gathering dust in a cupboard, because rereading it traumatised me each time I tried to proofread it and the nightmares started again, I gained my PhD studying psychological and sociological factors implicated in teenage suicide. Wanting to help as many teenagers as possible, I found numerous risk factors that when combined could increase the likelihood that a teenager could attempt suicide. It became a natural progression after finishing "The Right Thing," to continue to write, so I took each risk factor and wrote the "I Only Said" series of therapeutic novels, to help teenagers and young adults address the problems that could drive them to such despair that they could contemplate suicide. Writing the series was a challenge, being dyslexic myself and finding reading difficult, and I wrote them very simply so that even the poorest reader could manage them and learn coping skills.

I wish with all my heart that Greta could have found help while she was a troubled teenager. Her level of pathology wouldn't allow herself to commit suicide, but with help maybe she could have understood herself and why she felt the way she did. With knowledge and understanding perhaps Greta could have learned to love herself, and then ultimately her mother, who gave her life and did the best she could with what *she'd* learned as a child.

# Appendix

As mentioned previously, Sir Winston Churchill stated that the United States and The United Kingdom were "two nations separated by a common language." As one of the objectives of this book was to explore cultural differences and the way in which our two countries use the English language, the following appendix explains some English words or phrases I've used in my pursuit to remain "English." I hope you find them amusing.

Blanks me:            Totally ignores the space one occupies.

Car boot sale:           Like a garage sale but all the personal items for sale are in the "trunk/boot" of your car, and the sale is usually held on a Sunday in a field along with hundreds of other cars.

Cotton on:            Suddenly understand through intuition rather than verbal explanation.

Cream-tea:            An afternoon snack, originating from South West England, particularly Devon and Cornwall, of a scone (very similar to a "biscuit" yet less greasy), local clotted cream (lumpy and yellow) and strawberry jam (preserves). Usually a treat for holiday makers (vacationers) as it's very fattening. Must be served with a pot of tea, not coffee!

| | |
|---|---|
| Esplanade: | The road that runs parallel to the beach, just feet away from the sand. The road is usually lined with fancy hotels, cafes and amusement arcades. |
| Frock: | A full-skirted dress. |
| Had up: | Accused and arrested by the police. |
| Het-up: | Stressed out and manic. |
| Homely: | Comforting childhood memories of home; cosy and warm feelings. |
| Jackdaw treasures: | Random, non-matching items of sentimental value that catch the eye. Usually sparkly. |
| Judder: | Vibrate. The shaking of a structure. |
| Like a thing possessed: | Manic energy. |
| Loo: | A toilet (bathroom), lavatory, WC— Water Closet. |
| Nineteen to the dozen: | Excessive speed. Trying to cram too much work or activity into too small a time. |
| Paddy: | Temper tantrum (children) or acting out by being very dramatic (adults). |
| Pavement: | Raised tarmac at either side of a road where pedestrians can walk safely (sidewalk?). |

| | |
|---|---|
| Queues up: | Stands in "line" waiting. |
| Remains insitu: | Remains in place. Normally referring to medical apparatus... IVs or catheters. |
| Rings off: | Hangs up the phone. |
| Sick to the back teeth: | Slang term for "utterly fed up" and exhausted through trying to endure or fix something. |
| Slips round a treat: | Easily without a problem. |
| Sussed out: | Figured out through intuition. |
| Tucking into: | Eating greedily without reserve. |
| Vicar: | A pastor, Father or priest. Leader of church and congregation. |
| Washing up liquid: | Dish detergent. |

# About the Author

DYSLEXIA WASN'T HEARD OF when I was a child and I just thought I was slow, yet I was inspired by my brother, the composer Philip Feeney, who was younger than me and very clever. So armed with my stubbornness and determination, I sought to educate myself in spite of my dyslexia and conventional learning methods feeling alien to me. Over twenty years I went from failing miserably at school to becoming a Registered Nurse, obtaining an Honours degree in psychology, a Masters degree in Applied Social Studies (social work), five years training in psychotherapy, and finally earning a PhD researching teenage suicide attempts. I developed a risk assessment tool to identify those who slipped through the net using current screening methods.

While I love to learn, there's no denying that it is hard for me, and for many years I cursed my dyslexic brain, until my husband and I took our large family on a "pirate" camp and I wrote eight short pirate stories to amuse my grandchildren and other children who gathered around. It was then that I began to appreciate thinking differently and being able to "paint pictures with words" through writing. Since then I've written numerous short stories in the "Funny Thing Happened Today," and the "Windows of Wisdom" series. I also wrote a novel addressing racism called "Shades of Ebony" several years ago, with a sequel as well.

"The Right Thing" is the first autobiographical work I've done and it is a true story that has to be told for all the forgotten elderly and infirm, and for all the children who suffer at the hands of those who are supposed to love them.

An autobiography is about the self but this is one with a difference. Yes, it shows my personal journey through a four-month period when I was terrified, but it's mainly about those who have touched my life: my courageous mother who tried to teach me what "the right thing" meant, and whose sustaining currency in our home was education and creativity; my two loving foster mothers who loved me unconditionally and balanced my life; and the greatest gift in mine and my whole family's lives, my brother Philip Feeney. He epitomizes the "right thing," humbly putting everyone before himself, yet still adhering to our mother's principles—education and creativity.

# WIGHITA PRESS ORDER FORM

| Book Title | Price | Qty. | Total |
|---|---|---|---|

### I Only Said I Had No Choice
ISBN 0-9786648-0-9      $14.99 x \_\_\_\_\_    $ _____

Shane learns how to control his anger and make positive life choices; and he gains understanding about adult co-dependency.

### I Only Said "Yes" So That They'd Like Me
ISBN 0-9786648-1-7      $14.99 x \_\_\_\_\_    $ _____

Melody learns how to cope with being bullied by the in-crowd at school and explores the emotional consequences of casual sex. She raises her self-esteem and learns what true beauty is.

### I Only Said I Couldn't Cope
ISBN 0-9786648-2-5      $14.99 x \_\_\_\_\_    $ _____

Adam learns how to deal with grief and depression. He works through the grieving process and explores his perceptions of death and life.

### I Only Said I Didn't Want You Because I Was Terrified
ISBN 0-9786648-3-3      $14.99 x \_\_\_\_\_    $ _____

Hannah experiences peer pressure to drink alcohol. She learns about teenage pregnancy, birth, and caring for a new baby. Hannah faces the consequences of telling lies and learns how to repair broken trust.

### I Only Said I Was Telling the Truth
ISBN 0-9786648-4-1      $14.99 x \_\_\_\_\_    $ _____

Ruby embarks upon a journey to rid herself of the damaging emotional consequences of sexual abuse.

### I Only Said I Could Handle It, But I Was Wrong
ISBN 9780978664855      $14.99 x \_\_\_\_\_    $ _____

Simon embarks upon the most challenging journey of his life—to give up drugs, understand why he takes them and reclaim his life.

### I Only Said It Didn't Hurt
ISBN 9780978664862      $14.99 x \_\_\_\_\_    $ _____

Marsha cuts herself. As she learns how to cope with stress safely, she discovers a secret about herself that makes it impossible to ever cut again.

### I Only Said I Wasn't Hungry
ISBN 9780978664879      $14.99 x \_\_\_\_\_    $ _____

Ellie is bullied about her weight and sees food as her enemy. She learns to resist the voice of anorexia and explores the reasons for her poor self-image.

continued on reverse

# WIGHITA PRESS ORDER FORM

| Book Title | Price | Qty. | Total |
|---|---|---|---|

**I Only Said I Wanted to Kill Myself;**
**I Didn't Really Mean It**
ISBN 9780978664886        $14.99   x _____    $ _____

    Kenny is angry and hates authority figures, but he forms
    a relationship with Miss Tina who teaches him how to
    get his needs met without acting up. He eventually understands
    why adults have to set rules.

**I Only Said Leave Me Out of It**
ISBN 9780978664893        $14.99   x _____    $ _____

    Maizy's parents divorce and she learns that, although
    it hurts when others are unkind or unjust, everyone has
    a choice as to how to respond. She finds a valued place
    in her new blended family.

Sub Total    $_____

Sales Tax 7.5% ($1.13 per book)    $_____

Shipping/handling    $_____
1st book, $2.50; each add'l. book $1.00 / U.S. orders only.
(For orders outside the United States, contact Wighita Press.)

**TOTAL DUE**    $_____

PLEASE PRINT ALL INFORMATION.

Customer name: _____

Mailing address: _____

City/State/Zip: _____

Phone Number(s): _____

E-mail address: _____

**Make check or money order payable to Wighita Press and**

**mail order to:** P.O. Box 30399, Little Rock, Arkansas 72260-0399

✦ ✦ ✦

Look for us on the web at: www.wighitapress.com

(501) 455-0905 or after office hours: (501) 952-1321